CHARLES STEWART PARNELL

VOL. I.

W. Lawrence, photo.

Walker & Boutall, ph. sc.

Charles Stewart Parnell

London, Published by Smith, Elder & Co. 15, Waterloo Place.

THE LIFE

OF

CHARLES STEWART PARNELL

1846–1891

BY

R. BARRY O'BRIEN

OF THE MIDDLE TEMPLE, BARRISTER-AT-LAW

IN TWO VOLUMES—VOL. I.

GREENWOOD PRESS, PUBLISHERS
NEW YORK

Originally published in 1898
by Smith, Elder, & Co.

First Greenwood Reprinting 1969

Library of Congress Catalogue Card Number 68-57635

SBN 8371-2358-5

PRINTED IN UNITED STATES OF AMERICA

CONTENTS

OF

THE FIRST VOLUME

THE LIFE

OF

CHARLES STEWART PARNELL

——◦◇◦——

CHAPTER I

PARNELL'S ANCESTORS

THE founder of the Parnell family was Thomas Parnell,
'mercer or draper,' who became Mayor of Congleton,
Cheshire, in the reign of James I. He had four sons—
William, Thomas, Richard, and Tobias. Of William
and Thomas little is known, but Richard seems to have
been the most remarkable of the brothers. He was a
staunch Cromwellian, the friend of Bradshaw, and thrice
mayor of the town. Tobias was a gilder and decorative
painter, and also stood high in the esteem of his fellow-
citizens. He passed away with the Commonwealth.
At the Restoration, his son Thomas, quitting the old
home, purchased an estate in Ireland, and took up his
abode there. This Thomas Parnell—the first of the
Irish Parnells—was the ancestor of an illustrious off-
spring. Dying probably in 1685, he left two sons—
Thomas, the poet, the friend of Swift, Pope, Gay,
Bolingbroke, and other famous wits; and John, who

died one of the judges of the Irish Court of King's Bench.[1]

Thomas, the poet, was born in Dublin in 1679. A bright lad with a remarkable memory, he attracted the special attention of Dr. Jones, to whose school he was first sent, and afterwards sustained his early reputation by a distinguished career at college. Matriculating at Dublin University in 1693, he took his degree in 1697. Then, entering the Church, he was ordained Deacon in 1700, and Priest in 1703. In 1704 he became Minor Canon of St. Patrick's, and in 1706 Archdeacon of Clogher. Soon afterwards he married Miss Anne Minchin, of Tipperary—a beautiful girl, to whom he was passionately attached. His life was soon divided between literary pursuits and Church affairs. In 1709 Convocation appointed a committee to consider the best means for converting the Irish Catholics, and Parnell was made its chairman. But his heart was in literature. He now paid frequent visits to London, and mingled in the society of the wits of the day. He was very popular, prized for his conversational gifts and scholarly attainments. With Pope he was a special favourite, while Swift held him in high esteem. The former was always impatient of his absence in Ireland, and would often write to urge his return to his English friends.

'Dear sir,' says Pope in one of these letters, 'not only as you are a friend, and a good natured man, but as you are a Christian and a divine, come back speedily and prevent the increase of my sins; for at the rate I have began to rave, I shall not only damn all the poets and commentators who have gone before me, but be

---

[1] Head, *Congleton, Past and Present.*

damned myself by all who come after me. To be serious, you have not only left me to the last degree impatient for your return, who at all times should have been so (though never so much as since I knew you in best health here), but you have wrought several miracles upon our family. You have made old people fond of a young and gay person, and inveterate papists of a clergyman of the Church of England. Even nurse herself is in danger of being in love in her old age; and, for aught I know, would even marry Dennis for your sake, because he is your man, and loves his master. In short come down forthwith, or give me good reasons for delaying, though but for a day or two, by the next post. If I find them just, I will come up to you, though you must know how precious my time is at present; my hours were never worth so much money before; but perhaps you are not sensible of this, who give away your own works. You are a generous author; I, a hackney scribbler. You are a Grecian and bred at a University; I a poor Englishman, of my own educating. You are a reverend parson, I a wag. In short, you are a Doctor Parnelle (with an *e* at the end of your name), and I your obliged and affectionate friend and faithful servant.'

In August 1711 Parnell lost his wife, and her death seems to have overwhelmed him with grief. Nearly a year later Swift wrote in his 'Journal to Stella': 'On Sunday Archdeacon Parnell came here to see me. It seems he has been ill for grief of his wife's death, and has been two months at Bath. He has a mind to go to Dunkirk with Jack Hill, and I persuaded him to it, and have spoke to Hill to receive him, but I doubt he won't have spirit to go.'

Towards the end of 1712 Parnell wrote a poetical

essay on the 'Different Styles of Poetry.' Swift made him insert 'some compliments' to Bolingbroke, and then seized the opportunity of introducing him to the Minister. On December 22 the Dean notes in his 'Journal to Stella': 'I gave Lord Bolingbroke a poem of Parnell's. I made Parnell insert some compliments in it to his lordship. He is extremely pleased with it, and read some parts of it to-day to Lord Treasurer, who liked it much; and, indeed, he outdoes all our poets here a bar's length. Lord Bolingbroke has ordered me to bring him to dinner on Christmas Day, and I made Lord Treasurer promise to see him, and it may one day do Parnell a kindness.'

'*Dec. 25th.*—I carried Parnell to dine at Lord Bolingbroke's, and he behaved himself very well, and Lord Bolingbroke is mightily pleased with him.'

'*January* 31*st.*—I contrived it so, that Lord Treasurer came to me and asked (I had Parnell by me) whether that was Dr. Parnell, and came up and spoke to him with great kindness, and invited him to his house. I value myself on making the ministry desire to be acquainted with Parnell, and not Parnell with the ministry. His poem is almost fully corrected, and shall be out soon.'

February 19*th.*—I was at Court to-day, to speak to Lord Bolingbroke to look over Parnell's poem since it is corrected, and Parnell and I dined with him, and he has shown him three or four more places to alter a little. Lady Bolingbroke came down to us while we were at dinner, and Parnell stared at her as if she were a goddess. I thought she was like Parnell's wife, and he thought so too.'

But despite Parnell's literary distractions, the death of his wife still seriously affected his health and spirits.

On March 6, 1713, Swift says in his 'Journal': 'I thought to have made Parnell dine with him (Lord Treasurer), but he was ill; his head is out of order like mine, but more constant, poor boy.' And again, on March 20: 'Parnell's poem will be published on Monday, and to-morrow I design he shall present it to Lord Treasurer and Lord Bolingbroke, at Court. The poor lad is almost always out of order with his head.' The poem was now published. '[It is],' says Swift, 'mightily esteemed; but poetry sells ill.'

In 1714 we find Parnell, who was still in precarious health, at Bath with Pope. In 1715 he was once more in Ireland. In 1716 he was presented to the Vicarage of ·Finglass, which he retained until his death two years later. Towards the close of his life he seems to have suffered more acutely from fits of depression, to which he was apparently subject for many years. At these times he kept himself away from his friends, withdrawing to a remote part of the country, and there enjoying a 'gloomy kind of satisfaction in giving hideous descriptions of the solitude' by which he was surrounded. In the summer of 1718 he paid his last visit to London, and met some of his old friends. But his health was now rapidly failing, and, on his way to Ireland in October, he fell suddenly ill at Chester and there died: pre-deceased by two unmarried sons, and leaving one daughter, who, it is said, lived to a ripe old age. His remains rest in Holy Trinity churchyard, not far from the home of his ancestors.[1]

In 1721 Pope raised the most enduring monument to his fame by bringing out an edition of his works,

---

[1] Goldsmith, *Life of Thomas Parnell*; Johnson, *Lives of the Poets* (ed. Cunningham); Swift's *Journal to Stella*; *The Dictionary of National Biography*.

and dedicating the volume in immortal lines to the
Earl of Oxford :

> ' Such were the notes, thy once-loved poet sung,
> 'Till death untimely stopp'd his tuneful tongue.
> Oh, just beheld, and lost ! admired and mourn'd,
> With softest manners, gentlest arts, adorn'd !
> Blest in each science, blest in every strain !
> Dear to the muse, to Harley dear in vain !
> For him thou oft hast bid the world attend,
> Fond to forget the statesman in the friend :
> For Swift and him, despis'd the farce of state,
> The sober follies of the wise and great ;
> Dext'rous the craving fawning crowd to quit,
> And pleas'd to 'scape from flattery to wit.
> Absent or dead, still let a friend be dear
> (A sigh the absent claims, the dead a tear) ;
> Recall those nights that closed thy toilsome days,
> Still hear thy Parnell in his living lays :
> Who careless, now, of int'rest, fame, or fate,
> Perhaps forgets that Oxford ere was great,
> Or, deeming meanest what we greatest call,
> Behold thee glorious only in thy fall.'

The family property (including land in Armagh,
which the poet inherited from his mother) now descended
to the poet's brother John.   Beyond the fact that he
was a barrister, a member of Parliament, and a judge,
little is known of the details of John Parnell's life.
Married to the sister of Lord Chief Justice Whitshed,
he died in 1727, leaving one son, John, who became
member for Bangor in 1761, and was created a baronet
in 1766.   He married the second daughter of the Hon.
Michael Ward, of Castleward, in the County Down, one
of the judges of the Court of King's Bench, and, dying
in 1782, was succeeded by his famous son, Sir John
Parnell, Chancellor of the Exchequer in Grattan's
Parliament.

Sir John Parnell was born about 1745. At first intended for the diplomatic service, he ultimately gave himself up wholly to Irish politics. Becoming a student of Lincoln's Inn in 1766, he was never called to the Bar either in England or Ireland; though elected, many years later, a bencher of the King's Inns, Dublin. He entered the Irish Parliament about 1776, and was appointed a Commissioner of Customs and Excise in 1780.

Parnell's position was now unique. Holding office under the Crown, he possessed the confidence of Grattan and the Nationalists; a supporter of the Government, he was in touch with popular feeling. He commanded a volunteer corps during the great crisis of 1780–82, and cordially identified himself with the struggle for legislative independence. In 1783, however, he opposed Flood's Scheme of Parliamentary Reform, and later still he declined, like many other patriotic Irishmen of the time, to follow Grattan's lead on the Catholic question. Standing high in favour with the authorities, he became Chancellor of the Exchequer in 1785, and Privy Councillor in 1786. In 1788 he won popular applause by reducing the interest on the National Debt from 6 to 5 per cent. After the admission of the Catholics to the parliamentary franchise in 1793, he was drawn more into sympathy with them, and apparently looked upon complete emancipation as inevitable.

In 1794 he, Grattan, and some other Irish politicians visited London and conferred with Pitt on Irish affairs. At a dinner party at the Duke of Portland's, Parnell, who sat next to Pitt, took the opportunity of introducing the subject of Catholics and Protestants in Ireland. He said that the old feeling of ill-will was

disappearing, and that he looked forward hopefully to
the establishment of more cordial relations between
the members of both creeds.   'Yes, Sir,' said Pitt,
'but the question is, whose will they be?'   A union
between Catholics and Protestants in the English
interest would have been gratifying enough to the
English Minister, but a union for the purpose of
building up an Irish nation was not to his taste.   It
was, however, rather of the Irish nation than the
English interest that both Grattan and Parnell were
thinking, and Pitt no doubt shrewdly suspected the
fact.   'What does Ireland want?' he said to Grattan.
'What would she have more?'   'Mr. Pitt does not
like Ireland,' Grattan observed afterwards.   'She is
not handy enough for him.'   And handy enough, indeed,
she was not for Mr. Pitt, nor has she been for any
other English Minister.   Before leaving England
Grattan told Pitt that the time had come when the
Catholics should be completely emancipated, and, as we
know, in 1795 Lord Fitzwilliam was sent as Viceroy
to emancipate them.   Parnell, at Grattan's urgent
request, was retained in office, a fact which shows how
thoroughly the Nationalist leader believed in the
Chancellor of the Exchequer.   The sudden recall
of Lord Fitzwilliam and the breach of faith with the
Catholics are amongst the best known and the most
discreditable transactions in the history of the English in Ireland.   Rebellion followed, and when it
was crushed Pitt determined to destroy the Irish
Parliament.

In November 1798 Sir John Parnell was in London,
and Pitt broached the subject of the Union to him.   Parnell dealt cautiously with the subject, saying, 'that
before any decided step was taken communications

ought to be opened with the leading men in Ireland and public opinion sounded.'

In December 1798 Lord Cornwallis wrote to the Duke of Portland : 'I trust that the Speaker [Sir John Foster] and Sir John Parnell will not have left London before Lord Castlereagh's arrival, as I consider it highly important that he should have an opportunity of hearing them state their opinions before the king's minister on the question. Some of the king's servants appeared to be amongst the most impracticable in their opinions ; and I feel confident that your Grace will leave no means untried to impress these gentlemen more favourably before they return to this kingdom.' But Sir John Parnell was not 'impressed favourably,' for we find Cornwallis writing to Portland on January 16, 1799 : 'On my finding from a conversation which I had with Sir John Parnell soon after he landed that he was determined not to support the Union, I have notified to him his dismission from the office of Chancellor of the Exchequer.' Parnell now flung himself heart and soul into the struggle against the Union. On January 22 he opposed the measure *in limine*, though in what Cornwallis described as a 'fair and candid' speech, avoiding 'topics of violence.' 'I have only now to express my sincere regret,' Cornwallis wrote to Portland on January 23, 'to your Grace that the prejudices prevailing amongst the members of the Commons, countenanced and encouraged as they have been by the Speaker and Sir John Parnell, are infinitely too strong to afford me any prospect of bringing forward this measure with any chance of success in the course of the present session.'

In 1800 the struggle was renewed, and Parnell fought against the Government with increasing vigour

and vehemence. On February 17, 1800, we learn
from Cornwallis that ' Sir John Parnell rose at eleven
and went into the details of the measure, on which he
commented with severity.' On March 13 he moved
that ' an address be presented to his Majesty, to request
his Majesty to dissolve the present Parliament and call
a new one before the measure of legislative Union
should be concluded.'

After a fierce debate the motion was defeated at
three o'clock in the morning by a majority of 150
to 104.

On May 26 we find Parnell defending Grattan from
the imputation of treason cast upon him by Lord
Castlereagh. Grattan had said that the Union was a
measure of slavery, but that liberty was immortal, and
that the nation would yet rise to recover its rights.
' Rebellion, treason,' cried Castlereagh. ' No,' retorted
Parnell, ' for we shall recover our rights by constitutional means. The Sovereign himself will yet appeal
to the people to vindicate the freedom of which they have
been robbed.' But there was no such appeal. The
people were not consulted. The Parliament was destroyed by force and fraud. The nation was cheated by
intrigue and falsehood. Immediately after the Union
Parnell took his seat in the English House of Commons
as member for the Queen's County. But he did not long
survive the Irish Parliament, dying somewhat suddenly
in Clifford Street, London, on December 5, 1801. There
were few members of the old Irish Parliament more
universally esteemed than Sir John Parnell. Frank,
upright, honourable, courageous, he won the confidence
of friends and the admiration of foes. Moderate in
opinion, firm in resolve, he entered every struggle with
deliberation and fought every issue without flinching.

Called to high office in corrupt days, he never used his position for the advancement of a single member of his family ; he never under any circumstances allowed personal considerations to interfere with his lofty conceptions of public duty. He was no orator ; but his speeches commanded the attention and respect always given to a man who speaks with the authority which knowledge, sense, and honesty confer. A short time after his death the Prime Minister, Mr. Addington, paid a just tribute of esteem to his memory, describing him as a man 'whose loss they deeply deplored and whose memory would be reverenced by all who set any value on a sound understanding, extensive information, and a benevolent heart.'

Sir John married Letitia Charlotte, second daughter and co-heiress of Sir Arthur Brooke, Bart., of Cole-brooke, County Fermanagh, and had six children, amongst whom were Henry, the first Lord Congleton, and William, the grandfather of Charles Stewart Parnell.

Henry Parnell had a distinguished career. Born in 1776, he was educated at Eton, and Trinity College, Cambridge. In 1797 he entered the Irish Parliament, and took his place in the National ranks, in the struggle against the Union. On his father's death in 1801 he succeeded to the family estates which had been settled on him by Act of Parliament in 1789, owing to the incurable mental and physical disabilities of his eldest brother, John Augustus. Entering the English Parliament in April 1802, he retired before the end of the year; only, however, to return to active life early in 1806 as member for the Queen's County. Appointed a Commissioner of the Treasury in Ireland under the short-lived Grenville Administration (1806–7), he found himself again in Opposition after enjoying the sweets of office for less than a twelvemonth. In Opposition as in power he was a staunch supporter of the Catholic claims, and threw himself into the struggle for emancipation with persistence and energy.

In 1809 he called the attention of Parliament to the Tithe Question, and moved for an inquiry; but the motion was rejected by a large majority. In 1810 he returned to the subject, but again failed to awaken the interest of the House of Commons in it. During the hard fight for the removal of the Catholic disabilities, he stood side by side with Grattan until 1815, when the two friends for a time parted. Grattan had expressed his willingness to accept emancipation, subject to the condition that the Crown should have a veto on the appointment of the Catholic bishops. But O'Connell, who was now rapidly rising to power, demanded emancipation unfettered by any such restrictions, and carried the country with him. In this crisis Parnell supported O'Connell, and thenceforth became the representative of the Catholic Board in the House of Commons.

In July 1815 Sir Henry moved for a commission to inquire into the nature and effects of the Orange Society in Ireland. 'I voted for the question,' says Sir Samuel Romilly in his diary, 'and, as is always the case in important questions of this kind relative to Ireland, in a very small minority. We were only 20, the majority being upwards of 80.' We get some more glimpses of Parnell in Sir Samuel Romilly's diary :

'*May* 21, 1817.—Mr. Peel moved and obtained leave to bring in a Bill to continue the Irish Insurrection Act. I intended to oppose it, but, knowing that

Sir Henry Parnell meant to oppose it too, I waited for him to rise, as he meant to do. But the question having been put hastily, it was declared by the Speaker to be carried before he had risen ; and it was therefore passed without opposition.

'*May* 23.—I opposed on the second reading the further progress of the Bill for continuing the Irish Insurrection Act, on the ground that a measure of such extraordinary severity ought not to be continued, but in case of absolute necessity ; and that that necessity could not be apparent without an inquiry into the state of Ireland. That it was quite unjustifiable to persevere in such a system, upon no better grounds than the mere statements of the Irish Secretary. None of the members for Ireland supported me in this opposition except Sir Henry Parnell and General Matthew.

'*June* 13.—On a motion for going into committee on the Irish Insurrection Bill I again resisted the further progress of it, and supported a motion of Sir Henry Parnell for an inquiry into the facts which were stated as the grounds of proposing the measure. General Matthew and Sir William Burroughs were the only other members who opposed the Bill now, as they were the only members who had, together with myself and Sir Henry Parnell, opposed the second reading.'

In 1825 Parnell opposed the Bill for the suppression of the Catholic Association; urging that Ministers should adopt not a policy of coercion, but of redress.

After the concession of Catholic Emancipation in 1829, Parnell co-operated with the Liberal party ; and, indeed, it was on his motion to refer the Civil List to a Select Committee that the Government of the Duke of

Wellington was defeated and driven from office in November 1830. On the accession of the Grey Ministry, Parnell was made Secretary of War and Privy Councillor. But he proved a restive subaltern. He differed from the Postmaster-General on the subject of postal reform, he prepared army estimates which the Ministry would not accept, and, finally, he was dismissed from office in January 1832 for refusing to vote in favour of paying the dividend on the Russian-Dutch Loan, contrary to treaty stipulations.[1] On leaving office he wrote to Brougham, urging him to induce the Government of Lord Grey to come to terms with O'Connell and to take up the Irish question. 'Recurring to Ireland,' he said, 'I must press on you the urgency of your taking an active and decided part in its affairs. You are the only member of the Cabinet who at all comprehends the case. Most of your colleagues are not only ignorant of it, but, as it seems to me, incapable of understanding it.'

Parnell did not contest Maryborough at the general election of 1832, but in 1833 he was returned for Dundee.

In 1835 he became Paymaster-General of the Forces in the Melbourne Administration, a post which he held until his elevation to the peerage as Lord Congleton in 1841. He now ceased to take interest in public affairs. His health became seriously impaired. His mind was ultimately affected, and, in August 1842, he died by his own hand at his residence in Cadogan Place, Chelsea.

Sir Henry Parnell was an advanced Liberal of inde-

---

[1] During the French war Russia had borrowed from a Dutch house in Amsterdam the sum of 25,000,000 florins. After the war, the King of the Netherlands and Great Britain agreed to bear one-half of the charge until Holland and Belgium were separated—a contingency which happened in 1830.

pendent views and a sturdy spirit. At first interesting himself chiefly in Irish and financial questions, he soon pushed forward along the whole line of Liberal reform. He advocated the extension of the franchise and vote by ballot, the shortening of Parliaments, the repeal of the corn laws, and a rigorous policy of retrenchment in all public departments. Nearly half a century later his grand-nephew took a leading part in the agitation for the abolition of flogging in the army. But Sir Henry anticipated the movement, and, in office and out of office, condemned the lash with uncompromising hostility. Like his father, he was no orator, but a plain, businesslike, matter-of-fact speaker, who, however, possessed a complete mastery of every subject on which he touched, and was always listened to with attention and respect. His appearance in the House of Commons is thus described by a contemporary authority: 'Sir Henry Parnell is a respectable, but by no means a superior, speaker. He has a fine clear voice, but he never varies the key in which he commences. He is, however, audible in all parts of the House. His utterance is well timed, and he appears to speak with great ease. He delivers his speeches in much the same way as if he were repeating some pieces of writing he had committed to his memory in his schoolboy years. His gesticulation is a great deal too tame for his speeches to produce any effect. He stands stock still, except when he occasionally raises and lets fall his right hand. Even this he does in a very gentle manner. What he excels in is giving a plain, luminous statement of complex financial matters. In this respect he has no superior. Sir Henry is gentlemanly in his appearance; so is he also in reality. His manners are highly courteous. His stature is of the middle size, rather inclining to stoutness. His complexion is fair, his features are regular, with a mild expression about them; and his hair is pure white.'[1] Sir Henry published several books, the most important of which is a 'History of the Penal Laws against Irish Catholics from 1689 to the Union'—the best work, perhaps, on the subject.

He married Lady Caroline Elizabeth Dawson, eldest daughter of the first Earl of Portarlington, by whom he had five children, three daughters and two sons.

Sir Henry's youngest brother, William—the grandfather, as has been said, of Charles Stewart Parnell— was born about 1780. Of his early years little is known. But in 1801 he succeeded, under his father's will, to the property of Avondale, which had been settled on Sir John Parnell by a friend and admirer, Samuel Hayes, barrister-at-law. William Parnell was a modest, retiring man, fond of his books and his home; and, though keenly interested in political affairs, unwilling to take active part in public life. An enemy of the Union, a friend to the Catholics, a good landlord, a just magistrate, amiable, benevolent, sympathetic, he was very popular amongst the people in whose midst he lived, and whose welfare he studied. From his quiet retreat near the beautiful Vale of Avoca he watched the political struggle beyond, and even sometimes gave signs of the faith that was in him. In 1805 he published a pamphlet, entitled, 'An Enquiry into the Causes of Popular Discontent,' setting out the causes thus:

'1st. The recollections which exist in Ireland of being a conquered people.

'2nd. The great confiscation of private property.

---

[1] *Random Recollections of the House of Commons.*

' 3rd. The distinctions between Protestants and Catholics.

' 4th. The distinction between the members of the Church of England and the Presbyterians.

' 5th. Tithes.

' 6th. The degraded state of the peasantry.

' 7th. The influence of a Republican Party.

' 8th. The Union.'

He devotes many pages to a vigorous condemnation of the Union, putting the case at one point very happily, thus : ' The reasoning and practice of the Union was very like a transaction in " Mon Oncle Thomas." A grenadier sold his son's teeth to a dentist. The only difficulty was to persuade the child to part with them. The contracting parties took the favourable opportunity of a severe fit of toothache and reasoned the matter thus : " This tooth you are going to have drawn gives you a great deal of pain ; all the rest will decay in their turn, and give you as much pain ; therefore, while you are about it, you had better have them all drawn at once." " Oh, but," said the child, " how should I be able to chew my victuals ? " " That is easily settled," said the father ; " I will chew them for you." The English,' said Parnell, ' have the disposition of a nation accustomed to Empire. Anything that compromises their own dignity is out of the question. But the dignity of any other nation never makes any obstacle to their measures.' A few years later he published the work by which he is best known, ' An Historical Apology for the Irish Catholics.' This is a remarkable little book, showing an intimate knowledge of Irish history, and displaying both literary skill and logical acumen. Taking up the argument that Irish disaffection springs from religious causes, he proves that the Irish were rebellious before religious differences arose. The English came, he says in effect, to rob and kill, and the Irish fought for property and life. 'Contemporary writers never mentioned religion as a cause of rebellion till long after the Reformation; on the contrary, their fears are always expressed against the Irishry, not against the Papists. They found the greatest opposition in national pride, not in religion.' He thus deals with the Protestant oligarchy, though he himself belonged to that oligarchy : 'The Protestants, in their terror of persecution, have become persecutors, their alarm at Catholic atrocities has made them atrocious. To hear them speak, one would imagine that they had been the patient and uncomplaining sufferers, from the reign of William till George III.; that they had borne this long and cruel test with loyal resignation; that they had been deprived of property, of arms, of every legal and honourable right. No, it is not suffering, but it is power, it is pride of artificial ascendancy, it is the jealousy arising from exclusive privilege that corrupts the understanding and hardens the heart.' Sydney Smith reviewed the book very favourably in the ' Edinburgh,' saying : ' We are truly glad to agree so entirely with Mr. Parnell upon this great question; we admire his way of thinking, and most cordially recommend his work to the attention of the public.'

A warm friendship existed between William Parnell and Thomas Moore. It was at Avondale that the poet wrote ' The Meeting of the Waters,' and the exact spot from which he is supposed to have viewed the scene was pointed out to me by Mr. John Parnell some time ago.

' Tom Moore's tree '—under whose wide-spreading

branches the poet sat, it is said, when he penned his famous song—is still shown as one of the sights of Avondale. But there has always been uncertainty and mystery on the subject—uncertainty and mystery which, even at the request of William Parnell, Moore declined to clear up. Fourteen years after Parnell's death he revisited the scene, and notes with a touch of pardonable vanity in his journal: 'August 25, 1835. After breakfast the landau and four was again at the door, and with a most clear morning, promising a delicious day, we set out for the Vale of Avoca and the meeting of the waters. I had not been in this beautiful region since the visit (ages ago it seems) which gave birth to the now memorable song, "There is not in the wide world." How wise it was of Scott to connect his poetry with the beautiful scenery of his country. Even indifferent verses derived from such an association obtain a degree of vitality which nothing else could impart to them. I felt this strongly to-day while my companions talked of the different discussions there were afloat as to the particular spot from which I viewed the scene ; whether it was the first or second meeting of the waters 'I meant to describe. I told them that I meant to leave all that in the mystery best suited to such questions. Poor William Parnell, who now no longer looks upon those waters, wrote to me many years since on the subject of those doubts, and, mentioning a seat in the Abbey churchyard belonging to him where it was said I sat while writing the verses, begged me to give him two lines to that effect to be put on the seat. "If you can't tell a lie for me," said he, " in prose, you will, perhaps, to oblige an old friend, do it in verse." '

But Moore did not comply with the request.

Though little inclined to take an active part in politics, Parnell was induced to enter Parliament as member for Wicklow in 1817. But his public career was of brief duration. In 1821 he died in the prime of life, deeply mourned by true and loving friends, and keenly missed by a faithful and sorrowing tenantry. He married the eldest daughter of the Hon. Hugh Howard, of Castle Howard, County Wicklow, by whom he had two children, John Henry and Catherine.

John Henry Parnell led an uneventful life. Residing on his estate at Avondale and interesting himself chiefly in questions of agricultural improvement, he sought by every means in his power to promote the well-being and happiness of his people. A good landlord, a staunch Liberal, a kind friend, he was respected and esteemed by all classes in the country. In his youth he was fond of travel, and during a visit to the United States, in 1834, he met, loved, and married Miss Delia Tudor, the daughter of Commodore Charles Stewart, of the American Navy. This was the one notable event in the life of John Henry Parnell.

Delia Stewart was the daughter of a remarkable man. About the middle of the eighteenth century there were agrarian disturbances in Ulster; and thousands of tenants, smarting under a sense of wrong and despairing of the future, fled across the ocean to seek a refuge and a home in the British colonies of North America. Among these emigrants were the parents of Charles Stewart. They settled in Philadelphia, and there he was born on July 28, 1778. Two years afterwards his father died, and Mrs. Stewart was left to face the world alone with a young and helpless family. But her forlorn position excited the pity and the love of a generous man, and after the lapse of some

time she became the wife of Captain Britton, a member
of Congress and Commander of Washington's bodyguard. Britton was more than a stepfather to the
little Stewarts, and to Charlie he took special fancy, as,
growing up, the lad showed a brave spirit and a warm
heart. In 1790 Britton introduced him to President
Washington, an incident in his life which Charles
Stewart never forgot. In old age he often spoke of
this famous interview, dwelling particularly upon the
effect which it produced on his playmates at Philadelphia. 'Not one of them,' he would say, 'dare
knock a chip off my shoulder after that.' Britton
intended to have young Stewart trained for some quiet
and honourable post in the public service. But the lad
had his own plans. He resolved to go to sea. His
mother and stepfather protested; but Charlie settled
the question one day by running away from school and
becoming cabin boy in a coasting schooner. Britton,
like a sensible man, accepted the inevitable, and determined to help the youth along the lines he had marked
out for himself. With his own brains and grit, and by
Britton's influence, Charlie went rapidly ahead, and
before he was twenty-one rose to the command of an
Indiaman. Then he left the merchant service, and
in 1798 entered the navy as lieutenant on board the
frigate ' United States.' Thenceforth his success was
steady and remarkable.

In 1800 he was sent in the ' Experiment ' to deal with
French privateers in West Indian waters. During this
mission he displayed the fighting qualities which were
destined to make him famous, seizing privateers and
warships, re-capturing American vessels, scouring the
seas, and scattering his enemies. Nor was he less
mindful of works of humanity, for this same year he

rescued a number of women and childen who had
been wrecked while escaping from a revolution in San
Domingo.   This gallant action brought a despatch of
grateful acknowledgment from the Spanish Governor of
the island to the President of the United States.

In 1803 he was despatched on a graver mission.
The United States had made war on Tripoli for insults
offered to the American flag, and Stewart was sent to
co-operate with Captain Trible, who commanded the
American squadron in the Mediterranean.   In the
operations which followed (1803, 1804) Stewart again
distinguished himself; supporting Lieutenant Dicatur
in his successful efforts to re-capture the frigate
'Philadelphia,' which had fallen into the hand of the
Tripolitans; seizing a British and a Greek vessel,
which had attempted to run the blockade of the
harbour; and leading the attack on the enemy's flotilla
in the bombardment of the town.   For these services
he was promoted to the rank of master-commandant.

He was next sent in the 'Essex' to Tunis, where
fresh troubles had arisen.   The American Consul,
fearing an attack on the consulate, had fled to the fleet.
A council of war was held.   Operations against the
town were suggested.   But Stewart said, 'No.'   War
had not been declared by the United States against
Tunis, and the fleet, therefore, could not act.   The
fleet could not declare war.   Congress alone could do
that.   Negotiations, he urged, should be re-opened
with the Bey.   This advice was taken.   Negotiations
were re-opened.   They were carried to a successful
issue.   The Consul was sent back, and peaceful relations were established.   Thus Stewart proved himself
a skilful diplomatist as well as a hard fighter.   His
sound constitutional views and admirable tact on this

occasion won the high commendation of President Jefferson.

In 1806 he was promoted to the rank of captain, and, a season of peace having supervened, he returned to the merchant service. But on the breaking out of the war with England in 1812 he once more joined the navy. England claimed the right to search American vessels for English sailors. The United States repudiated this claim, and resolved to resist it by force. The Government at first decided to act on the defensive, collecting the fleet close to the American shore to await events. Stewart and Captain Bambridge, however, pointed out that this would be a fatal policy, and proposed instead that the vessels should put to sea and attack the Britisher wherever he was to be found. Their views finally prevailed, and in January 1813 Stewart was ordered to sail in the frigate ' Constellation ' from Washington to Norfolk, and thence to the open sea. But on reaching Norfolk he found a British fleet in the offing. Dropping down the river, the American captain anchored abreast of Craney Island, to cover the fortifications which were in course of construction. There he was greatly exposed to the enemy. But he prepared a plan of defence which baffled his foes and won the admiration of naval experts. The ' Constellation ' was anchored in the middle of a narrow channel. On each side of her were seven gunboats. A circle of booms protected the gunboats from being boarded, and enabled them at the same time to maintain a flanking fire on all assailants of the frigate. On board the frigate herself the greatest precautions were taken. The gun-decks were housed, the ports shut in, the stern ladders taken away, and the gangway cleats removed. Not a rope could be seen hanging over the side, while every means that ingenuity could suggest were devised for embarrassing, bewildering, and out-manœuvring the enemy, should he succeed in coming to close quarters. Then the carronades were charged to the muzzle with musket-balls and depressed to the nearest range, in order to sweep the water around the ship. 'As the frigate was light and unusually high out of the water, it was the opinion of the best judges that, defended as she would certainly have been under the officers who were in her, she could not have been carried without a loss of several hundred men to the enemy, if she could have been carried at all.' [1]

This was clearly the opinion of the English admiral too. For, after reconnoitring several times with great care, he came to the conclusion that no attempt could safely be made to attack the 'Constellation'; the English officers confessing that the vigilance of the ship was too much for them, and insisting that Captain Stewart must be a Scotchman, he was so actively awake.[2] So Stewart remained abreast of Craney Island until the fortifications were completed, when he returned to Norfolk Harbour.

Soon afterwards he was given the command of the 'Constitution,' and in the summer of 1813 sailed in her for the West Indies. In this cruise he captured the British war schooner 'Picton,' a letter of marque under her convoy, and several merchant vessels. Returning to America for repairs, he fell in with two British ships, which gave him chase, but, skilfully evading them, he ran his craft under the guns of Fort Marblehead, and a few days afterwards reached Boston Harbour in perfect safety. There, for a moment, he

---

[1] Fenimore Cooper, *History of the American Navy*.   [2] *Ibid.*

deserted the god of battles for the god of love, and
married Delia Tudor, 'the belle of Boston,' daughter
of Judge Tudor, who had fought against the British
in the War of Independence. But the wedding was
scarcely over when the 'Constitution' was once more
ready for sea, and Stewart bade farewell to his bride.
'What present shall I bring you home?' he asked as
they parted. 'A British frigate,' was the prompt
reply. 'I shall bring you two,' said Stewart. In
December 1814 he set sail for Europe, seizing two
British vessels on the way, destroying one, and sending
the other, which had a valuable cargo, to New York.
On February 19, 1815, at 1 P.M., the 'Constitution'
was off the coast of Spain. A sail was sighted some
twelve miles ahead. The first lieutenant reported that
she was probably a British ship of 50 guns. 'Whatever may be the number of her guns,' said Stewart,
'I'll fight. Set every stitch of canvas; lay me along-
side.' With studding sails alow and aloft the 'Constitution' sped through the waters, and by 4 P.M. she
had shortened the distance between herself and the
enemy by one-half. Then a second ship hove in sight,
and she was soon pronounced to be the consort of the
first. But the 'Constitution' sped on. 'Before sunset,
my lads,' said Stewart, 'we must flog these Britishers,
whether they have one or two gun-decks each.' The
'Constitution' now came up hand over hand, and it
was soon seen that the British ships—for so they
turned out to be—were ready for action. All three
vessels formed (as Stewart put it) an equilateral
triangle; the British ships—the 'Cyane,' 34 guns, and
the 'Levant,' 21 guns—making the base, the 'Constitution' the apex. Stewart began the action by firing
between the British ships. The British responded

with a broadside, which was, however, ineffective owing
to the American's excellent strategic position. Stewart
now concentrated his fire on the foremost vessel, the
' Levant,' raking her fore and aft. The British replied
gallantly, and a hot combat ensued. At this juncture
the sternmost ship, the ' Cyane,' crept up to the
' Constitution' and endeavoured to take her on the
weather side. But Stewart, handling his ship with
admirable skill, out-manœuvred the Britisher, and
getting to close quarters poured a tremendous broadside into her. Both ships now maintained a running
fire until about 6 P.M., when the enemy, raked, bat-
tered, and disabled, was forced to surrender. Stewart,
putting a crew on board the frigate, bore down on
the ' Levant,' passing under her stern and delivering
a well-directed broadside. The ' Levant ' briskly returned the fire, striking the ' Constitution ' amidships ;
but another broadside from the American brought
down the British colours, and made Stewart the victor
of the day. He had kept his word with his bride.
He had captured two British frigates in less than
two months since they had parted. When the battle
was over the British commanders sat in the cabin
of the ' Constitution ' and discussed the action in
the presence of Stewart, each blaming the other for
the disaster which had befallen them. ' Gentlemen,'
said Stewart, ' it is idle to discuss the question. You
both fought gallantly, and neither of you is to blame.
No matter what you had done the result would have
been the same. If you doubt it, go back to your ships
and we will fight the battle over again.'

Stewart now made for home with his two frigates.
On the way back he rested in neutral waters at Porto
Praya in Santiago, the largest of the Cape Verde

islands. But a British squadron soon hove in sight. Stewart knew that the British would not respect the neutral waters of a weak Power like Portugal ; so he slipped his cable and, followed by his prizes, set sail for America. The British squadron gave chase and quickly overhauled the Americans. Fighting was out of the question, for the ' Constitution' was under-manned, her crew being distributed in the prizes. Stewart's only plan, therefore, was to escape the enemy. Signalling the ' Cyane' and the ' Levant' to vary their courses so as to distract and scatter the pursuers, he succeeded in getting all three vessels out of range of the squadron's fire. The 'Constitution' and the 'Cyane' reached New York in safety, but the ' Levant,' pressed by two of the British ships, re-entered Porto Prayo and anchored under the shelter of the forts. The British squadron, ignoring neutral rights, sailed in and recaptured her, and thus the affair ended.

On reaching New York Stewart was welcomed with honours. Congress voted him thanks, a sword, and a gold medal, the State of Pennsylvania thanks and a sword, New York the freedom of the city, while the masses of the people greeted him with the appropriate sobriquet of ' Old Ironsides.' [1]

In September 1814 peace was made with England, and Stewart spent the rest of his life in tranquillity, although he remained still for nearly fifty years in the public service. From 1816 to 1820 he commanded the American squadron in the Mediterranean, from 1820 to 1825 he guarded American interests in the Pacific with characteristic tact, skill, and patriotism.

Afterwards he continued to fill important posts

[1] This was a name first given to the ' Constitution' ; it was now transferred to her captain.

afloat or ashore until 1862, when he was placed on the retired list as rear-admiral. The remainder of his days were serenely passed in his house at Bordentown, New Jersey, where he died, full of years and honour, on November 9, 1869. His personal appearance is thus described :

‘ Commodore Stewart was about five feet nine inches high and of a dignified and engaging presence. His complexion was fair, his hair chestnut, eyes blue, large, penetrating, and intelligent. The cast of his countenance was Roman, bold, strong, and commanding, and his head finely formed. His control of his passions was truly surprising, and under the most irritating circumstances his oldest seamen never saw a ray of anger flash from his eyes. His kindness, benevolence, and humanity were proverbial ; but his sense of justice and the requisitions of duty were as unbending as fate. In the moment of great stress and danger he was cool, and quick in judgment, as he was utterly ignorant of fear. His mind was acute and powerful, grasping the greatest or smallest subjects with the intuitive mastery of genius.’

Commodore Stewart was predeceased by his son-in-law, John Henry Parnell, who died in Dublin in 1859 ; but his daughter, Delia Tudor Stewart Parnell, lived until 1898. In the autumn of 1896 I called on her in Dublin. She had just arrived from America and was recovering from a severe illness. She looked pale and delicate, but was bright and even incisive in conversation, taking a keen interest in political affairs. Her face suggested no likeness to her remarkable son, but she had the calm, determined, self-possessed manner which always distinguished him. She knew her own mind, too. Her views might have been right or wrong,

sensible or the reverse, but she had no doubts. She
held her ground firmly in argument, and could not
easily be moved from her opinions. She was certainly
a woman of convictions, independent, fearless, resolute;
indifferent to established conventions and animated by
one fixed idea, a rooted hatred of England; or rather,
as she herself put it, of 'English dominion.' 'How
came it,' I said, 'that your son Charles had such an
antipathy to the English?' 'Why should he not?'
she answered, with American deliberation. 'Have not
his ancestors been always opposed to England? My
grandfather Tudor fought against the English in the
War of Independence. My father fought against the
English in the war of 1812, and I suppose the Parnells
had no great love for them. Sir John Parnell fought
against the Union and gave up office for Ireland, and
Sir Henry was always on the Irish side against
England, and so was my son's grandfather William.
It was very natural for Charles to dislike the English;
but it is not the English whom we dislike, or whom
he disliked. We have no objection to the English
people; we object to the English dominion. We would
not have it in America. Why should they have it in
Ireland? Why are the English so jealous of any outside interference in their affairs, and why are they
always trying to dip their fingers in everybody's pie?
The English are hated in America for their grasping
policy; they are hated everywhere for their arrogance,
greed, cant, and hypocrisy. No country must have
national rights or national aspirations but England.
That is the English creed. Well! other people don't
see it; and the English are astonished. They want
us all to think they are so goody goody. They are
simply thieves.'

Although there was no physical resemblance that I could discern between Mrs. Parnell and Charles Stewart Parnell, there were mental traits of likeness which could not be mistaken, and the opinions and sentiments of the mother were certainly the opinions and sentiments of the son.

The living members of the Parnell family are—

John Howard, who now resides at Avondale;

Henry Tudor;

Emily, who married Captain Dickinson;

Theodosia, who married Lieutenant Paget, R.N.;

Anna, who played an important part in the Land League agitation.

Those who have passed away are Fanny, a poetess of considerable ability; William; Hayes; Delia, who married Mr. Livingston Thomson; Sophia, who married Mr. MacDermott, and Charles Stewart, the story of whose life I have now to tell.

NOTE TO CHAPTER I

Parnell's Pedigree

Thomas Parnell, 1685.

Rev. Thomas Parnell, Archdeacon and Poet. Died 1717. Issue died before him. Succeeded by his brother.

John Parnell, Judge of the Court of King's Bench, Ireland; married Mary, sister of the Lord Chief Justice Whitshed. Succeeded in 1727 by his only surviving son

John Parnell, M.P. (first Baronet); married Anne, second daughter of the Hon. Michael Ward. Died 1782. Succeeded by his son

Sir John Parnell, who married Letitia Charlotte, second daughter and co-heiress of the Right Hon. Sir Arthur Brooke, Bart., Chancellor of the Exchequer, 1787. Died 1801. Issue

Henry, created Baron Congleton.

John Augustus.

William, of Avondale; married Frances, eldest daughter of the Hon. Hugh Howard. Died 1821, leaving a daughter and a son

John Henry Parnell, Justice of the Peace and Deputy-Lieutenant; married May 31, 1834, Delia Tudor, only daughter of Commodore Charles Stewart, U.S. Navy. Died 1859, leaving issue, amongst other children,

CHARLES STEWART PARNELL.

CHAPTER II

BIRTH AND EARLY DAYS

FROM Dublin to Rathdrum is a pleasant run of an hour and a half by the Dublin, Wicklow, and Wexford Railway along the edge of the sea.   Rathdrum is a neat little village, the centre for visiting the Vale of Avoca, Glendalough, and other scenes of infinite beauty in the county of Wicklow.

Avondale lies close by, and thither one day in the September of 1896 I drove to visit the home of Parnell.

The one pervading influence of this beautiful spot is melancholy.   Perhaps it is difficult to dissociate the place from the sorrowful memories which linger around the name of its late owner.   But, however that may be, a feeling of sadness and gloom possessed me as I drove up the avenue leading to the house—a spacious, even in some measure a noble, residence.   There was an appearance of neglect—a look, indeed, as if death had been there, and as if his shadow still overhung the stricken home.

As I alighted I was met at the door by the present owner, Mr. John Parnell—a quiet, courteous, hospitable, kindly gentleman.   He, too, looked sad and thoughtful, and there was for a moment in his eyes that far-away look which those who knew Charles Stewart Parnell will never forget.

On entering the hall, which has quite a baronial appearance in miniature, there was a warm, pleasant feeling. There was no fire to be seen, but a genial, comfortable atmosphere which made me at once think of what Parnell used often to say, 'I like a warm house.' In this respect Avondale is perfect. Above the hall is a little gallery, and hung all around are mementoes of the dead Chief. 'In the old days,' said Mr. Parnell, ' we used to have dances in this hall, and the band used to be placed in that gallery.' We lingered for a while in the hall. It is the distinguishing characteristic of the Parnells that they seem to be like no other people. They are absolutely unconventional. They all give you the idea of having pre-occupations quite outside their immediate surroundings. How often did one feel in walking with Parnell that he really was unconscious of your presence, that his thoughts were far, far away from you, and from anything of which you were think-ing or talking ! He did not strike you at these moments as a practical statesman. He looked a visionary, a poet, a dreamer of dreams—anything but the Charles Stewart Parnell that the world knew him to be. You felt that those eyes, with their inward look, took little notice of anything that was going on around. But, suddenly you said something that specially fixed the attention of the Chief. He at once woke up ; the eyes were turned full upon you, the whole body was swung round, and you soon found that not only had the immediate remark which produced this effect been fully taken in, but that all you had been saying for the past half-hour had been fully grasped and most thoroughly considered. Well, all the Parnells have that pre-occu-pied look that distinguished Charles, but they lack the practical skill and the genius which made him famous.

We walked through the house. Everywhere there
was an exceptionally warm, agreeable atmosphere (in
very pleasant contrast to the damp outside), but an
inexpressible air of sadness all the time. There was
absolute silence. The house might have been almost
deserted. Indeed, one felt as if one were being shown
over the castle or mansion of a great chief who had
passed away long ago, and as if nothing had been
touched since his death. There was furniture, there
were bookcases and books, all looking ancient, all apparently belonging to another time. In the hall hung a
picture of the Irish House of Commons. The scene
painted was an important debate. Curran was addressing the House. Around sat Grattan, Sir John Parnell,
and other well-known figures of the day. But the
memories which this picture awakened did not, as it
were, belong more completely to the past than did the
memories awakened in walking through the rooms at
Avondale. We stood at a window : what a beautiful
sight met our eyes ! The house stands on an eminence ;
around rise the Wicklow hills ; beneath runs the little
river Avonmore, through glens and dells that lend a
delightful charm to a glorious scene. For quite ten
minutes we exchanged not a word. It is the genius
of the Parnells to invite silence and to suggest thought.
I was thinking how beautiful everything was, and
how sad. I said at length exactly what I thought.
' It is most sad to wander through this house and to
think what might have been.'

We walked about the grounds, and new glimpses of
interest and beauty constantly caught the eye.

We passed through a wooded way close to the river's
side—a delightfully solitary spot to commune with one-
self. ' This,' said John, ' was Charlie's favourite walk.

He was fond of Avondale. "There is no place like
Avondale, Jack," he would say.'

After a ramble around the grounds we returned to
luncheon. We sat in the library. It was still a dampish
day outside, and there was a nice log fire which gave a
pleasant air of comfort to the room. When luncheon
was over, John rose, and said, 'Let us walk to the Vale
of Avoca. You have never seen it, and it is very beautiful.' To Avoca we strolled along the river-side, and
I beheld for the first time the charming spot which
Moore has made famous. Gleams of brightness lighted
up the beautiful scene, and valley and waters lay bathed
in the subdued light of the autumn sun. It was, indeed,
a glorious panorama, and Moore's lines were readily
recalled, not only by the picture on which we gazed,
but by the appropriateness of the concluding lines to
what might well have been the aspirations of Parnell
amid the storms which closed his checkered life.

> There is not in the wide world a valley so sweet
> As that vale in whose bosom the bright waters meet;
> Oh! the last rays of feeling and life must depart
> Ere the bloom of that valley shall fade from my heart.
>
> .   .   .   .
>
> Sweet Vale of Avoca! how calm could I rest
> In thy bosom of shade, with the friends I love best,
> When the storms that we feel in this cold world should
>   cease,
> And our hearts, like thy waters, be mingled in peace.

At Avondale, within ten minutes' walk of the Vale
of Avoca, Charles Stewart Parnell was born on June 27,
1846.

As a lad he was delicate but wiry, nervous but
brave, reserved but affectionate, thoughtful and deliberate, but bright and cheery. He was fond of home life,

and warmly attached to the members of his family, especially to Emily, Fanny, and John, he had few companions outside the home circle, and was very shy with strangers. Delighting in all sorts of games— outdoor and indoor—his favourite pastime was playing at soldiers. He never liked to be beaten at anything, and was resourceful and ingenious, though not too punctilious or scrupulous, in the adoption of means for out-manœuvring his opponents. One day he had a game of soldiers with his sister Fanny. 'He commanded one well-organised division, while she directed the movements of another and opposing force. These never came into actual conflict, but faced one another impassively, while their respective commanders peppered with pop-guns at the enemy's lines. For several days the war continued without apparent advantage being gained by either side. One morning, however, heavy cannonading was heard in the furthest corner of the room (produced by rolling a spiked ball across the floor). Pickets were called in, and in three minutes from the firing of the first shot there was a general engagement all along the line. Strange as it may seem, Fanny's soldiers fell by the score and hundred, while those commanded by her brother refused to waver even when palpably hit. This went on for some time until Fanny's army was utterly annihilated. It was learned, from his own confession, an hour after this Waterloo, that Charles had, before the battle began, glued his soldiers' feet securely to the floor.' [1] He also liked the game of 'follow-my-leader.' 'Charlie,' says a member of the family, 'liked playing the game of "follow-my-leader," but always insisted on being

---

[1] This story is told in Mr. Sherlock's clever little sketch of Parnell.

the leader.' 'He was very fond of fighting,' says his brother John, 'and would fight with me if he had nobody else.' But there was no malice in his combativeness. He liked fighting for fighting sake, and was quite good friends afterwards with the boy whom he might have thrashed or who might have thrashed him. Insubordinate and headstrong in the hands of those for whom he did not care, he was obedient and docile with the people he loved. Even as a boy he had a keen sense of justice, and was ever ready to assist the weak and helpless. ' As a little boy,' writes his sister, Mrs. Dickinson, ' he showed that consideration for all things helpless and weak, whether human beings or animals, for which he was distinguished in after years.' ' One day,' says his mother, ' he thought the nurse was too severe with his sister Anna. Anna was placed in a room to be punished. Charles got into the room, put Anna on a table, rolled the table into a corner, and, standing in front of it with a big stick, kept the nurse at bay.'

In 1853, when Charlie was just six years, Mr. Parnell took him to England, and put him in charge of a lady who kept a boarding-school for girls near Yeovil, in Somersetshire. It was not the custom to take boys in the school, but an exception was made in the case of little Parnell. Mr. Parnell, so he told the mistress of the school, was anxious that Charlie should ' spend some of his earlier years in England, with someone who would mother him and cure his stammering.' After returning from the mid-summer holidays of 1854 the boy fell seriously ill with typhoid fever. ' I nursed him,' says his schoolmistress, ' for six weeks, night and day, to an entire recovery,' and she adds : ' this formed a link between us which has made every event

of his life most important to me.' He was a special
favourite with this lady, who speaks of him as quick,
interesting to teach, very affectionate to those he loved
(a few), reserved to others ; therefore not a great favourite with his companions.' He remained at Yeovil
until 1855, and then returned to Avondale. For a time
afterwards he was taught by his sister's governess, and
later on by a tutor. But he got on with neither. He
argued with the governess, defied the tutor, made fun
of the clergyman who was engaged to give him religious
instruction, and generally infused a spirit of rebellion
into the household. Finally he was despatched once
more to England, taking up his abode first at the Rev.
Mr. Barton's, Kirk Langley, Derbyshire, and next at
the Rev. Mr. Wishaw's, Chipping Norton, Oxfordshire.
At both schools he was idle, read little, resisted the
authority of the under masters (though submissive to
the head of the establishment), disliked his fellow-pupils,
and was disliked by them.

On one occasion he was construing a Greek play
and mistranslated a word. Wishaw corrected him, but
Parnell argued the point. Wishaw said : 'Well, look
the word out in the Lexicon,' passing the book towards him. Parnell looked into the Lexicon, and saw
that it bore out Wishaw's views ; but coolly answered :
'Well, the Lexicon says what you say, but I expect
the Lexicon is wrong.' He cared only for two things,
cricket and mathematics, and was proficient in the
game and in the science. Still, he was not popular,
either with the masters or the boys, though the one
recognised his sharpness and ability and the other his
manliness and pluck. Even at school he showed the
reserve and aloofness which were among his traits in
after years ; and he was always glad when the vacation

came round to find himself back at Avondale free and among friends and favourites.

' I well remember,' says one who was at Chipping Norton with Parnell, ' the day the Parnells (for John accompanied Charles) came. Their mother brought them. She wore a green dress, and Wishaw came to me and said : " I say, B——, I have met one of the most extraordinary women I have ever seen—the mother of the Parnells. She is a regular rebel. I have never heard such treason in my life. Without a note of warning she opened fire on the British Government, and by Jove she did give it us hot. I have asked her to come for a drive, to show her the country, and you must come too for protection." So we went for a drive, but my presence did not prevent Mrs. Parnell from giving her views about the iniquities of the English Government in Ireland.'

My informant added : ' We liked John, who was a very good, genial fellow ; but we did not like Charles. He was arrogant and aggressive, and he tried to sit on us, and we tried to sit on him. That was about the state of the case.'

At this time, and for many years afterwards, he was subject to nervous attacks and would walk in his sleep. When the nervous attacks were on he never liked to be left alone, and would send for some person to remain with him. The feeling continued even when he had grown up to man's estate, and was, indeed, in Parliament.

One night, in the days when the British Ministers were at their wits' end to devise means for suppressing the terrible agitation, he was alone at Avondale. No one was in the house except the old housekeeper (who had been his nurse), her husband, and another servant. In the early morning the master's bell was vigorously rung, and old Peter and his wife came up. Parnell lay in bed wide awake, looking nervous and distressed. ' I am sorry,' he said, ' to ring you up, but the fact is I am not well, and have not slept all night. I am better now, but feel nervous, and would like someone to stop with me for a while.' Old Peter remained, and Parnell talked away on a variety of domestic topics until a couple of hours had passed, when he fell quietly asleep. His somnambulistic habits also continued after he left school and college. But he ultimately cured himself by tying his leg to the bed, an inconvenient but effectual remedy. He was at all times very fond of dogs, but very much afraid of hydrophobia. One day a favourite dog jumped on him in play, and pressed his teeth through the sleeve of his coat. Feeling the pressure he thought he was bitten, and ordered a car to drive for the doctor. ' But,' said his old housekeeper, ' perhaps the dog has not bitten you at all.' And on examination that was found to be the case. ' Ah! I am glad, Mary,' said he, ' for I would not like to kill him, which they say you should do if a dog bites you.' ' And foolish to say so,' urged Mary, ' for the harm is done.' ' You are very wise, Mary,' said Parnell, and he went off with the dog for a ramble over the fields.

In July 1865 Parnell went to Cambridge University. ' He was entered,' says a correspondent, ' as a pensioner on the boards of Magdalene College, Cambridge, July 1, 1865, and came into residence the following October. The rooms allotted to him were on the ground floor of the right cloister in the Pepysian buildings, looking out on the college close and immediately beneath the famous Pepysian Library. Before Parnell came up, Mrs. Parnell forewarned the tutor (Mr. Mynors Bright) that her son was given to somnambulism. The tutor accordingly instructed the college servant to sleep in an adjacent gyp-room. On the first night of his residence, however, Parnell, walking round, but not in his sleep, to take stock of his new tenement, discovered the intruder, and promptly expelled him.

'Parnell showed considerable aptitude for mathematics. One of his tutors, Mr. F. Patrick, whose lectures he attended, used often to describe how Parnell, when he had been given the ordinary solution of a problem, would generally set about to find whether it could not be solved equally well by some other method.

'On one occasion, after the college gates were closed, there being some town and gown commotion in the street outside, Parnell ran up to Mr. Patrick as he was going to ascertain the cause, exclaiming : "Sir, do let me go out to protect you." ' But his career was undistinguished at Cambridge ; and indeed the place was utterly uncongenial to him. Whether he would have taken more kindly to Irish schools and colleges may be a matter of doubt. But he certainly regarded his school and college days in England with peculiar aversion. The English he did not like. ' These English,' he would say to his brother John, ' despise us because we are Irish ; but we must stand up to them. That's the way to treat the Englishman— stand up to him.'

Parnell's English training had undoubtedly something to do in the making of him, and if it did not make him very Irish, it certainly made him very anti-English.

In 1869 he left Cambridge without taking a degree.

He was, in fact, 'sent down,' under circumstances
which have been related to me by Mr. Wilfrid A. Gill,
Fellow and Tutor of Magdalene College, Cambridge :
' The story of Parnell's being sent down from college
has never been authoritatively told, and has often been
misstated or exaggerated. The case came (at first)
before the Cambridge County Court on May 21, 1869,
and the course which the college subsequently took
was the usual one in such instances of misconduct.
A Mr. Hamilton, a merchant of Harestone, sought to
recover 33*l.* as compensation for alleged assault. To
avoid the appearance of blackmailing, he undertook, if
successful, to devote the proceeds of the suit to Adden-
brooke's Hospital. He stated in court that on Saturday,
May 1, about 10 P.M., he saw a man lying across the
path in the station road drunk, another man (Mr.
Bentley) standing over him. Asking if he could be
of any assistance, Bentley replied to him, " We want
none of your d——d help." Parnell then, springing up,
struck witness on the face and collarbone, and kicked
him on the knee. Hamilton's man retaliated by striking
Parnell.

' This was the plaintiff's statement.

' Parnell's statement in reply was as follows. He,
with three friends, drove in a fly to the station between
9 and 10 P.M. to take some light refreshment, " sherry,
champagne, and biscuit," at the restaurant. In half
an hour they prepared to return home. Parnell, with
one of them, sat down and waited in the station road,
while the others went in search of a fly. Meanwhile
two men passing by exclaimed: " Hullo, what's the
matter with this 'ere cove," or words to that effect.
Bentley replied that he wanted no interference.
Hamilton answered in gross language. Then he

(Parnell) first interposed, striking at Hamilton but missing him. Hamilton next struck Parnell, whereupon Parnell knocked him down. Hamilton's man then attacked Parnell, who knocked him down also, though he at once offered a hand to raise him. Parnell never kicked Hamilton. A police constable corroborated Parnell's statement that he (Parnell) was perfectly sober. After other evidence had been called, Parnell's counsel admitted to some fault on his client's part, and stated that he would not resist a verdict. He asked, however, for nominal damages, little harm really having been done; and there also seemed to be some attempt at extortion.

'The judge held that, the assault being admitted, the damages should be substantial. The jury, after some consideration, found damages for twenty guineas.

'On May 26 a college meeting was convened, at which it was resolved to send down Parnell for the remainder of the term in consequence of the misconduct proved against him. There being only two weeks before the end of the term, the actual punishment was not a severe one, and, had Parnell wished it, there was nothing to prevent his resuming residence in the following term. He did not, however, return to Cambridge.'

Up to this time Parnell had paid no attention to Irish affairs. He had probably never read an Irish history or political tract. He knew nothing of the career of his great-grandfather, Sir John Parnell, or his grand-uncle, Sir Henry, or his grandfather, William Parnell. At Avondale politics were tabooed, and when Charles was there he spent his time fishing or shooting, riding or playing cricket. Ireland was almost a closed book to him. Something he had certainly heard of

the rebellion of 1798 from the peasants in the neighbourhood, but the effect of these stories was transient.

How came Parnell, then, to turn his attention to
Irish affairs ?   He has himself answered this question.
He has told us that it was the Fenian movement that
first awakened his interest in Ireland.

Most of my readers know that about the year 1859
two men who had taken part in the Young Ireland
rising—John O'Mahony and James Stephens—formed
a political organisation for the purpose of separating
Ireland from England and of establishing an Irish
republic.   This organisation, called by its founders
and members the Irish Revolutionary Brotherhood,
was popularly known as the Fenian Society.   It grew
steadily in numbers and influence.   Fenian bodies
were scattered throughout Ireland, Scotland, England,
and America, and within five years of its formation it
had already become a power in the land.

In 1863 a Fenian newspaper, the ' Irish People,'
was founded, under the management of John O'Leary,
assisted by Thomas Clarke Luby and Charles Kickham.   Its office was within a stone's-throw of Dublin
Castle, and there, under the very shadow of the
authorities, it preached week by week a crusade of
insurrection and war.   Among the contributors to the
' Irish People ' was a handsome young girl, who used
to come to the office accompanied by a tall lanky youth.
Entering the editor's room, she would place her ' copy '
in his hands and depart.   The ' copy' generally consisted
of some stirring verses which breathed a spirit of treason
and revolt.   The girl was Miss Fanny Parnell, and
the youth her brother John.   Fenianism soon invaded
Avondale. The political indifference which had hitherto

prevailed there gradually disappeared, and Ireland came to have a foremost place in the thoughts of the family. Mrs. Parnell especially took a keen interest in the movement, and did not hesitate to express her views and sympathies in the Government circles in which she moved. Lord Carlisle, the Lord Lieutenant in 1864, was a friend of the Parnell household. Mrs. Parnell, both at his table and at her own, felt no hesitation in condemning British misrule and justifying Irish discontent. In 1865 there was a crisis: the Government swooped down on the 'Irish People,' and arrested the editor and some of the leading members of the staff. State trials, the suspension of the Habeas Corpus Act, and an abortive insurrection followed. Fenianism was the question of the hour. People thought and spoke of nothing else. The whole empire watched the Fenian trials with interest and anxiety. In the dock the Fenian prisoners demeaned themselves like men of faith, courage, and honesty. They neither faltered nor flinched. Baffled for the moment, they believed that their cause would yet triumph, and they boldly told their judges that they neither repented nor despaired. 'You ought to have known,' said Judge Fitzgerald, in passing sentence on O'Leary, 'that the game you entered upon was desperate—hopeless.'

O'Leary. 'Not hopeless.'

Judge. 'You ought further to have known that insurrection in this country or revolution in this country meant not insurrection alone, but that it meant a war of extermination.'

O'Leary. 'No such thing.'

Judge. 'You have lost.'

O'Leary. 'For the present.'

Judge. 'It is my duty to announce to you that the

sentence of the court is such as may deter others—we
hope it will.'

O'Leary. ' I hope not.'

Judge. ' The sentence of the court is that you be
detained in penal servitude for twenty years.'

'As long as there are men in my country,' said
Luby, 'prepared to expose themselves to every difficulty
and danger, and who are prepared to brave captivity—
and even death itself, if need be—this country cannot
be lost.'

Years afterwards Isaac Butt, the advocate who
defended almost all the Fenian prisoners, wrote of
them :

' Whatever obloquy gathered round them at first,
there are few men who now deny to the leaders of the
Fenian conspiracy the merits of perfect sincerity, of a
deep and honest conviction of the righteousness of their
cause, and of an unselfish and disinterested devotion to
the cause. I was placed towards most of them in a
relation which gave me some opportunity of observing
them, in circumstances that try men's souls. Both I
and those that were associated with me in that relation
have often been struck by their high-mindedness and
truthfulness, that shrunk with sensitiveness from sub-
terfuges which few men in their position would have
thought wrong. No mean or selfish instruction ever
reached us. Many, many, many messages were conveyed to us which were marked by a punctilious and
almost over-strained anxiety to avoid even a semblance
of departure from the strictest line of honour. There
was not one of them who would have purchased safety
by a falsehood, by a concession that would have brought
dishonour on his cause, or by a disclosure that would
have compromised the safety of a companion. It seems

like exaggeration to say this, but this is a matter on
which I can write as a witness, and therefore am bound
by the responsibility of one. I know that my testimony
would be confirmed by all who had the same means of
observing them as myself. The conviction was forced
upon us all, that whatever the men were, they were no
vulgar revolutionists disturbing their country for any
base or selfish purpose ; they were enthusiasts of great
heart and lofty minds, and in the bold and unwavering
courage with which one and all they met the doom
which the law pronounced upon their crime against its
authority, there was a startling proof that their cause
and their principles had power to inspire in them the
faith and the endurance which elevated suffering into
martyrdom.'

No one followed the Fenian trials with keener
interest than Mrs. Parnell. But her interest was not
merely of a passive character. Her house in Temple
Street, Dublin, was placed under police surveillance.
One night a batch of detectives paid a surprise visit
and insisted on searching the premises. Mrs. Parnell
(who was alone with her daughter) protested, but the
police remained ; the daughter left, and spent the night
at Hood's Hotel, Great Brunswick Street. The police
went on with their work, and were rewarded for their
pains by finding a sword, which they carried off in
triumph. The sword belonged to Charles, who was at
that time an officer in the Wicklow Militia. 'D——
their impudence in taking my sword,' he said afterwards, on hearing the news, ' but I shall make them give
it back precious soon ' (which he did). ' Perhaps one
day I will give the police something better to do than
turning my sister into the street. I call it an outrage
on the part of the Government of this country.'

But the event which was destined to turn Parnell's thoughts fully to Irish politics now occurred. In September 1867 two Fenian leaders, Kelly and Deasy, were arrested in Manchester. Their comrades in the city resolved to rescue them. Accordingly, as the van conveying them was on its way from the police court to the jail at Bellevue it was attácked. The prisoners were liberated, and a policeman, Sergeant Brett, was shot dead in the struggle. Many Fenians were arrested for complicity in this affray, including Allen, Larkin, Condon, and O'Brien, who were tried, convicted, and sentenced to death. In the dock they showed a bold front, a dauntless spirit, and an abiding faith in their cause. All protested their innocence of the crime of murder, but did not shrink from the charge of treason. Indeed, they gloried in it. 'No man in this court,' said Allen, 'regrets the death of Sergeant Brett more than I do, and I positively say in the presence of the Almighty and ever-living God that I am innocent— ay, as innocent as any man in this court. I don't say this for the sake of mercy. I want no mercy, I'll have no mercy. I'll die, as many thousands have died, for the sake of their beloved land and in defence of it.' 'I was not even present,' said Condon,[1] 'when the rescue took place. But I do not accuse the jury of wilfully wishing to convict, but I believe they were prejudiced. We have, however, been convicted, and, as a matter of course, we accept our death. We are not afraid to die. I only trust that those who are to be tried after us will have a fair trial, and that our blood will satisfy the craving which, I understand, exists. You will soon send us before God, and I am perfectly prepared to go. I have nothing to regret, or

[1] Condon was afterwards reprieved.

to retract, or take back. I can only say, " God save
Ireland ! " ' ' God save Ireland ! ' repeated all the prisoners, and ' God save Ireland ! ' has since become a
political watchword in the country.

All England was profoundly moved by this Manchester affair. Irish discontent and Irish treason were
painfully brought home to the English people. But
the first feeling was one of vengeance and retaliation,
when the mob which gathered round the gaol the night
before the execution, shouting, cheering, and reviling
the men within, singing ' Rule, Britannia,' performing
break-down dances, and bursting into yells of glee, only
too faithfully represented the general feeling of triumph
and satisfaction at the fate of the doomed men. On
the morning of November 23, 1867, Allen, Larkin, and
O'Brien perished on the scaffold. Nothing can, perhaps, better show the chasm which separates English
from Irish political opinion than the way in which the
news of their execution was received in each country.
In England it awoke a pæan of joy: in Ireland it
produced a growl of indignation and horror. In the
one country they were regarded as murderers and
traitors, in the other as heroes and martyrs. Up to
this time a section of the Home Rulers was more or less
out of sympathy with the Fenian movement. But the
Manchester executions brought all Irish Nationalists
into line. ' Commemorative funerals' were held in
almost every principal city in Ireland, and Consti-
tutional-Nationalists and Revolutionists marched side
by side in honour of the Manchester martyrs. ' The
Dublin procession,' says Mr. A. M. Sullivan, himself a
persistent opponent of Fenianism, ' was a marvellous
display. The day was cold, wet, and gloomy, yet it
was computed that 150,000 persons participated in the

demonstration, 60,000 of them marching in a line over a route some three or four miles in length. As the three hearses, bearing the names of the executed men, passed through the streets, the multitudes that lined the streets fell on their knees, every head was bared, and not a sound was heard save the solemn notes of the "Dead March in Saul" from the bands, or the sobs that burst occasionally from the crowd. At the cemetery gate the procession formed into a vast assemblage, which was addressed by Mr. Martin in feeling and forcible language, expressive of the national sentiment on the Manchester executions. At the close once more all heads were bared, a prayer was offered, and the mourning thousands peacefully sought their homes.' To Englishmen these demonstrations were only a proof of Irish sympathy with crime. A policeman had been killed by a gang of Irish revolutionists, and Ireland went mad over the transaction. That was all that Englishmen saw in the Manchester celebrations. But Parnell, despite his English surroundings, caught the Irish feeling on the instant. 'It was no murder,' he said, then and afterwards. It was not the intention of Allen, Larkin, and O'Brien to kill Sergeant Brett. Their sole object was to rescue their comrades. And why not? Was England to sit in judgment on Fenianism, or upon anything Irish? The Irish were justified in overthrowing the English rule, if they could. The Fenians who rescued Kelly and Deasy had a better case than the English Government which punished them. They acted with pluck and manliness. What they did they did in the open day. A few Irishmen faced the police and mob of a hostile city, and snatched their comrades from the clutches of the law—the law to which they morally owed no allegiance. The rescue

was a gallant act, the execution a brutal and a
cowardly deed. A strong and generous Government
would never have carried out the extreme penalties of
the law. But the English people were panic-stricken.
The presence of Fenianism in their midst filled them
with alarm, and they clamoured for blood. The killing
of Sergeant Brett was no murder; the execution of the
Fenians was.[1]

That was the Irish view of the case, and that was
the view of Parnell. But, though the execution of
Allen, Larkin, and O'Brien made Parnell think about
Ireland, he did not for several years afterwards take an
active part in Irish politics. He never did anything in
a hurry. He thought out every question. He looked
carefully around before taking any forward step. But
when once he put his hand to the plough he never
turned back. When I was at Avondale in 1896 I met a
middle-aged man, a retainer of the family, who remembered Parnell as a boy and a man. He said to me : ' You
see, sir, if it was only the picking up of that piece of
stick (pointing to the ground), Master Charles would
take about half an hour thinking of it. He never would
do anything at once, and when he grew up it was just
the same. I would sometimes ask him to make some
alterations about the place. " I will think of that,
Jim," he would say, and I would think he would forget
all I said; but he would come back, maybe in two
days' time, and say, " I have considered it all," and
would do what I asked, or not, just as he liked.'

---

[1] It is quite clear that it was not the intention of the Fenians to kill
Sergeant Brett. Brett was on guard inside the van. He was asked to
give up the keys, but refused. Allen then fired to force the lock of the
door. The ball penetrated, and killed Brett. Shaw, a police-constable,
swore at the trial that it was his impression that Allen fired to knock
the lock off.—*Annual Register*, 1867.

Parnell's favourite pastime was cricket. He became captain of the Wicklow Eleven, and threw himself with zest into the game. A strict disciplinarian, always bent on victory, and ever ready to take advantage of every chance (which the rules allowed) to outwit his opponents, reserved, uncompromising, self-willed, he was obeyed and trusted rather than courted or liked.

'Before Mr. Parnell entered politics,' says one who knew him in those days, 'he was pretty well known in the province of Leinster in the commendable character of cricketer. We considered him ill-tempered and a little hard in his conduct of that pastime. For example, when the next bat was not up to time, Mr. Parnell, as captain of the fielders, used to claim a wicket. Of course he was within his right in doing so, but his doing it was anything but relished in a country where the game is never played on the assumption that this rule will be enforced. In order to win a victory he did not hesitate to take advantage of the strict letter of the law. On one occasion a match was arranged between the Wicklow team and an eleven of the Phœnix Club, to be played on the ground of the latter in the Phœnix Park. Mr. Parnell's men, with great trouble and inconvenience, many of them having to take long drives in the early morning, assembled on the ground. A dispute occurred between Mr. Parnell and the captain of the Phœnix team. The Wicklow men wished their own captain to give in, and let the match proceed. Mr. Parnell was stubborn, and, rather than give up his point, marched his growling eleven back. That must have been a pleasant party so returning without their expected day's amusement, but the Captain did not care. In later years Mr. Parnell used to use the Irish party much as he used the Wicklow eleven.'[1]   He was very fond of taking long rides in the country with his sister, Mrs. Dickinson.   'Used he ever,' I asked her, 'to talk politics upon these occasions?' She said: 'No. He was completely wrapped up in his family, and our conversations were chiefly about family matters and country life.   The only political incident which seemed to affect him was the execution of the Manchester martyrs.   He was very indignant at that. It first called forth his aversion for England, and set him thinking of Ireland.   But he rarely talked politics to any of us.   He brooded a great deal, and was always one to keep things to himself.'   'Did you ever see him read in those days?' I asked another member of his family.   'The only book I ever saw him read,' he said, 'was that (pointing to Youatt's " The Horse "), and he knew that very well.'

Within a few miles of Avondale was Parnell's shooting - lodge, Aughavannah.   Aughavannah was originally a barrack, built in 1798 for the soldiers who scoured that part of the country for rebels.   The barrack ultimately fell into the hands of the Parnells, and was converted into a shooting-lodge ; here Parnell spent several weeks in the autumn of each year.   At the back of the barrack was a granite stone, where —so runs the tradition—the rebels sharpened their pikes.   Parnell was very fond of showing this stone to his friends, and would, when in the humour, tell them stories of '98.   Here is one of them.   A rebel was seized by the soldiers.   He was court-martialled, and ordered to be whipped to death.   The sentence was carried out, but the lashes were inflicted on his belly instead of on his back.   The old lodge-keeper at

[1] *Pall Mall Budget.*

Avondale, who had witnessed the scene, would say
how the man shrieked in his agony and cried for
mercy, calling upon the colonel of the regiment,
Colonel Yeo, until his lacerated body fell, bleeding and
torn, lifeless to the ground. Parnell seems to have
had some knowledge of the rebel Holt, picked up, no
doubt, from the tradition of the peasants rather than
the memoirs of the insurgent himself. Holt was a
Wicklow man and Protestant, and had led the rebels
in his native county with courage, skill, and chivalry.
Parnell always felt that if there had been many chiefs
like Holt the rebellion might have had a different
termination. But Parnell was very proud of Wicklow
and Wicklow men. 'I am,' he would say, ' an Irishman first but a Wicklow man afterwards.'

In 1871 he went to America on a visit to his
brother John, who had settled in Alabama, and there
he remained a twelvemonth. ' While he was with you
at that time,' I asked John, ' did he show any inclina-
tion to go into politics or take up any career ? ' John
said : ' No, he never talked politics. But he was never
a good man at conversation ; and you could never very
easily find out what he was thinking about. If something turned up to draw him, then he would talk ; and
I was often surprised to find on those occasions that he
knew things of which he never spoke before. Something practical was always necessary to draw him.
One day we called to see a State Governor. When we
came away, Charlie surprised me by saying, " You see
that fellow despises us because we are Irish. But the
Irish can make themselves felt everywhere if they are
self-reliant and stick to each other. Just think of that
fellow, where he has come from, and yet he despises
the Irish." That always stuck in Charlie—that the Irish

were despised. You see,' continued John, 'none of
us take in many things at once. But we are awful to
stick to anything we take up. The idea that the Irish
were despised was always in Charlie's mind. But you
would never know it if some particular thing did not
happen to stir him up at the moment. In those days
he was ready to take offence, and was even quarrelsome,
though he worked himself out of all that afterwards.
One day I took him to see a house I was building for a
man, an Irishman too. The man complained of something I had done. I did not object. It was quite fair,
and we were very good friends. While he was pointing
out these things to me, Charlie went quietly over the
house, and then, coming back, walked up to the man
and said very coolly : "I tell you what it is, the house
is a deal too good for you." "You're a d——d liar," said
the man. In an instant Charlie's coat was off, and it
was only by the greatest effort that I prevented them
from flying at one another. We then all went off to
luncheon, and were as hearty as possible. We all
laughed at the row, and I said there was no doubt but
we were all Irishmen. The man—his name was Ryan,
a very good fellow—told us that in America they always
say "it takes two Irishmen to make a row, three to
make a revolt, and four to make an insurrection."
Charlie said if we knew our powers we could make
ourselves felt in America and everywhere else.'

While in America Parnell was nearly killed in a
railway accident. He and John were travelling
together. There was a collision on the line. John
was flung to the bottom of the car with great violence,
and there he lay bruised and unconscious. Parnell
was unhurt. Seeing John on the ground, he said to
the other occupant of the car, ' My brother is killed.

I expect we shall be killed next, for this car is certain
to tumble down the embankment.'   The car, however,
did not tumble down the embankment, and Parnell
escaped without a scratch.   John was laid up with a
severe illness after the accident, and Parnell nursed
him all the time.   'No one,' said John, 'could have
been a better nurse than Charlie; he was thoughtful,
patient, and gentle as a woman.'

In 1872 Parnell, accompanied by John, returned to
Avondale.   Vote by ballot had just been extended to
Ireland.   The measure drew Parnell's attention once
more to politics.   He thought it was of greater practical importance than either the Irish Church Act or
the Land Act, for it emancipated the voters. 'Now,' he
said, 'something can be done if full advantage will be
taken of this Ballot Act.'   His sympathies had gone
out to the Fenians after the Manchester executions.
But he did not see how Fenianism was to be practically
worked.   The Ballot Act first suggested to him a
mode of practical operation.   The Irish voter was now
a free man.   He could send whom he liked to Parliament.   He was master of the situation.   An independent Irish party, free from the touch of English
influence, was the thing wanted, and this party could
be elected under the Ballot Act.

One morning in 1873 the two brothers were at
breakfast at Avondale.   John, who was essentially a
Democrat, said, 'Well, Charlie, why don't you go into
Parliament?   You are living all alone here, you represent the family, and you ought to take an interest
in public affairs.   Our family were always mixed up
with politics, and you ought to take your place.   Go
in and help the tenants, and join the Home Rulers.'
Parnell answered—knocking the tip of an egg and

peering into it suspiciously, as if its state was much
more important to him than Parliament—'I do not
see my way. I am in favour of the tenants and Home
Rule, but I do not know any of the men who are
working the movement.' John replied : 'It is easy to
know the men. Go and see them.' 'Ah,' replied
Parnell, 'that is what I don't quite see. I must look
more around for myself first ; I must see a little more
how things are going ; I must make out my own way.
The whole question is English dominion. That is
what is to be dealt with, and I do not know what the
men in these movements intend.' Then, with a little
banter, in which he occasionally indulged, he added,
'But, John, why don't you go into Parliament ? Why
should not we make a start with you ? You are the
head of the family. In fact, Avondale is more yours
than mine. Do you lead the way.'

This little conversation satisfied John that Parnell
had been thinking more of politics than his family at
all suspected, though with characteristic reticence he
kept his own counsel. Nor did he even after this
show any disposition to resume the subject. He
relapsed into his old state of apparent indifference,
devoting himself mainly to family and local affairs.

He had, indeed, become a member of the Synod of
the Disestablished Church, but he took more interest
in the mining operations which he had then commenced on his estate than in the affairs of that
institution. And so the last days of the year 1873
found Parnell still living the life of a quiet country
gentleman, still leaving politics severely alone.

CHAPTER III

THE HOME RULE MOVEMENT

'WELL,' said an Old Irelander to me towards the end
of the year 1870, 'out of evil comes good. The unfortunate Fenians have made the English disestablish
the Church (1869) and pass the Land Act (1870).
But, poor devils! what good have they done for themselves? Penal servitude and the gallows.' 'You are
right enough, sir,' said a Fenian who was standing
by. 'The difference between the Whigs and Fenians
is, the Fenians do good for Ireland but no good for
themselves, the Whigs do good for themselves and no
good for Ireland.' 'Begad, I believe you are right,'
said the Old Irelander, who was a frank and genial old
fellow.

Old Irelander and Fenian were both right. Fenianism had roused the English conscience, had 'rung the
chapel bell,' and the result was disestablishment and the
first great measure of land reform. Mr. Gladstone has
made the matter very plain. 'It has only been since
the termination of the American war,' he said, 'and the
appearance of Fenianism that the mind of this country
has been greatly turned to the consideration of Irish
affairs. . . . In my opinion, and in the opinion of
many with whom I communicated, the Fenian conspiracy has had an important influence with respect to
Irish policy; but it has not been an influence in

determining, or in affecting in the slightest degree, the
convictions which we have entertained with respect to
the course proper to be pursued in Ireland. The
influence of Fenianism was this—that when the
Habeas Corpus Act was suspended, when all the consequent proceedings occurred, when the overflow of
mischief came into England itself, when the tranquillity of the great city of Manchester was disturbed,
when the Metropolis itself was shocked and horrified
by an inhuman outrage, when a sense of insecurity
went abroad far and wide—the right honourable
gentleman [Mr. Gathorne-Hardy] was, better than we,
cognisant of the extent to which the inhabitants of the
different towns of the country were swearing themselves in as special constables for the maintenance of
life and property—then it was when these phenomena
came home to the popular mind, and produced that
attitude of attention and preparedness on the part of
the whole of the population of this country which
qualified them to embrace in a manner foreign to their
habits in other times the vast importance of the Irish
controversy.'

Again, answering Mr. Gathorne-Hardy in the
House of Commons on April 3, 1868, he said:

'The right hon. gentleman says, "Why did you
not deal with the Irish Church in 1866, when you
asked for the suspension of the Habeas Corpus Act?"
My answer is, for a perfectly plain and simple reason.
In the first place, circumstances were not ripe then as
they are now. Circumstances, I repeat, were not ripe,
in so far as we did not then know so much as we know
now with respect to the intensity of Fenianism.'

But though Fenianism forced disestablishment and
land reform, the Fenians cared little either for the

Church or the land.   Their movement was purely
political, and none of the leaders at that time saw any
advantage in associating a struggle for national freedom with an agitation for the redress of material
grievances.   Accordingly, while the Constitutionalists
pushed forward their demands for Church and land
reform, the Fenians concentrated themselves on a
movement for the release of their comrades who had
been sent to penal servitude in the years 1865, 1866,
and 1867.

In 1868 the first Amnesty Association was formed.
Isaac Butt became its president.

Butt was one of the most remarkable men who
have appeared in Irish politics during the past half-
century.   Born at Glenfin, in the County Donegal, in
1813, he was educated at the Royal School, Raphoe,
and entered Trinity College, Dublin (as a scholar) in
1832.   He took his degree in 1835, became LL.B. in
1836, and M.A. and LL.D. in 1840.   As one of the
founders and for a time editor of the Dublin ' University Magazine,' he showed the culture and literary
skill which always distinguished him.   In 1836 he was
appointed Whately Professor of Political Economy at
Dublin University, and in 1838 he was called to the Bar.
In 1841 he gave up his professorship, and thenceforth
devoted himself absolutely to law and public affairs.
Chosen in 1840 by the Municipal Corporation of
Dublin—then a Tory stronghold—to defend their
privileges before the House of Lords and to oppose
the Irish Municipal Reform Bill, he was, in recognition
of his able but unsuccessful efforts, elected an alderman of the Reformed Corporation.   He now became
one of the leading champions of Conservatism in the
City, and was singled out to confront O'Connell in

the famous three days' debate on Repeal, which took place in the City Hall in February 1843.

In 1844 he was called to the Inner Bar, and in the same year he founded the 'Protestant Guardian,'[1] which became a leading Tory organ in the Press. But his Toryism did not prevent him from defending the Young Ireland leader, Gavan Duffy, in 1848, or indeed from showing a general appreciation of the Nationalist position. He first entered Parliament in 1852 as the Tory member for Harwich; but in the general election of the same year he was returned as a Liberal Conservative for Youghal, which borough he continued to represent until 1865.

In 1865, when the Fenian prisoners looked around for leading counsel to defend them, they at once fixed on Butt. He stood in the front rank of his profession, he had been associated with the Young Ireland trials, and his politics were nothing to men who despised Whig and Tory alike. Butt flung himself zealously into the cause of his clients. He practically gave up all other business at the Bar, and his advocacy of the hopeless case of the rebels was among the most earnest and brilliant of his forensic efforts. From 1865 to 1869 these Fenian trials dragged on, and towards the end Butt became the friend as well as the advocate of the prisoners. The purity of their intentions, the uprightness of their aims, their courage, their honesty, their self-sacrifice, produced a deep impression on the generous and impulsive advocate, and made him feel that there was something essentially rotten in the State when such men were driven to such desperate courses.

[1] Afterwards incorporated in the *Warder*. See article on 'Butt' in *Dictionary of National Biography*.

'Mr. Gladstone,' he exclaimed, 'said that Fenianism taught him the intensity of Irish disaffection. It taught me more and better things. It taught me the depth, the breadth, the sincerity of that love of fatherland that misgovernment had tortured into disaffection, and misgovernment, driving men to despair, had exaggerated into revolt.' And again he says : ' The conviction forced itself upon everyone that the men whom they saw meet their fate with heroism and dignity were not a mere band of assassins actuated by base motives, but real earnest patriots, moved by unselfish thoughts, and risking all in that which they believed to be their country's cause. The lofty faith of their principles and their cause which breathed through the words of many of them as they braved the sentence which closed upon them all hope made it impossible for anyone to doubt their sincerity—difficult even for those who most disapproved of their enterprise to withhold from them the tribute of compassion and respect.'

Butt was not content with advocating the cause of the Fenian prisoners when they stood in the dock. He followed them to the prison cells, and finally led the movement which was initiated towards the end of 1868 to obtain their release. One of the first of the great amnesty meetings was held at Cabra, near Dublin, in October 1868. Butt took the chair. It was an extraordinary gathering. Quite 200,000 people were present. Butt himself describes the scene : ' Words of far more power than any I can command would fail to give expression to emotions I can but faintly recall, when I stood in the presence of 200,000 human beings, and was conscious that every eye in that vast assemblage was turned upon me, and felt that every heart in that mighty multitude—far, far beyond the limit to which the human voice could reach—was throbbing with the belief that I was giving utterance to the one thought that was actuating all. That scene was worth the memories of a life. Into every human form in that great multitude God had breathed the breath of life as each of them became a living soul. In the voice of that multitude spoke the spirit which that breath had sent into the heart of man. There was an awe and solemnity in the presence of so many living souls. Dense masses of men, outnumbering the armies that decided the fate of Europe on the field of Waterloo, covered a space of ground upon the far-off verge of which their forms were lost in distance. Around that verge the gorgeous banners of a hundred trades' unions, recalling to the mind the noblest glories of the Italian free republics, glistened in the brightness of a clear autumn sun. Words fail to describe—imagination and memory fail in reproducing—the image of a scene which, like recollections of Venice, is so different from all the incidents of ordinary life that it seems like the remembrance of a vision or a dream.'

Amnesty meetings were now held throughout the country. Amnesty became a rallying cry. Constitu- tional-Nationalists and Fenians stood shoulder to shoulder on the amnesty platforms. No word was now raised against the Fenians by any Home Ruler; and even outside the Nationalist ranks altogether there was a feeling of admiration and pity for the men who had shown their readiness to sacrifice liberty and life in the cause they held dearer than both. Many people did not see that these amnesty meetings were making all the time for Home Rule. They were bringing all Irish Nationalists, constitutional and revolutionary, together. They were inspiring Isaac Butt, they were inspiring

the whole country, with intense national feeling. The
farmers might be content with land reform; the old
Catholic Whigs might be content with disestablishment; but outside there was a new generation who
believed that all would be lost if national freedom were
not gained. Accordingly, neither disestablishment nor
land reform checked for one moment the flowing
tide. Indeed, the first measure served only to accelerate
it by driving discontented Protestants into the National
ranks. The upshot was the establishment of the
' Home Government Association of Ireland.' [1]   On
May 19, 1870, a remarkable gathering met at the
Bilton Hotel, Dublin. There were Protestants and
Catholics, Tories and Liberals, Orangemen and
Fenians—all come together to protest against the
legislative union with Great Britain.

Speaking, some years afterwards, to a Fenian
leader who was at this meeting, he said to me : ' I went
under an assumed name to watch the proceedings.
The suppression of the rising in 1867 and the imprisonment of our people did not damp our energies a bit.
We kept working away just the same as ever, with this
difference, that we had thousands of sympathisers in

[1] To show the influence that Fenianism had gained in the country
the case of the Tipperary election of November 1869 may be cited. The
Liberal candidate was Mr. Heron, a popular Catholic barrister. The
Fenians suddenly started in opposition a Fenian convict, O'Donovan
Rossa, who was actually undergoing his term of penal servitude. Of
course he was an impossible candidate, and everyone knew it. But he
was started as a protest against Whiggery, to rally the Fenians. He
was elected, to the amazement of the loyalists, by 1,311 votes to 1,028.
Of course the election was declared void, and in January 1870 a new
election took place. Mr. Heron stood again. There was a difference of
opinion now among the Fenians. Some said enough had been done for
honour in Rossa's candidature. Others said ' No '; and these latter put
up Kickham, who had just been liberated on account of serious illness.
However, Kickham declared he would never enter the English Parliament.
Nevertheless, the Fenians demanded a poll, with the result—Heron,
1,668 ; Kickham, 1,664.

1870 who would not touch us at all in 1865. In fact, we had a stronger hold on the country after the rising than we had before. We were anxious to follow the new movement carefully. Even at that date the idea of the "new departure" had occurred to some of us. We felt that we might have a long time to wait before we could put 20,000 or 30,000 men into the field to fight England; but we thought that by taking part in every political or semi-political movement that was going on we could exercise much influence, and mould these movements to our own ends. An Irish Parliament was certainly the next best thing to absolute separation, and many of us would be quite content to close the account with England on the basis of legislative independence. But then we had to see that this Parliament would not be a sham. If the Home Rule movement were a genuine affair, we would help it all we could. But we had to take care it should be genuine; we had to take care that there should be no backsliding on the part of the Parliamentarians. So I went to watch and report. I gave the name of James Martin, and I was greatly amused afterwards to find myself figuring in A. M. Sullivan's book as "James Martin," J.P., ex-High Sheriff. I believe Martin, who is an old Catholic Whig, was very indignant at finding his name in such doubtful company. What would he have said if he had known that it had been used as a blind by a Fenian centre?" [1]

The first resolution of the meeting—carried by acclamation—was:

> 'That it is the opinion of this meeting that the true remedy for the evils of Ireland is the establish-

[1] Before the meeting at the Bilton Hotel 'Mr. Martin' met Butt at the lodgings of another Fenian, when an understanding was arrived at

ment of an Irish Parliament with full control over our domestic affairs.'

The objects of the new association were then defined specifically thus :

I.—This association is formed for the purpose of obtaining for Ireland the right of self-government by means of a National Parliament.

II.—It is hereby declared, as the essential principle of this association, that the objects, and THE ONLY OBJECTS, contemplated by its organisation are :

> To obtain for our country the right and privilege of managing our own affairs, by a Parliament assembled in Ireland, composed of her Majesty the Sovereign, and her successors, and the Lords and Commons of Ireland ;

> To secure for that Parliament, under a federal arrangement, the right of legislating for and regulating all matters relating to the internal affairs of Ireland, and control over Irish resources and revenues, subject to the obligation of contributing our just proportion of the Imperial expenditure ;

> To leave to an Imperial Parliament the power of dealing with all questions affecting the Imperial Crown and Government, legislation regarding the Colonies and other dependencies of the Crown, the relations of the United Empire with foreign States, and all matters appertaining to the defence and the stability of the empire at large ;

> To attain such an adjustment of the relations between the two countries, without any interference with the prerogatives of the Crown, or any disturbance of the principles of the constitution.

III.—The association invites the co-operation of all Irishmen who are willing to join in seeking for Ireland a federal arrangement based upon these general principles.

IV.—The association will endeavour to forward the object it has in view, by using all legitimate means of influencing public sentiment, both in Ireland and Great Britain, by taking all opportunities of instructing and informing public opinion, and by seeking to unite Irishmen of all creeds and classes in one national

---

that the Fenians would at least assume an attitude of benevolent neutrality towards the ' open movement.'

movement, in support of the great national object hereby contemplated.

V.—It is declared to be an essential principle of the association that, while every member is understood by joining it to concur in its general object and plan of action, no person so joining is committed to any political opinion, except the advisability of seeking for Ireland the amount of self-government contemplated in the objects of the association.

Thus was the Home Rule movement launched. The words 'Home Rule' were the invention of Butt. He thought the old cry of 'Repeal' would frighten the English; but that the phrase 'Home Rule' would commend itself to everyone as reasonable and innocent.

The new movement was opposed by the orthodox Liberals and the orthodox Tories; by the 'Freeman's Journal,' the most powerful newspaper in the country; and, more important than all, by the Catholic Church. But it nevertheless grew and prospered. In 1871 came the first trial of strength. There were four by-elections—Meath, West Meath, Galway (city), and Limerick (city). Home Rulers were returned for all: John Martin for Meath, P. J. Smyth for West Meath, Mitchell-Henry for Galway, and Butt himself for Limerick. In 1872 there were two more important by-elections, Kerry and Galway (county). Home Rulers were once more put forward for both, and were returned—Mr. Blennerhassett for Kerry, and Colonel Nolan for Galway.

Great preparations were now made for the General Election, which it was felt would soon come. In November 1873 a Home Rule Conference was held in Dublin; the name of the organisation was changed from the 'Home Government Association' to the 'Home Rule League.' The 'Freeman's Journal' and the Church gave in their adhesion to the movement;

and further resolutions were passed defining the object
of the society.   It was declared, among other things :

'That as the basis of the proceedings of this conference we declare our conviction that it is essentially
necessary to the peace and prosperity of Ireland that
the right of domestic legislation on all Irish affairs
should be restored to our country.

'That in accordance with all ancient and constitutional rights of the Irish nation we claim the privilege
of managing our own affairs by a Parliament assembled in Ireland, composed of the Sovereign, the
Lords, and the Commons of Ireland.

'That in claiming these rights and privileges for
our country we adopt the principle of federal arrangement which would secure to the Irish Parliament the
right of legislating for and regulating all matters relating to the internal affairs of Ireland ; while leaving
the Imperial Parliament the power of dealing with all
questions affecting the Imperial Crown and Government, legislation regarding the Colonies and other
dependencies of the Crown, the relations of the empire
with foreign States, and all matters appertaining to
the defence and stability of the empire at large, as
well as the power of granting and providing the
supplies necessary for Imperial purposes.

'That such an arrangement does not involve any
change in the existing constitution of Imperial Parliament, or any interference with the prerogatives of the
Crown, or disturbance of the principles of the constitution.

'That to secure to the Irish people the advantages
of constitutional government it is essential that there
should be in Ireland an Administration of Irish affairs,
controlled according to constitutional principles by the

Irish Parliament and conducted by the Ministers constitutionally responsible to that Parliament.'

In February 1874 the General Election came like a bolt from the blue. The Home Rulers were taken by surprise, but they rallied vigorously, and, to the astonishment of everyone, carried over fifty-nine seats all told.

Four Fenians were subsequently returned.

The return of these Fenians was not pleasing to the leaders of the I. R. B., who believed that an oath of allegiance to the Queen (which every member of Parliament was bound to take) was inconsistent with the oath of allegiance to the Irish republic (which all those men had taken) ; but some of the rank and file were not troubled by scruples about the double oath. The Fenian members were, however, all ultimately expelled from the organisation by the chief executive authority.

The General Election of 1874 was, then, a great Home Rule victory. While it was pending Parnell resolved to enter public life.

CHAPTER IV

PUBLIC LIFE

ONE night during the General Election of 1874 Parnell
dined with his sister, Mrs. Dickinson, in Dublin.
After dinner Captain Dickinson said : ' Well, Charles,
why don't you go into Parliament ? Why don't you
stand for your native county ? ' To the surprise of
everyone at the table, Parnell said quickly : ' I will.
Whom ought I to see ? ' ' Oh ! ' said Dickinson, ' we
will see about that to-morrow. The great thing is you
have decided to stand.' ' I will see about it at once,'
said Parnell. ' I have made up my mind, and I won't
wait. Whom ought I to see ? ' ' I think Gray, of
the " Freeman's Journal," ' said John, who was also
present. ' Very well,' said Parnell, rising from the
table, ' I shall go to him at once. Do you come with
me, John.' The two brothers then went away together.
It was now eleven o'clock, and they found Gray at
the ' Freeman's ' office. He was amazed when Parnell
entered and said : ' I have come to say, Mr. Gray, that
I mean to stand for Wicklow as a Home Ruler.'
Gray was much pleased with the intelligence, and he
and the two Parnells sat down to consider the situation.
' You know,' said Parnell, ' I am High Sheriff of the
county, but then I can be relieved from the office by
the Lord Lieutenant.' ' Then,' answered Gray, ' the

first thing to do is to see the Lord Lieutenant. See
him in the morning, and if he releases you start at
once for Wicklow, and the Home Rule League will
send you all the help they can. We have already a
candidate in the field, Mr. O'Byrne.' Next day Parnell
and John went to Dublin Castle and saw the Lord
Lieutenant. But his Excellency would not relieve
Parnell from his duty as Sheriff. 'Very well,' said
Parnell, as he and John walked away from the Castle,
'but we shall not be baulked. You shall stand, John.
We shall start for Rathdrum this evening, and begin
the campaign at once.' Having advised the Home
Rule League of their intentions, they proceeded that
evening to Rathdrum. The news of John's candidature had travelled before them, and a crowd was
collected at the village to give them a hearty reception. 'Charlie,' says John, 'mounted a cart or a barrel
and made a speech. He was not much of a speaker
then, but he said things which caught on. I was
rather surprised at his trying to speak at all. But
he knew what to say, though he said little, and they
cheered him. It struck me at the time that what he
said was rather wild, and on the way to Avondale I
said to him: "You know you ought not to make
speeches, you ought not to interfere at all. You will
get into trouble." "What can they do to me?" he
asked. "Turn you out of the office of Sheriff, for one
thing," I replied. "What I want," said he, smiling.
However, he finally agreed not to interfere again, and
to act properly as Sheriff, and this he did. Well, the
election came off, and I was left at the bottom of the
poll.' [1]

But the Wicklow election was practically the

[1] Mr. O. Byrne (H.R.) and Mr. Dick (Liberal) were elected.

beginning of Parnell's public career. He was now
bent on plunging headlong into politics at the first
opportunity.

The opportunity soon came. Colonel Taylor, one
of the members for Dublin County, had become Chancellor of the Duchy in Mr. Disraeli's Ministry, and
had to seek re-election on his appointment to office.
The Home Rule League, of which Parnell was now
a member, resolved to contest the seat. It would,
they knew, be a hopeless battle. Still they felt that
the contest would rally the Home Rulers of the county,
and be an incentive to action as well as a test of
strength. But who would enter the list for this
desperate conflict? A strong candidate, a candidate
of means, was essential. Parnell offered to jump into
the breach. But his offer was not quite regarded with
satisfaction. He was a landlord and a Protestant, and
he came of a good old stock; in addition, he would be
able to pay his own election expenses. These things
were in his favour. But would he in other respects
make a good candidate? Personally he was hardly
known to the council of the League. A few Home
Rulers had, indeed, met him. But they had formed an
unfavourable opinion of him. He was at this time a
tall, thin, handsome, delicate, young fellow; very diffident, very reticent, utterly ignorant of political affairs,
and apparently without any political faculty. His
whole stock of information about Ireland was limited
to the history of the Manchester martyrs. He could
talk of them, but he could not talk of anything else.
Still, it must be allowed that even this limited knowledge helped him. 'Did Parnell,' I asked one who was
familiar with Irish politics, 'ever meet any Fenians
about this time?' 'Yes,' was the answer, 'I some-

times saw him with ——. They used to talk about
the amnesty movement, so far as Parnell ever talked
at all, but he was a better listener than a talker. He
knew nothing about Home Rule, but he was interested
in Fenianism. For that matter,' my friend added,
' so was Butt. Butt often said to me at the beginning of the movement that the Fenians were the best
men in Irish politics.' Fenianism and Home Rule
were certainly a good deal mixed up ; and at a dinner
party at Butt's, when the question of the Wicklow
candidature was practically decided, —— was present
and supported Parnell, though a leading Constitutional-
Nationalist said ' he would never do.' Butt himself
was favourable to Parnell.

One morning about this time I called on Butt at his
residence in Henrietta Street, Dublin. He came into
the library in his usual genial radiant way, looking well
pleased and in excellent humour. Without any formal
words he rushed up to me and said : ' My dear boy, we
have got a splendid recruit, an historic name, my friend,
young Parnell, of Wicklow ; and unless I am mistaken,
the Saxon will find him an ugly customer, though he is
a good-looking fellow.' But the council of the Home
Rule League had yet to pronounce judgment. When
the question came formally before them there was
much misgiving. ' Will he go straight ? ' one of the
members asked. ' If he gives his word,' said the '48
veteran, John Martin, ' I will trust him. I would
trust any of the Parnells.' ' Still,' says Mr. A. M.
Sullivan, who was present, ' there was hesitancy, and
eventually we said, " Let us see him." The general
council adjourned for the purpose, and on re-assem-
bling I saw Mr. C. S. Parnell for the first time. I do
not wish to pretend that I possessed any marvellous

power of divination, but when the young neophyte
had retired I not only joined John Martin in espousing
his cause, but undertook to move his adoption at a
public meeting which it was decided to hold in the
Rotunda.'

At this public meeting Parnell made his *début*.
Mr. Sullivan describes the scene. ' The resolution
which I had moved in his favour having been adopted
with acclamation, he came forward to address the
assemblage. To our dismay, he broke down utterly.
He faltered, he paused, went on, got confused, and, pale
with intense but subdued nervous anxiety, caused everyone to feel deep sympathy for him. The audience saw
it all, and cheered him kindly and heartily ; but many
on the platform shook their heads, sagely prophesying
that if ever he got to Westminster, no matter how
long he stayed there, he would either be a "silent
member " or be known as "single-speech Parnell." '
' What was thought of Parnell at that time,' I asked
another prominent Nationalist. ' Well,' he answered,
' we thought him a nice gentlemanly fellow who would
be an ornament but no use.' ' I first met Parnell,' said
Mr. T. W. Russell, ' in 1874, when he was standing
for Dublin. I was then struck by what I thought his
extraordinary political ignorance and incapacity. He
knew nothing, and I thought he would never do anything. I interviewed him on behalf of the Temperance
people. He promised to vote for the Sunday Closing
Bill, and he kept his word. I found him very straight
in what I had to do with him.'

' I met Parnell,' says Mr. O'Connor Power, ' in 1874,
the time of the Dublin election. He seemed to me a
nice gentlemanly fellow, but he was hopelessly ignorant, and seemed to me to have no political capacity

whatever. He could not speak at all. He was hardly
able to get up and say, " Gentlemen, I am a candidate
for the representation of the county of Dublin." We
all listened to him with pain while he was on his legs,
and felt immensely relieved when he sat down. No
one ever thought he would cut a figure in politics. We
thought he would be a respectable mediocrity.' So
much for early promises.

On March 7 Parnell issued his address to the
electors of the county of Dublin, and on March 9 the
parish priest of Rathdrum wrote supporting his candidature, saying : ' His coolness, sound judgment, great
prudence and moderation, as well as capacity as a
practical man, will be a great acquisition to the
National Party should he be returned for the county
of Dublin.'

A few days later the Tories circulated a report
that Parnell had treated some of his tenants with
harshness.

' It has been sought,' Parnell said in a public letter
dealing with the matter, ' to connect me with some
difference between Mr. Henry Parnell and his tenants.
In reply to this transparent electioneering trick, I in
the most emphatic manner publicly declare that I
was in no way, directly or indirectly, connected with
or mixed up in any manner with the said dispute,
nor could I in any way control or influence the
matter.'

As John had been left at the bottom of the poll in
the Wicklow election, so Charles was left at the bottom
of the poll in the Dublin.[1]

---

[1] Parnell received 300*l.* from the Home Rule League to contest this
election. When the election was over he handed back the 300*l.* to the
League. The contest cost him 2,000*l.*

'I well remember,' said one of the retainers of the Parnell family at Avondale, 'the day Master Charlie came home when he was beaten at the Dublin election. He walked up here, looking so handsome and grand and devil-may-care. "Well, boys," he said, "I am beaten, but they are not done with me yet." The driver, sir, who brought him home said to us afterwards, "That's a regular devil. He talked all the way about fighting again and smashing them all, and he looked wild and fierce." And, sir, Master Charles was a regular devil when his blood was up, and no mistake.'

Parnell now resumed once more his quiet life at Avondale, attending to his mines, his sawmills, and his other country avocations, and so he remained for a twelvemonth. Then an event occurred which drew him from his retreat.

John Mitchell returned to Ireland. He had been sentenced to fourteen years' transportation in 1848 for treason-felony. In 1850 he escaped from Tasmania, and fled to the United States. There he remained for twenty-four years. Just about the time of his arrival in Ireland in February 1875 a vacancy occurred in the representation of Tipperary. The Nationalists resolved to nominate Mitchell, and he was elected without opposition. The House of Commons quashed the return on the ground that Mitchell was a felon who had neither received a free pardon nor purged his crime by serving the term of his imprisonment. A new writ was accordingly issued in March 1875. But the Nationalists resolved to defy the House of Commons, and to nominate Mitchell again. In this crisis Parnell reappeared.

Writing to the 'Freeman's Journal,' and inclosing

a cheque for 25*l.* towards Mitchell's expenses, he said
he hoped that Mitchell would again be returned for
Tipperary, and that the 'party vote of the House of
Commons' would be thus 'reversed,' adding, ' Let the
legal question be fought out calmly and fairly afterwards.'

The second Tipperary election took place on March
11. Mitchell was opposed by a Tory, but was returned
by an overwhelming majority. He, however, never
took his seat. A few days afterwards he fell seriously
ill, and died in his native town, Newry, on March 20.
Nine days later his old friend and comrade, John
Martin, passed away, and a vacancy was thus created
in the representation of County Meath. Parnell, who
was now a member of the council of the Home Rule
League, was put up by the Nationalists.

A short time prior to the election Sir Gavan Duffy
arrived in Europe from Victoria. He had scarcely
landed at Brindisi when he received the following telegram from an old friend, Father Peter O'Reilly :

' John Martin dead, telegraph will you stand for
Meath. At a conference in Kells on Monday twenty-
four priests present, much enthusiasm, the bishop not
disapproving. Come home, success certain.'

This telegram was followed by another, purporting
to be signed by William Dillon, the son of John Blake
Dillon, one of Duffy's colleagues in the '48 movement :

' John Martin dead. Parnell, candidate of Home
Rule League, would probably retire if you join League
and stand. Wire reply. Wm. Dillon, 15 Nassau Street,
Dublin.'

This telegram was a forgery. It was never signed by Mr. William Dillon, nor in any way authorised by him. But Sir Gavan Duffy naturally believed it to be genuine, and sent the following reply :

'Thanks. I do not seek a constituency, but I am a repealer, as I have been all my life, and if Meath elect me I will do my best in concert with the Irish members to serve the Irish cause. Should the constituency be dissatisfied with me at any time I will resign. But if it be made a condition that I shall join the League and adopt its novel formula instead of the principles held by me in common with O'Connell, O'Brien, Davis, Dillon, Dr. Maginn, Meagher, and all the Nationalists in my time, that I cannot do.'

This telegram was read immediately to the Home Rule League. A rumour was spread that Duffy meant to repudiate the League, and to destroy it ; and in order to avoid a split in the Nationalist ranks, his friends in Meath did not press his candidature.

Parnell, however, was opposed by a Tory and by an Independent Home Ruler. But in April 1875 he was placed at the head of the poll, amid a storm of popular enthusiasm. 'There was tremendous rejoicing in Royal Meath,' says a contemporary writer, 'over the victory. Enthusiastic crowds assembled in thousands to give vent to a common feeling of delight. Bonfires blazed in many quarters ; and the populace of Trim, in which town the declaration of the poll had been made, having discovered Mr. Parnell walking down from the parochial house to his hotel, laid lovingly violent hands on him, carried him in triumph round their own special bonfire in the Market Square, and

finally set him standing on a cask,' where he said a
few words of thanks for his return and of congratu-
lation for the Nationalist victory. The hour of the
future leader had at length come.[1]

[1] Sir Gavan Duffy objected to Butt's Home Rule plan as a retreat
from the historical position taken up by O'Connell and the Young
Irelanders, and complained that the policy of independent opposition,
initiated by him and the Tenant Right Leaguers of 1852, was not carried
out. 'I strove,' says Sir Gavan Duffy, 'to familiarise the people with
the policy by which alone the cause might be carried to success—the
policy of independent opposition; a policy which meant union with no
English party, and hostility to none which was prepared to advance our
cause.'—*North and South.*

CHAPTER V

IN PARLIAMENT

PARNELL took his seat in the House of Commons on April 22, 1875. He was introduced by Captain Nolan, member for Galway, and Mr. Ennis, senior member for Meath.

There were at this time, as we have seen, fifty-nine Home Rulers. The parliamentary attitude of the great majority of these may be described as active rather than aggressive. Butt himself was a model of courtesy and moderation. He tried rather to win English sympathy than force English opinion. He addressed the House as he would address a jury. He sought to persuade, conciliate, humour, never saying or doing aught to shock the susceptibilities of his audience. He argued, he appealed, he based his case on facts and reason, he relied on the justice and fairness of England. He respected English sentiment, and hoped by moderation and friendliness to remove English prejudice. He scrupulously observed parliamentary forms, and conscientiously kept the law of the land. He was, indeed, a perfect type of the constitutional agitator, seeking by legal methods to change the law, but doing no violence to it. 'The House of Commons,' said the late Mr. Henry Richards, 'is like the kingdom of Heaven in one respect, though it is very unlike it in other respects ; but it is like it in this, it suffereth violence and the violent take it by force.' These, however, were not the views of Isaac Butt. 'I am not,' he once said, 'in favour of a policy of exasperation.' The House cheered the sentiment ; and for the rest treated Butt with gentle contempt. There was at this time a member of the Irish party who did not sympathise with the tactics of his leader. He believed in a policy of blood and iron. 'All nonsense, sir,' he would say, 'the way Butt goes on. He thinks he will get something out of the English by rubbing them down. Nonsense ; rub them up, sir, that's the thing to do ; rub them up. Make them uncomfortable. That's the right policy.' This amiable individual was Joseph Gillis Biggar.

Biggar was a wealthy Ulster merchant and a member of the supreme council of the I. R. B. He came to the British Parliament practically to see how much mischief he could do to the British Empire. He had no respect for the House of Commons ; he had no respect for any English institution. Of course he had no oratorical faculty, no literary gifts ; indeed, he could hardly speak three consecutive sentences. He had little political knowledge, he despised books and the readers of books ; but he was shrewd and businesslike, without manners and without fear. He regarded parliamentary rules as all 'rot,' delighted in shocking the House, and gloried in causing general confusion. He had but two ideas—to rasp the House of Commons, and make himself thoroughly hated by the British public. It must be confessed that in these respects he succeeded to his heart's content.

Curiously enough, the very day on which Parnell took his seat Biggar made his first formidable essay in

parliamentary debate.   A Coercion Bill was under consideration.   It had just reached the committee stage.
Biggar rose to move an amendment.   It would be
absurd to say that he made a speech.   But he was on
his feet for four hours by the clock.

'We shall not,' wrote the ' Times,' in commenting
on this performance, ' attempt to inflict on our readers
a *réchauffé* of Mr. Biggar's address, and as it was,
indeed, to a large extent inaudible, it must be lost to
the world, unless it be printed in some Dublin newspaper.'

But Biggar's speech is not 'lost to the world.'
It is enshrined in the pages of ' Hansard ' to the
extent of seven columns, and has gained a good
deal—as many another address has gained—at the
hands of a friendly reporter.   But as a matter of
fact the oration was mainly inaudible and wholly
irrelevant.

Drawing at the start upon his internal resources,
but finding that they did not carry him very far, the
member for Cavan literally took away the breath of
the House by plunging into Blue Books, newspapers,
and strewing *disjecta membra* over his discourse.   There
is much unconscious humour in ' Hansard's ' account
of this part of the performance :

' The hon. member then read, in a manner which
made it impossible to follow the application, long
extracts from reports and evidence of the West Meath
Commission, and from the Catholic newspapers of
Ireland, and from statements and resolutions of various
public bodies and meetings.   The general purport
appeared to be to denounce the necessity for any
exceptional legislation in regard to Ireland, to assert
the general tranquillity and good order of the country,

and the absence of Ribbonism, and to protest against the invasion of the liberties of the people.'

Having inflicted these documents on the House until the assembly groaned under their weight, Biggar once more varied the entertainment by falling back on original resources, jerking out a number of incoherent and irrelevant sentences, but still keeping on the even tenor of his way with imperturbable calmness and resolution. The more the House groaned, the more delighted was the orator. He was sparing, however, of original matter, and soon took refuge in literature again. This time, to show the variety of his knowledge, he abandoned the Blue Books and the public Press, and gave the House a touch of the 'statutes at large.'

'The hon. member,' says the dignified 'Hansard,' 'who was almost inaudible, was understood to recapitulate some of the arbitrary enactments of older statutes, and to point out that they were in substance or effect re-enacted in the various Arms Acts and Peace Preservation Acts of the present reign.'

Having completely overwhelmed the House with this legal lore, Biggar again dropped into a lighter vein, and treated his listeners once more to some original observations. The House was now almost empty ; and an hon. member called attention to the fact that 'forty members were not present.' Biggar immediately resumed his seat, beaming benevolently —for be it known that Biggar was one of the most benevolent-looking men in the House, and his face was almost one perpetual smile—and observing to an Irish member by his side, 'I am not half done yet.' The House soon filled, and Biggar again rose. He had now come absolutely to an end of all original ideas ; he had exhausted his knowledge of the statutes, but

the Blue Books were still before him. 'The hon.
member,' says 'Hansard,' with delightful gravity,
' proceeded to read extracts from the evidence before
the West Meath Commission—as was understood—
but in a manner which rendered him totally unin-
telligible.' The Speaker at length interposed, saying
that the rules of the House required that an hon.
member should address himself to the Chair, and that
this rule the hon. member was at present neglecting.
This was the crisis ; but Biggar was equal to it.
He expressed great regret that he had not observed
the rule in question, but said the fact was that feeling
fatigued after speaking so long, and being so far away
from the Chair, he could not make himself heard.
This state of things, however, could be easily remedied,
and he would, therefore, with the permission of the
House, take up a more favourable position. Accordingly,
leaving his place behind the gangway, he marched right
up to the Treasury Bench, taking with him Blue Books,
Acts of Parliament, newspapers, and in fact a perfect
library of materials, from which, to quote once more
the decorous 'Hansard,' 'he continued to read long
extracts with comments.' But the longest day must
have an end, and even Biggar at length released the
House from bondage, and sank complacently into the
nearest seat.

'If Mr. Biggar,' said the 'Times,' 'had devoted
but one hour out of his four to the resolution upon
which he was nominally speaking, he might have said
something effective.' But it was not Biggar's intention
to say anything effective. He wanted to do something
offensive, and he did. He proved that one member
could stop the business of the House for four hours,
and make its proceedings absolutely ridiculous. The

lesson was not lost on Parnell, who sat calmly by and watched the performance with interest and amusement. Four days later he himself took part in the discussion, and made his maiden speech. It was short, modest, spoken in a thin voice and with manifest nervousness. However, he got out what he wanted to say, and what he said, briefly and even spasmodically, was the kernel of the whole matter. 'I trust,' he said, 'that England will give to Irishmen the right which they claim—the right of self-government. Why should Ireland be treated as a geographical fragment of England, as I heard an ex-Chancellor of the Exchequer call her some time ago? Ireland is not a geographical fragment. She is a nation.'

The year 1875 passed quietly away in Parliament and in Ireland. Parnell remained chiefly a calm spectator of the proceedings of the House of Commons, watching, learning, biding his time. He was ignorant of public affairs, and he read no books. But he was not ashamed to ask for information, and to pick up knowledge in that way. 'How do you get materials,' he asked one of the Irish members, 'for questioning the Ministers?' 'Why,' said his friend, smiling at the simplicity of the novice, 'from the newspapers, from our constituents, from many sources.' 'Ah,' said Parnell, 'I must try and ask a question myself some day.'

With his eminently practical turn of mind he soon saw that it was absolutely necessary, for the purpose of parliamentary warfare, to obtain a complete mastery of the rules of debate. But he did not, as some suppose, read up the subject laboriously. He never did anything laboriously. What he knew, he knew intuitively, or learned by some easy method of his own devising. Books he avoided. 'How am I to learn the rules of the House?' a young Irish member asked him in after years. 'By breaking them,' was the answer. 'That's what I did.' It was true enough. Parnell learned the rules of debate by breaking them himself, or by seeing others break them. But he was very quiet, very unobtrusive, very diffident, during the session of 1875. He came, he saw, and was for the time content. He did not, however, altogether remain a silent member. He asked some questions; he made some speeches, short, sharp, and to the point.

Before the session closed he had formed his own views of the House of Commons and of the position of Irishmen in it; and he gave expression to these views during the recess in two brief and pithy sentences. Speaking at Navan on October 7, he said: 'We do not want speakers in the House of Commons, but men who will vote right.' Ten days later he said, at a meeting at Nobber: 'The Irish people should watch the conduct of their representatives in the House of Commons.' These sentences summed up the Parnell gospel: a vigilant public opinion outside, and practical rather than talking members inside Parliament. From the beginning to the end Parnell disliked speechifying. The process was absolutely painful to him. Talking was sometimes necessary to get things done (or to prevent their being done), and he was forced to put up with it. But he took no pleasure in oratory, and had not the least ambition to become a great public speaker. The only occasion on which he made or listened to speeches with any degree of satisfaction was when talking obstructed the business of the House. Biggar was, perhaps, his ideal of a useful public speaker—a man who was silent when business had to be done, but who could hold the floor for four hours at a strétch when business had to be prevented.

Parnell from the outset seems to have thought that the atmosphere of the House of Commons was fatal to Irish activity, and that a healthy and vigorous public opinion in the country was absolutely necessary to save the Irish representation from inertia and collapse. He did nothing during the session of 1875 which fixed the public attention on him; but it is abundantly clear that even then he had resolved on his line, and that he only waited the opportunity to take it. His faith was not in mere Parliamentarians, but in forces outside, stronger than Parliamentarianism, which he determined to influence, and by whose help he hoped to dominate the parliamentary army. From the moment he first thought seriously of politics he saw, as if by instinct, that Fenianism was the key of Irish Nationality; and if he could or would not have the key in his hand, he was certainly resolved never to let it out of his sight. We shall therefore see him as the years roll by standing on the verge of treason-felony, but with marvellous dexterity always preventing himself from slipping over. Perhaps this was the secret of his power. But the year 1875 ended without that power being revealed, or, indeed, even dreamt of. No one saw into the future. On the surface Ireland was tranquil; there seemed no signs of coming storm in any part of the political horizon; all was apparently quiet, peaceful, prosperous. The Dublin correspondent of the 'Times' summed up the situation thus: 'The present circumstances of Ireland may be briefly summed up in the statement that at no period of her history did she appear more tranquil, more free from serious crime, more prosperous and contented. But few of the disquieting elements of former times are now at work. Political excitement has all but died out with Mitchell and Martin, whose last effort to revive it exhausted its impotent fury. There is no longer the agitation which convulsed the country in days gone by. Home Rule still keeps a little cauldron simmering, but there is no fear that it will ever become formidable; for, though there is no want of a Hecate to practise the old spells, they have lost their power over the people. An organised attempt is made to fan into a general flame the dissatisfaction which is felt in some parts of the country with the working of the Land Act; but its success has hitherto been slight, and confined to certain localities. The relations between landlord and tenant continue to be generally friendly, and both parties are, with some remarkable exceptions, adapting themselves with prudence and good feeling to the change consequent upon the application of a new law. In the north a determined struggle is made to obtain a larger concession of tenant-right than the Act has given, and in the other provinces corresponding advantages are sought; but the tenants whom it is sought to arouse and combine in general action are giving but a faint response to the call of their leaders. The truth is that it is by no means so easy as it was formerly to make them discontented, and they are unwilling to be drawn away from more profitable pursuits to engage in an agitation which offers but little chance of success.'

These were strange words, written on the eve of a great convulsion.

CHAPTER VI

GATHERING CLOUDS

IT is unnecessary to say that the opening of the year 1876 found all England united against the Irish Nationalist demand. The Tories were in power. Mr. Disraeli was Prime Minister, Sir Michael Hicks-Beach was Chief Secretary for Ireland.

Mr. Gladstone had retired from the leadership of the Liberal party, and Lord Hartington had taken his place. Differing on almost all other points, Liberals and Tories were united in their hostility to Home Rule. The fact that nearly sixty Irish members had been returned pledged to the question made no impression on the House of Commons. The great majority of these members were moderate, respectable men, anxious to conciliate English opinion, careful not to wound English sentiment. I have said that Butt was a perfect type of a constitutional agitator. The Irish party was a perfect type of a constitutional party. But it was laughed at and despised by the House of Commons. Home Rule was regarded as a supreme joke; the Home Rulers were looked upon as a collection of foolish but harmless 'gentlemen from Ireland.' Biggar alone stood out in bold relief from the whole *crowd*, and his efforts to seize every opportunity for outraging English opinion not only made him hateful to the

English members, but even brought him under the displeasure of the majority of his own party.

'Whigs, sir, Whigs, every one of them,' he said, speaking of his colleagues in moments of relaxation. No Irish Nationalist, be it said, can apply a more opprobrious epithet to another than to call him a Whig. To call him a Tory would be almost praise in comparison. In Ireland the Tory is regarded as an open enemy ; the Whig as a treacherous friend. It is the Whigs, not the Tories, who have habitually sapped the integrity of the Irish representation. So at least the Irish think, and in 1876 there was a growing suspicion in the country that the Irish party was gliding into Whiggery. Indeed, the Irish members themselves used sometimes to twit each other on the subject. 'You know you are a Whig,' I heard one Irish member say to another in the lobby in 1876. 'To be sure I am,' said S., 'and you are a Whig, and your father was a Whig, and Butt is a Whig, and Sullivan is a Whig, and Mitchell Henry is a Whig—we are all Whigs.' Poor S. was naked but not ashamed ; he had indeed been the most orthodox of Whigs all his life, until 1874, when the flowing tide swept him into Home Rule. The Irish parliamentary party was not, however, as a whole a party of Whigs. There were no doubt Whigs in its ranks, men who had been forced by their constituents to take the Home Rule pledge, but who did not believe in it. The majority of the party, however, were true Nationalists, albeit sincerely constitutional agitators. 'We shall fight England,' one of them said, 'not with bullets, but with ballot-boxes '; and this was practically the creed of the whole body. They believed that the House of Commons could be convinced by reason and moderation, that the battle

could be fought within the lines of the constitution
and in accordance with the usages which obtain in a
society of gentlemen. 'I think,' said one of them,
animadverting on Biggar's activity, 'that a man should
be a gentleman first and a patriot afterwards,' and the
sentiment was cheered by Irish members. They did
not think that the House of Commons would 'suffer
violence,' and they certainly had not the most remote
notion of 'taking it by force.' If a body of Irishmen
bent on constitutional agitation pure and simple, eager
to cultivate friendly relations with Englishmen, and
desirous of treating opponents with the courtesy and
respect which they expected for themselves, could have
made way in the English Parliament, then the followers
of Butt ought to have succeeded. But they did not
succeed. They made no way whatever. They not
only failed in pushing Home Rule to the front, but
they failed in pushing any Irish question to the front,
though their attention was given to every Irish question. They were voted down by 'brutal majorities' or
out-manœuvred by skilful parliamentary tacticians, and
thus their efforts were unavailing.

On the opening of the Session of 1876 the Irish
members mustered in full strength, and notices were
given of a goodly array of Bills. The Land question
and Education question were taken in hand. Measures
were announced for dealing with the subjects of
Union Rating, Electoral County Boards, Deep-sea
Fishing, Reclamation of Waste Lands, Grand Jury
Reform, Municipal Reform, Parliamentary Reform.
But none of the Irish Bills found their way to the
Statute Book.

Butt's Land Bill, a very moderate measure indeed
compared with recent enactments, was rejected by an

overwhelming majority, 290 to 56 votes.[1] The House
of Commons considered that the Land question had
been settled in 1870, and that it was simply an imperti-
nence to revive it. The Irish were not to have a
Parliament of their own, and the English Parliament
did not think it worth while to consider seriously an
Irish demand which went to the very root of the well-
being of the people. Such was the sagacious attitude of
British statesmanship towards Ireland in the year 1876.

Biggar, be it said, 'thoroughly disapproved of the
tactics of the Irish parliamentary party. He looked on
the introduction of all these Bills as "mere moon-
shine."' 'What's the good?' he would say. 'We
can't get them through, we know we can't get them
through. The English stop our Bills. Why don't we
stop their Bills? That's the thing to do. No Irish
Bills; but stop English Bills. No legislation; that's
the policy, sir, that's the policy. Butt's a fool, too

---

[1] The Land Act of 1870, it may be said, provided that tenants
should, on eviction, receive compensation for improvements, and in
certain cases for disturbance. That Act had not worked well, and Butt
now proposed to amend it. 'I propose,' he said, in introducing his Bill,
' that every tenant shall have permission to claim from the chairman of
his county the benefit of his improvements, and if he does that I propose
that a certificate shall be given him protecting him against eviction
by his landlord. That will in point of time establish a perpetuity of
tenure. The great difficulty in anything of this kind is to get a tribunal
which will fairly value the land. I confess that it is a difficulty which
I have found very hard to meet. This idea of a valued rent seems to be
getting largely hold of some of the landlords, and I see that some of
them suggest the valuation should be fixed by a Government valuer.
There are, I admit, some attractions in that proposal. Another suggestion is that the appointment of the arbitrators should be vested in three
Privy Councillors, and some time ago I proposed that the judges of
assize should appoint them. It is, however, the most difficult thing in
the world to find a tribunal to which you can entrust this task. I
therefore propose, by this Bill, that the landlord and tenant should each
select one arbitrator, and the two arbitrators thus appointed shall agree
on a third. In cases where the landlord should not appear I suggest
that the rent should be assessed by a jury, composed of three special
and three common jurors.'

gentlemanly; we're all too gentlemanly.' There was at this time an Irish member who shared Biggar's views, or perhaps it might be more accurate to say that Biggar shared his views. Any way they thought alike on the subject of parliamentary tactics. This member was Joseph Ronayne.

Ronayne had been a Young Irelander, and had sat for the city of Cork since 1872. He was a shrewd, business-like man, of quiet and retiring manners. Unwilling to take a prominent part in debate, he was helpful and earnest in council, always advising energetic action, but, as he would say, too old—he was only fifty-four—to put his views into practice. After three years' experience in the House of Commons he came to the conclusion that Irish business could never be done by the adoption of Butt's conciliatory tactics. ' We will never,' he urged in 1874, 'make any impression on the House until we interfere in English business. At present Englishmen manage their own affairs in their own way without any interference from us. Then, when we want to get our business through, they stop us. We ought to show them that two can play at this game of obstruction. Let us interfere in English legislation ; let us show them that if we are not strong enough to get our own work done, we are strong enough to prevent them from getting theirs.'

But, with a single exception, the Irish party were at this time unwilling to take Ronayne's advice. Butt would not listen to it. He thought such tactics would be undignified, useless, mischievous. Ronayne did not press the point, but he would say to the younger men of the party : ' Well, it is for you to do the work. I am too old. But Englishmen will never pay attention to you until you make yourselves a nuisance to them.'

'Ronayne is quite right,' Biggar would say. 'We'll never do any good until we take an intelligent interest in English affairs.' As Biggar preached, so he practised to the best of his abilities.

Parnell had heard of Ronayne's advice. He had seen Biggar at work. He knew that Butt objected to obstruction. But, without a moment's hesitation, he backed Ronayne's words and Biggar's deeds. It was one of the characteristics of this remarkable man that he never seemed to be taken unawares. If you suggested what you conceived to be a new idea, you found that apparently it was an old idea with him. 'Yes,' he would say to you, as you came up brimful of brilliant thoughts, 'I have thought that over.' This would, perhaps, have been unpleasant coming from another man, as it would in a sense take away the credit of the initiative from you—and we are all very vain—but it was never unpleasant coming from Parnell. After talking the matter over with him, he sent you away with the two-fold feeling: (1) that it was impossible to anticipate him in anything; (2) that you had done good service in bringing the subject under his notice, as the result might be to quicken his thoughts into action. He never wearied of impressing men with a sense of their usefulness, though you never spoke to him without feeling his absolute superiority as a political leader. The one idea which above all others he fixed in the minds of those who had intercourse with him was that he could lead them, and that they could not lead him.

When the subject of obstruction was brought before him, he was ready for it, and went briskly into action. Biggar was uncouth and brutal, and could scarcely succeed in getting members of his own party to stand

by him in his ' assaults ' on the House. But Parnell
was polished and skilful, had a happy knack of putting
other people in the wrong, and used not only to win
Irish support, but would occasionally obtain English
sympathy.

Parnell's first really notable utterance in the House
was made on June 30, during the debate on Butt's
motion for an inquiry into the Home Rule demand.
Sir Michael Hicks-Beach, the Chief Secretary for
Ireland, was speaking ; Parnell looked coldly and impassively on. How far the speech of the Chief Secretary
interested him, how far he was paying any attention
to the subject, it would be difficult to tell. At length
Sir Michael Hicks-Beach said : ' Of all the extraordinary delusions which are connected with the
subject, the most strange to me appears the idea that
Home Rule can have the effect of liberating the Fenian
prisoners, the Manchester murderers——.' ' No ! No !'
cried Parnell, with a suddenness and vehemence which
startled everyone. The House was shocked at what
seemed to be a justification of murder, and there was
an indignant murmur of disapprobation. Sir Michael
Hicks-Beach paused, and then, looking straight at
Parnell and amid sympathetic cheers, said solemnly :
' I regret to hear that there is an hon. member in this
House who will apologise for murder.' The House
thought that the young member for Meath was crushed,
and the cry of ' Withdraw !' ' Withdraw !' rang from
all quarters.

But Parnell rose with great dignity and great
deliberation, and said in clear and icy accents : ' The
right hon. gentleman looked at me so directly when
he said that he regretted that any member of the
House should apologise for murder that I wish to say

as publicly as I can that I do not believe, and never shall believe, that any murder was committed at Manchester.' This rejoinder was received with loud cheers from the Irish benches, and Sir Michael Hicks-Beach passed from the subject of the 'Manchester murderers.' [1]

[1] On August 1, 1876, a motion for the release of the Fenian prisoners was brought forward by Mr. O'Connor Power. Mr. Bright took part in the debate, and dealing with the case of the Manchester men, said : 'I have regretted that on a former occasion when this matter was before us I did not take the opportunity of saying what I have long thought with regard to the case which is called "The Manchester Outrage." There was in that case one man killed—one man shot—one fatal shot fired, and therefore it may be urged positively that only one man in a certain sense was guilty of murder. I had, living in that neighbourhood, a very painful interview with the relatives of one of the three men who were hanged, and they were not willing to lay the blame upon either of the other two, but they felt very confidently that there were no sufficient grounds for believing that the prisoner in whose fate they were particularly interested was the one who fired the fatal shot. One of the three, I presume, was the guilty person, but the three were hanged. Now, it always appeared to me that the course pursued by the Home Office on that occasion was an unwise one. I am averse to capital punishment, as most members of the House know, but in a case of this kind I think to hang three men for one fatal shot was a mistake—a mistake according to the order and practice of our law, and a great mistake when we look at it in its political aspect. On the occasion I have alluded to, when representations were made, it was denied that this was strictly a political case, or that severity was resorted to because it was a political case ; but I have always held the opinion that I held then, and hold now, that it was solely because it was a political case that three men were hanged for the murder of one man. I recollect urging it in this way : If these three men had been out on a poaching expedition, and in the conflict that took place one keeper was killed by one shot, and three men were tried for it, I believe there is no judge who would have sentenced, and no Home Secretary who would have thought it his duty to advise that, these three men should be hanged for the offence. I believe that the three men were hanged because it was a political offence, and not because it was an ordinary murder of one man, committed by one man and by one shot. The other day there was a case in my neighbourhood of an outrage committed by persons connected with a trade union in the neighbourhood of Bolton. Unfortunately a man was attacked by a number of his fellow-workmen and was killed. No doubt all who were present and maltreated the man were guilty of an illegal act, but it is difficult to say who it was that was guilty of the offence of destroying that man's life. Three, I think, were convicted, not of murder, but of manslaughter.

This utterance first fixed the attention of the Fenians on Parnell. Four years later I met a number of Fenians in a town in the North of England. I asked how it came to pass that Parnell gained the confidence of so many Fenians. One of them answered: 'In 1876 we no longer believed in Butt; we thought his way of dealing with the House of Commons was absurd. The House showed no deference to the Irish members, yet Butt was always showing deference to the House. Of course we had no belief in parliamentary agitation, but we wished to see Irish members stand up to the House. The humiliation of England anywhere was, of course, a pleasure to us, and there were some of us who thought that she might be humiliated even in the House of Commons. But it was quite clear that Butt's methods could lead to nothing but the humiliation of Ireland. We had grown quite tired of Butt, though we always liked him for his defence of our people in the State trials. What we wanted was a fighting policy. Even constitutional agitators who would defy England, who would shock English sentiment, who would show a bold spirit of resistance to English law and English custom, would help to keep the national feeling alive. But we knew pretty well that no Irish member would keep up a sustained fight against England unless he was in touch with us. A Constitutionalist could only do good by drawing inspiration from Fenianism, and Fenianism had ceased

---

It was an illegal act, and they were punished by various terms of imprisonment—from, I think, three to fifteen years. Unless this was a political offence, the evidence of murder was not very much different from the case I am now describing. I believe it was a great mistake. I said it then, and I say it now, and I have, I say, always believed that the extremity of the law was put in force against three men, only one of whom—supposing the one who committed the offence was captured—caused the death of the unfortunate and lamented policeman.'

to inspire Butt. We did not know very much about Parnell at this time. His defence of the Manchester men in the House of Commons was a revelation to us; but we never lost sight of him afterwards, and I think he never lost sight of us.'

Parnell certainly did not lose sight of the Fenians; and he ultimately rode into power on their shoulders. But up to the end of 1876 he continued undistinguished, and almost unnoticed. He had not yet, so to say, drawn out of the ruck, and no one anticipated his extraordinary future.

Parnell hated England before he entered the House of Commons; and his hatred was intensified by his parliamentary experience. He thought the position of the Irish members painfully humiliating. They were waiters on English providence; beggars for English favours. English Ministers behaved as if *they* belonged to the injured nation; as if, indeed, they showed excessive generosity in tolerating Irishmen in their midst at all. This arrogance, this assumption of superiority, galled Parnell. It was repugnant to his nature to approach anyone with bated breath and whispering humbleness; and he resolved to wring justice from England, and to humiliate her in the process. He wanted not only reparation, but vengeance as well.

In those days he would sometimes sit in one of the side galleries, and look down serenely on the performers below. He regarded the whole proceedings, so far as Irish business was concerned, as purely academic. The House of Commons seemed to him to be nothing better than a mere debating society, where Irishmen had an opportunity of airing their oratory, and were, apparently, satisfied when that was done. A distinguished Irish advocate once said that a 'speech was all very

good in its way, but that the verdict was the thing.'
In the House of Commons the speech was 'the thing,'
and Parnell despised the speech. He wanted 'the
verdict.' One night an Irish Bill was under discussion.
The member in charge of it acquitted himself with
skill and ability. Butt sat near him, and was manifestly much pleased with the performance. When the
member sat down the Home Rule leader patted him
paternally on the back and beamed satisfaction. Parnell
smiled on the scene. When the debate was over, and
when the Bill had been handsomely defeated, he met
the member in the Lobby, walked up to him, patted
him on the back in imitation of Butt, and said: 'You
have been a very good boy, you did that very well, and
you may now go home—and you won't hear any more
about your Bill for another twelvemonth.' Then (in a
more serious tone), 'Ah, it is not by smooth speeches
that you will get anything done here. We want rougher
work. We must show them that we mean business.
They are a good deal too comfortable in that House,
and the English are a good deal too comfortable everywhere.'

In the autumn a meeting of 'advanced Nationalists'
was held at Harold's Cross, near Dublin. Among other
business transacted, an address was voted to President
Grant, congratulating the American people on the
centenary of American independence. Parnell and
Mr. O'Connor Power were deputed to present this
address to General Grant.

They arrived at New York in October. It so happened that the President was in the city at the time.
Parnell suggested that they should see him at once.
Grant received them, expressed himself personally
grateful for the address, but said it would be necessary

for him to learn what was the etiquette in matters of this kind, and that he would communicate with them on his return to Washington. Grant immediately returned to Washington, whither the delegates proceeded too. There they were informed that it would be necessary to have the address presented through the English Ambassador, but they declined to take this course.

A correspondence then took place between the delegates and the American Secretary of State, they urging that the intervention of the British Minister was unnecessary and objectionable, he insisting that it could not be dispensed with.

Parnell returned to England in November, leaving Mr. O'Connor Power in charge of the address, which was ultimately accepted by the Legislative Assembly over the head of the President. Immediately on his arrival at Liverpool Parnell addressed a Home Rule meeting. He said:

'You have also another duty to perform, which is to educate public opinion in England upon Irish questions, which I have looked upon as a difficult and almost impossible task—so difficult that I have often been tempted to think that it was no use trying to educate English public opinion. The English Press encourage prejudice against Ireland. Englishmen themselves are in many respects fair-minded and reasonable, but it is almost impossible to get at them —it requires intelligence almost superhuman to remove the clouds of prejudice under which they have lived during their lives. I know the difficulties of the position of the Irish people in England. It is not easy for people, living as they are in friendship with their English neighbours, to keep themselves separated from

English political organisations, but they have never been
afraid to lay aside private and local considerations in
favour of supporting their fellow-countrymen at home.
Our position in Ireland is peculiar. One party says we go
too far in the Home Rule agitation, while another party
says we do not go far enough.   You have been told we
have lowered the national flag—that the Home Rule
cause is not the cause of Ireland a nation, and that we
will degrade our country into the position of a province.
I deny all this.   There is no reason why Ireland under
Home Rule would not be Ireland a nation in every
sense and for every purpose that it was right she
should be a nation.   I have lately seen in the city of
New York a review of the militia, in which five or six
thousand armed and trained men took part, at least
half of them being veterans of the war. They marched
past with firm step, and armed with improved weapons.
They were at the command of the legislature of New
York, and they could not budge one inch from the
city without the orders of the governor.   If in Ireland
we could ever have under Home Rule such a nationa
militia, they would be able to protect the interests o.
Ireland as a nation, while they would never wish to
trespass upon the integrity of the English Empire, or
to do harm to those they then would call their English
brothers.   It was a foolish want of confidence that
prevented Englishmen and the English Government
from trusting Ireland.   They know Ireland is determined to be an armed nation, and they fear to see her
so, for they remember how a section of the Irish
people in 1782, with arms in their hands, wrung from
England legislative independence.   Without a full
measure of Home Rule for Ireland no Irishman would
ever rest content.'

One who was present has given me the following account of how Parnell delivered this speech. He says :

'I remember that he came once to speak for us in Liverpool. It was in 1876. He was a bad speaker then—had a bad, halting delivery. In fact, it was painful to listen to him. You would think he would break down every moment. He seemed to be constantly stuck for want of a word. It was horribly awkward for the people listening to him, but, oddly enough, it never seemed awkward to him. I remember a number of us who were on the platform near him would now and then suggest a word to him in the pauses. But he never once took a word from any one of us. There he would stand, with clenched fists, which he shook nervously until the word he wanted came. And what struck us all, and what we talked of afterwards, was that Parnell's word was always the right word, and expressed exactly the idea in his head ; our word was simply makeshift, for which he did not even thank us.'

By the end of 1876 Parnell regarded Butt's movement as an absolute failure. Of the innumerable Bills and resolutions which had been introduced by the Irish party since 1871 only one measure of any importance had become law—the Municipal Privileges Act, which enabled municipal corporations to confer the freedom of their cities and to appoint sheriffs. The failure of the parliamentary party was, he thought, in some respects attributable to a want of energy and boldness. The majority of Butt's followers were too apathetic, too deferential to English opinion and sentiment, too fond of English society—in a word, too 'respectable.' Biggar was Parnell's ideal of an

Irish member—a political Ishmael, who would not
conciliate and who could not be conciliated. Butt's
policy was a policy of peace. Biggar's was the embodiment of a policy of war, and Parnell believed in a
policy of war. His faith was centred in a policy of
'aloofness' from all English parties, and indeed from
all Englishmen. He regarded them as enemies, and
he would treat them as enemies. He did not believe
in negotiations. He believed in fighting. The fighting
force in Ireland was the Fenians. Any man, Constitutionalist or Revolutionist, who was prepared to fight
England anywhere or anyhow was sure of Fenian
sympathy, though his methods might not always meet
with Fenian approval.

Were the Fenians to be fought on the one hand,
and the English on the other? Could any party of
Constitutionalists hope to succeed if the Fenians
were actively against them? Butt himself had
leant on the Fenians in founding the Home Rule
movement. What would become of him if the Fenian
support were withdrawn? There was the Church,
certainly. But what would become of Home Rule if
there were to be an open struggle between the Church
and the Fenians? The one thing Parnell hated
throughout his whole career was quarrels among Irishmen. 'Parnell's great gift,' Mr. Healy once said,
'was his faculty of reducing a quarrel to the smallest
dimensions.' He was, in truth, a centre of unity and
strength. He was able, if not to reconcile, certainly to
neutralise the antagonism of opposing forces and hostile characters. He was, indeed, a great peacemaker
as well as a great fighter, and herein lay his power.
'No war' was, we are told, a favourite expression of
Elizabeth's at the council board. 'No quarrels' was cer-

tainly a favourite thought, if not a favourite expression,
of Parnell. To have any single force which made for
Irish nationality in conflict with any other force which
made in the same direction, or which could by any possibility be brought to make in the same direction, was
utterly abhorrent to him. And yet danger of such a
conflict there was in 1876. The Fenians were getting
thoroughly tired of Home Rule. They had given the
movement a fair trial, and nothing had come of it. It
was now time, many of them thought, to look to
their own organisation and to that alone. Within the
parliamentary ranks there were divisions and dissensions. Butt had ceased to be a power. The
constitutional movement was drifting on the rocks.
It was a period in the history of the country when
everything depended on the appearance of a man.
O'Connell would have got the Church at his back,
broken with the Fenians, and inaugurated a mighty
constitutional agitation. A Stephens would have
reorganised Fenianism on a formidable basis, fought
the Church and Constitutionalists, and drawn the
country into insurrection. But there was no O'Connell,
no Stephens. Parnell came; he was unlike both the
great agitator and the great conspirator. He was not
a son of the Church. He was not a son of the revolution. But he believed profoundly in the power of the
one and of the other, and resolved to combine both.
This was a herculean labour, but it was not above the
stature of Charles Stewart Parnell. 'Ireland,' he once
said, 'cannot afford to lose a single man.' That was
his creed. To combine all Irishmen in solid mass and
hurl them at the Saxon, that was his policy. In the
ensuing pages we shall find him pursuing that policy,
steadily, skilfully. We shall find him gradually winning

the confidence of the Church and of the Fenians—the two great forces, be it said, in Irish politics—and ultimately obtaining an ascendency over both. We shall find him forming and dominating a strictly disciplined parliamentary party, and at length reaching that position of eminence well described by the title which the people gave him—the ' uncrowned King of Ireland.'

CHAPTER VII

WAR

THE Queen's Speech in opening the parliamentary session of 1877 contained the following paragraph about Ireland :

'You will be asked to constitute one Supreme Court of Judicature for Ireland, and to confer an equitable jurisdiction in the county courts of that country.'

Every question that stirred the nation was calmly ignored — land, education, parliamentary franchise, Home Rule. The people had asked for bread in the shape of legislative freedom ; they were offered a stone in the shape of a Judicature Bill. Yet Butt showed no disposition to harass the Government. He was resolved to bring forward his Irish measures, to fight them through the House of Commons in accordance with the ordinary rules of the game, and to abide the result. But Parnell and Biggar were now practically in revolt and on the war track. 'If we are to have parliamentary action,' said the former in one of those short, sharp, and decisive sentences which always meant business, 'it must not be the action of conciliation, but of retaliation,' and on the policy of retaliation he was now more than ever inexorably bent.

In 1876 Parnell had already fleshed his sword. In the spring of 1877 he regularly opened the obstruction campaign. He singled out the Mutiny Bill and the Prisons Bill for attack. Anyone reading 'Hansard' now would see nothing unusual in his proceedings. For anything that appears to the contrary, he might have been influenced by a *bonâ-fide* desire to improve both measures. 'Parnell excelled us all,' said one of his obstructive colleagues, 'in obstructing as if he were really acting in the interests of the British legislators.' He was cool, calm, business-like, always kept to the point, and rarely became aggressive in voice or manner. Sometimes he would give way with excellent grace, and with a show of conceding much to his opponents ; but he never abandoned his main purpose, never relinquished his determination to harass and punish the 'enemy.' The very quietness of his demeanour, the orderliness with which he carried out a policy of disorder, served only to exasperate, and even to enrage, his antagonists. One night an Irish member proposed that the committee on the Irish Prisons Bill should be put off, as the Irish members ' would shortly have to attend the grand juries at the assizes in Ireland.' This was barefaced obstruction. But Parnell would have none of it. Rising with the dignity of a Minister responsible for the despatch of public business, he said: 'I think the business of the nation should be attended to before local affairs, and therefore the attendance at the grand juries is no reason for postponing the committee.' Who could charge this man with obstruction ? Upon another occasion he moved an amendment to the English Prisons Bill. Mr. Newdigate (who had sometimes gone into the same lobby with him in the divisions on the Bill, for

Parnell drew his amendments with so much skill that he often caught an English vote) asked him to withdraw the amendment. Biggar (who used to say that *he* never withdrew anything) urged Parnell to persevere; but Parnell, with much show of grace, said: ' Out of deference to the committee I will not press my amendment, although I consider I shall be doing wrong in abandoning it. I must, however, say that it is incorrect for any hon. member to say that I am chargeable with obstructing the business of the House. My opinion on obstruction is that when it is employed it should be like the action of the bayonet—short, sharp, and decisive.'

From February 14, when his Bill for facilitating the creation of a peasant proprietary under the operation of the Church Act was rejected, up to April 12 Parnell was constantly in evidence, constantly interfering in the business of the House, constantly obstructing, constantly seeking to turn everything upside down with tantalising politeness and provoking tenacity. 'How came Parnell,' I asked one of his obstructive colleagues, 'to lead you all in these fights ? He was not an able speaker, he was deficient in intellectual gifts, which many of you possessed, he had little parliamentary experience.' ' By tenacity,' was the answer. ' Sheer tenacity. He stuck on when the rest of us gave way.'

' What was Parnell's distinguishing characteristic ? ' I asked another of his colleagues who loved him not. He answered, ' He was a beautiful fighter. He knew exactly how much the House would stand. One night I was obstructing. S—— was near me. He was generally timid, afraid of shocking the House. He said : " O ——, you had better stop or you will be suspended."

" Oh, no," quietly interjected Parnell, who was sitting
by us, " they will stand a good deal more than this.
You may go on for another half-hour." I did go on
for another half-hour or so. Then there was an awful
row, and I stopped. Parnell had gauged the exact
limit. Another night I was obstructing again. Parnell
came in suddenly and said, " Stop now, or there will
be an explosion in five minutes, and I don't want
a row to-night." In all these things Parnell was
perfect.'

It is needless to say that in all these fights Mr.
Biggar was his right-hand man. It was a rule of
the House that no opposed business should be taken
after half-past twelve at night. Biggar used this rule
to block every Bill, important or unimportant, which
was introduced after the prescribed hour. 'After
every order of the day,' wrote the London correspondent of the 'Liverpool Daily Post' in March
1877, 'there is this announcement. "Mr. Biggar:
That this Bill be read a second time this day six
months."'

Butt was sadly perplexed by the tactics of his two
unruly lieutenants. He hated obstruction. He believed
it was discreditable and mischievous. And yet the
House by its constant rejection of Irish Bills exposed
itself to this policy of retaliation. Parnell and Biggar
were not without justification. Butt felt this as well
as anybody else. Yet he thought, upon the whole,
that the policy of ' retaliation ' was undignified and
useless, and that the proper remedy was more con-
centration on Irish measures and more persistence in
pushing them to the front. He had, however, this
difficulty to contend with : the Moderate Home Rulers
could not be kept up to the collar, the energetic Irish

members were unruly, the orderly Irish members were
apathetic. This was Butt's difficulty. While the
House was smarting under Parnell's attacks, much
pressure was used by the Moderate Home Rulers and
by the English members to induce Butt to crush
him. Parnell was aware of this, but he stuck to
his guns, and was resolved, in the last resort, to fight
it out with his leader rather than abandon the policy
of obstruction. In justice to the young member for
Meath this much must be said. While in the main
his object was obstruction pure and simple, yet he did
introduce some amendments with a sincere desire of
improving the measures under consideration. I will
give an instance. On April 5 he moved an amendment
on the Prisons Bill to the effect that any prisoners
convicted of treason-felony, sedition, or seditious libel
should be treated as first-class misdemeanants. 'It is
high time,' he said, 'that an attempt was made to
remove from England the reproach that she treated
her political prisoners worse than any other country
in the world. In France even the Communards,
who half burnt Paris, and to whom were attributed
the most atrocious designs, were not sent to the
hulks or the galleys, but simply expatriated. When
history comes to be written there is nothing for which
the children of Englishmen now living would blush so
much as for the treatment of the [Fenian] men convicted in 1865. . . . I hope that this Bill when it
leaves the committee will be so framed that political
prisoners will not be treated as murderers, demons,
and culprits of the worst order.' A long debate
followed, and Parnell ultimately, on the suggestion
of Sir Henry James, withdrew the words 'treason-
felony,' retaining the words 'sedition' and 'seditious

libel,' and with this alteration the clause was added to
the Bill.

But there was more of pure obstruction in his
opposition to the Mutiny Bill on April 12. He,
Captain Nolan, and Biggar fought many clauses, and
at length, about twelve o'clock, Biggar moved to
'report progress.' 'It was quite too late,' he said, 'to
go on with the Bill, as there were several important
amendments to be proposed.'

Mr. Gathorne-Hardy. 'I hope the committee will
pass the unopposed clauses.'

Parnell. 'Will the Government undertake to report
progress when Clause 55 is passed?'

Mr. Gathorne-Hardy. 'I propose to take the clauses
up to Clause 93.'

Parnell. 'The Government are unreasonable. I
have endeavoured to facilitate business. But an example of obstruction was set the other night by hon.
members opposite, who would not allow the Bill of the
hon. member for Sheffield (Mr. Mundella) to proceed,
and not only so, but the Government followed their
disorderly supporters into the lobby.' (Cries of 'Order.')

The Chairman. 'The expression just used is certainly one that should not be used by hon. members.'

The unimpassioned page of Hansard gives no notion
of the state of excitement into which the House (a full
House) was plunged during this altercation. Most of
the clauses in question were unopposed. Members were
impatient, and anxious to get the business through
quickly. There was really nothing which needed
serious discussion. But Parnell inexorably blocked
the way. The House stormed and raged, but the
member for Meath held his ground defiantly. The
Moderate Home Rulers were as much shocked at his

conduct as any English member. Butt was not
present. He was sitting quietly in the smoking-room.
Thither several Irish members hastened to tell their
leader what was going on, and to urge him to interfere.
English members came to him too, and implored him
to save the dignity of Parliament and suppress his
unruly follower. Butt, after some hesitation, at length
yielded to these importunities, rushed into the House
flushed with passion and indignation, and pounced on
the member for Meath. 'I regret,' he said, 'that the
time of the House has been wasted in this miserable
and wretched discussion. If at this hour of the night
any member really wished to propose a serious amendment, I would support the motion to "report progress,"
and so also, I think, would the Secretary for War. But
when there was no amendment to a number of clauses,
I must express my disapproval of the course taken by
the hon. member for Meath. It is a course of obstruction, and one against which I must enter my protest.
I am not responsible for the member for Meath, and
cannot control him. I have, however, a duty to discharge to the great nation of Ireland, and I think I
should discharge it best when I say I disapprove
entirely of the conduct of the hon. member for
Meath.'

This speech was received with ringing cheers from
all parts of the House. But how did the member for
Meath take his castigation? He sat calmly, cynically
by, watching his leader with a placid smile. Well he
knew that the English cheers which greeted Butt only
sounded the political death knell of the Home Rule
leader. No Irishman who had attacked a comrade in
the face of the 'common enemy,' and because he fought
the common enemy, could ever again command the

sympathy of the Fenian organisations; and without
the help of the Fenians no man could lead the Home
Rule movement.   But Butt had allowed himself to be
carried away by the English cheers, and had for the
moment thought only of the House of Commons.
Parnell cared nothing for the House of Commons, and
thought chiefly of the extreme men in Ireland and in
England.

Parnell disposed of Butt's oration in a single
sentence: 'The hon. and learned gentleman,' he said,
'was not in the House when I attempted to explain why
I had not put down notice of my amendments.'   That
was enough.   Butt had attacked him without having
heard him in justification of his position.   Parnell
knew that the single sentence he had spoken in reply
would filter through the Fenian mind and would arouse
Fenian sympathies; and, as subsequent events proved,
he did not count without his host.   Four days later
he was again in evidence, obstructing as vigorously
and persistently as ever.

On April 16 the Marine Mutiny Bill was under
consideration.   Parnell protested against the clause
dealing with crime punishable by death.   He suggested that there should be some classification of
offences, and that any offence which did not involve
any moral depravity, or any injury to an officer, or
any other person, might be punished by imprisonment with or without hard labour instead of penal
servitude.

All his amendments on the Mutiny Bill (Marine
and Army) and on the Prisons Bill were directed to
mitigate their severity, and several of them were
adopted.   There was obstruction—plenty of obstruction, wilful obstruction—in his tactics; but I feel I am

doing him only the barest justice in saying that many of the amendments were inspired by humane and manly considerations.[1]

On June 5 he said, speaking on an amendment moved by Mr. O'Connor Power, that it was unnecessary for him to go further into the question, for the complaints of the Fenian prisoners were fully established before the Devon Commission ; but before he sat down he wished to say that the Irish people were deeply interested in this question, that it was a question on which they could go to extremities as they could not go on any other Irish question.

On June 14, 1877, he returned to the subject. He reminded the House that the Devon Commission had recommended that certain relaxations should be made in the treatment of political prisoners, and that they should be kept apart from other convicts ; and he trusted the Home Secretary would see his way to give effect to that recommendation.

The breach between Butt and Parnell had now widened much ; and before the end of May the struggle for the mastery had commenced.

A lengthy correspondence between them appeared in the 'Freeman's Journal.' Parnell wrote on April 13 complaining of Butt's action in the House of Commons on the previous day : [2]

---

[1] On the motion of Parnell the following clauses were added to the Prisons Bill on June 14, 1877 : 'It shall not be lawful for any jailor to order any prisoner to be confined in a punishment cell for any term exceeding twenty-four hours, nor shall it be lawful for the Visiting Committee of Justices to order any prisoner to be punished by confinement in a punishment cell for any term exceeding fourteen days.' 'In a case where an inquest is held on the body of a person who dies in prison, no person engaged in any sort of trade or dealing with the prison shall be a juror on such inquest.'

[2] *Ante*, p. 112.

Parnell to Butt

'On that occasion I yielded my judgment to your opinion upon a matter regarding which full individual liberty of action had always been left to each member of our party. You will recollect that upon the only occasion when you suggested that our party should follow you on a question of Imperial policy it was, after a long discussion, decided that each individual should act for himself. I must then, in future, claim for myself that liberty of action upon Imperial and English matters which has hitherto been granted to every member of the party, while I shall continue to follow your lead in regard to Irish questions.'

Butt replied on April 21 in a very long letter, the import of which may, however, be gathered from the following extracts :

'If I rightly interpret your letter, I understand you to say that, while you owe to me in relation to Irish measures that which you are good enough to call "allegiance," your conduct in all Imperial and English measures is free from obligation either to me or the party in whose ranks you have enrolled yourself. . . . I must dissent from your view of the relation in which each member of our party stands to the rest.

'The pledge which we take is clear, plain, and distinct :

' "That, deeply impressed with the importance of unity of action upon all matters that can affect the parliamentary position of the Home Rule party, or the interests of the Home Rule cause, we engage to each other and the country to obtain that unity by taking counsel together, by making all reasonable concessions to the opinions of each other, by avoiding as far as

possible isolated action, and by sustaining and supporting each other in the course that may be deemed
best calculated to promote the grand object of self-
government which the nation has committed to our
care.''

'This pledge carefully defines the limits of our
obligations. The application of that engagement to
our conduct in the House does not depend upon the
point whether it relates to Irish or English or Imperial
questions, but whether it is such as can affect the parliamentary position of the Home Rule party or the interests
of the Home Rule cause. In all matters that affect the
parliamentary position of the Home Rule party or the
interests of the Home Rule cause we have solemnly
bound ourselves to avoid setting up any private opinions
of our own, to defer to the judgment of our colleagues,
and to sustain and support each other in the course
that may be deemed best calculated to promote the
great object we have in view. I am sure you will, on
reflection, see that to limit the effect of this pledge to
our conduct on Irish measures would be an evasion of
its plain and direct terms. Were such a construction
possible, it would reduce the pledge to an absurdity.
It would enable any professing Home Rule member to
intrigue with any English party, to give his vote on
every Imperial or English question to serve the interests
of the faction of which he might be the minion, and to
fulfil his pledge to his country by voting two or three
times in the year on questions on which his vote could
not do his masters any harm.'

Butt went on to say that he had no objection to see
Parnell and other Irish members take part in debates
on English and Imperial affairs, provided they acted
bonâ fide in the public interests. 'But,' he added, 'it

is impossible not to see that your action in the House is considered both by friends and enemies as an organised system of policy adopted not for English but for Irish purposes, and one which both friends and enemies do not hesitate to describe as a policy " of obstruction."

' I feel that I am in a position in which I can judge of the effect that is likely to be produced by any " policy of obstruction." It must tend to alienate from us our truest and our best English friends.

' It must waste in aimless and objectless obstruction the time which we might, in some form or other, obtain for the discussion of Irish grievances. It must expose us to the taunts of being unfit to administer even the forms of representative government, and even of discrediting and damaging every movement we make.

' But, if I urge these grounds of prudence, I am not insensible of that which is higher than all prudence— the duty of maintaining before the civilised world the dignity of the Irish nation and the Irish cause. That will only be done while we respect ourselves and our duties to the assembly of which we are members—an assembly to degrade which is to strike a blow at representative institutions all over the world, a blow that will recoil with terrible severity on the very claims we make for our own country, but which, whatever be its effects, would be unworthy of ourselves and our cause.'

Parnell's reply (which I am also obliged to abridge) was written on May 24, 1877 :

' Your interpretation of the views which I expressed in my last letter regarding my obligations to yourself (not to the Home Rule party, as you state) is not a correct one, and does not accurately convey either the expressions used by me or their sense. I did not say, or in any measure convey, that my conduct on all Imperial and English measures is free from any obligation to the Irish party ; but I did intend you to understand that I should preserve my individual liberty of action, unfettered by your control, upon those English and Imperial questions upon which the Irish party are agreed not to act as a party; while I have always been ready cheerfully to surrender my own opinion to the majority upon any of those questions that our party decided to take up. You remark that " were the pledge only to embrace our conduct on Irish measures " (which I certainly never argued) " it would enable any professing Home Rule member to intrigue with any English party, to give his vote on every English and Imperial question, to serve the interests of the faction of whom he might be the minion, and to fulfil his pledge to his country by voting two or three times in the year on questions on which his vote could not do his masters any harm."

'Now, unfortunately, all these things are precisely what many Home Rule members are constantly doing, and apparently without remonstrance or even attempt at restraint by you. It has been rendered perfectly evident by the experience of four sessions that "any professing Home Rule member may intrigue with any English party," either Whig or Tory, and yet bring upon himself neither your denunciation nor those of that Irish journal which is supposed to be devoted to your interests. . . .

'Now [to go to another point], my clause on the Prisons Bill regarding the treatment of the political

prisoners was supported by all sections of the English
Liberal party, and the Government were compelled to
accept it lest they should be defeated on a division.
Here, then, no adverse effect as regards the support of
Englishmen was produced by my course of action.
Subsequently, on the Marine and Army Mutiny Bills,
amendments that I moved were supported by the full
strength of all sections of the Liberal party present, as
many as 146 and 150 voting for some of the amendments, although at this very time the English Press
was teeming with complaints of my " obstruction," and
you had yourself thought proper to denounce me publicly in the House on similar grounds a night or two
previously.   Here again no English votes were lost to
me owing to my action.   Furthermore, by our action
on the Mutiny Bills I obtained some important restrictions of power to inflict cruel punishments, and
the Government also agreed to submit these Bills to
the consideration of a select committee—Bills that for
many years had been adopted as a matter of course
almost without discussion.

' The hours at or after midnight are always reserved
for Irish Bills, and it is a physical impossibility that it
could be otherwise.   Consequently no action of mine
can diminish the chances of Ireland obtaining what
she has never had—a share in the Government time.
On the other hand, nothing that I have done interferes
with the time at the disposal of private members, as I
have not interfered with measures brought in by ˙ such
members.

' I cannot sympathise with your conclusions as to
my duty towards the House of Commons.   If Englishmen insist on the artificial maintenance of an anti-
quated institution which can only perform a portion of

its functions by the " connivance " of those intrusted
with its working, in the imperfect and defective
performance of much of even that portion—if the continued working of this institution is constantly attended
with much wrong and hardship to my country, as
frequently it has been the source of gross cruelty and
tyranny—I cannot consider it is my duty to connive in
the imperfect performance of these functions, while I
should certainly not think of obstructing any useful,
solid, or well-performed work.'

While this correspondence was going on Parnell
wrote the following letter to Dr. Kenny with reference
to the Tipperary election, then pending :

'MY DEAR DR. KENNY,—I do not think ———
would be much use. We have too many men of his
stamp already, who consider that they are sent here
to make a parliamentary reputation and not to attend
to the interests of the country. I quite agree with
you, it is best to let Mr. Biggar, myself, and others
work along quietly for the present. If Butt can only be
induced to let us alone, we are quite equal to the task
we have set ourselves, which is not a very difficult one.

'Yours very truly,
'CHAS. S. PARNELL.'

Parnell now resolved to carry on the fight with
Butt to the bitter end. The Home Rule leader had
the Moderate Home Rulers at his back. The member
for Meath relied on the advanced men. The Home
Rule Confederation of Great Britain—a body influenced
by Fenians—took him up, and under its auspices he
addressed public meetings in England and Scotland.
'We got Parnell a platform,' said the founder of this

organisation—himself a member of the Fenian brother-hood—to me some years ago ; ' we made him.' It would not be accurate to say that the Fenians made Parnell. Parnell made himself. But it would be accurate to say that in Fenianism he found the lever on which his power turned. Here it will be necessary to add a few words about the Home Rule Confederation of Great Britain.

In 1873 a member of the supreme council of the I. R. B., whom I shall call X., asked Butt if he intended to take any steps for pushing forward the Home Rule cause in England. Butt said that he was rather puzzled to know what to do ; he was anxious to found an English organisation, but afraid that the Fenians might smash it. X. said that he did not think they would smash it ; that they certainly looked suspiciously on Home Rule and disbelieved in parlia-mentary agitation, but that nevertheless they would not place themselves actively in opposition to Butt. It was ultimately agreed between Butt and X. that a Home Rule organisation should be formed in England ; and X. set to work to form it. He found many difficulties in the way. Many Fenians did not take kindly to the notion of co-operating with the Constitutionalists ; they said that union with the Parliamentarians would only weaken their movement. The minds of the people would be fixed on parlia-mentary agitation and drawn away from Fenianism. Parliamentary agitation would end, as it always had ended, in failure ; the upshot of the whole business would be collapse, both of Fenianism and Constitutionalism. X. took a different view. He said : ' We need not give up our own principles by joining the Home Rulers. They go part of the way in our direction ;

why not help them so far? In addition we will stiffen
their backs by joining them. Here are the Irish in
England—a great force; but absolutely lost at present.
It is our policy to make the English feel the presence
of the Irish everywhere. They don't know what a
power the Irish can be made in their midst. The
English only recognise power. We must make ourselves troublesome. We can make ourselves troublesome by organising the Irish vote in Great Britain,
and by forcing the English candidates to take the
Home Rule pledge. We can control the parliamentary
movement if we go into it. At all events, let us
try.'

X.'s arguments at length prevailed among a certain
number of the rank and file of the Fenians, and
the Home Rule Confederation of Great Britain was
formed.

Butt had promised to attend the inaugural meeting
at Manchester. Some of the Moderates, however, got
at him, saying that the association was in the hands
of the Fenians. He became uneasy, and wrote to
X. just on the eve of the meeting to say that he
was afraid he could not attend. X. wired back a
telegram of nearly 1,000 words, urging Butt not to
fail, saying that the meeting had been got up on
the strength of his promise to attend, that delegates had been summoned from all parts of Great
Britain, and that his absence would be nothing short
of an insult. Butt subsequently related to X. the
circumstances under which he received the monster
telegram:

'I was in court at the time; I was addressing the
judges. The telegram was placed in my hands. I
opened the envelope—in itself a formidable document

—and out tumbled a package the like of which was
certainly never seen in telegraphic form before. The
judges looked at it ; everybody looked at it. I said :
" My lords, will you allow me to read this message ? It
may be of importance." They said, " Certainly," and
I sat down and waded through the telegram, turning
over sheet after sheet, to the amazement of the on-
lookers. But it was not your arguments that made
an impression on me—it was the length of the telegram.
" The man," I said, " who has sent me this telegram of
1,000 words must be terribly in earnest, and the men
behind him must be terribly in earnest too," and so I
sent off a reply to you at once.' Butt's reply was short
and to the point. ' Shall be with you if I am alive.'
And so Butt attended the meeting, and the Home
Rule Confederation of Great Britain sprang into being.
' Was the Confederation always under the control of
Fenians ? ' I asked X. ' Always,' he answered. ' They
were well represented on the council ; our best workers
and best organisers were Fenians. Of course, there were
plenty of members who were not Fenians, but the
Fenians were the masters of the situation.' The Home
Rule Confederation of Great Britain did excellent work
for the Home Rule cause in Great Britain. The Irish
vote was perfectly organised ; the Irish voter was
made formidable. Every candidate who stood for a
constituency where the Irish vote was strong had the
following pledge submitted to him : ' To vote for the
appointment of a select committee to inquire into and
report upon the motive, extent, and the grounds of
the demand made by a large proportion of the Irish
people for the restoration to Ireland of an Irish Parliament with power to control the internal affairs of the
country.'

Between 1874 and 1877 several English candidates took this pledge and were returned to Parliament.[1] 'Did the candidates who took the pledge really believe in Home Rule?' I asked X. 'Not at all,' he said; 'they took it to get the Irish vote. The first man who took it was Jacob Bright. They wired to him from the central Liberal offices in London not to take it, and he refused at first. But we held him firm; "the pledge or no Irish vote," we said. Then we went to the Tory, Powell, and he took it right off. The Liberals were in a devil of a fix; but Jacob turned round and took the pledge too. Then we were in a fix, because as the Tory promised first we ought to have supported him; but the Irish preferred the Liberals, and they particularly liked Jacob Bright. Butt came and made a speech. He said that as both candidates had taken the pledge, the Irish might go for whichever they pleased. They voted for Jacob and put him in. Jacob was a good fellow, and would just as soon take the pledge as not, though of course he wouldn't take it if it wouldn't get him in. That's all that most of them thought about—getting in. Wilfrid Lawson and Joe Cowen were exceptions. We had practically no influence in Lawson's constituency (Carlisle), but he went Home Rule all the same. He believed in it. We had influence in Cowen's constituency (Newcastle), but it was not our influence that weighed with Cowen. He would have voted for Home Rule anyway. He was thoroughly Irish in feeling. There was another respectable man who took the pledge—Joseph Kay, of Salford. He took the pledge at the by-election at

---

[1] In 1877 the following were the English Home Rulers in the House of Commons: Barran (Leeds), Jacob Bright (Manchester), Gourley (Sunderland), Hibbert (Oldham), Sir W. Lawson (Carlisle), Macdonald (Stafford), R. N. Philips (Bury), Cowen (Newcastle).

Salford in April 1877. Of course we meant Home
Rule by the pledge. It was the thin edge of the
wedge. It was as far as we could then go. But I
don't know that Kay meant Home Rule. He probably
meant exactly what the pledge said, an inquiry.'

Joseph Kay, Q.C., was the author of two remarkable
books, ' Education of the Poor in England and
Europe,' published in 1846, and ' Social Condition and
Education in England and Europe,' published in 1850.
In the latter work Mr. Kay showed a keen appreciation
of the evils produced by the Irish system of land tenure.
In fact he was an advanced reformer on all subjects,
and felt a deep sympathy for Ireland and the Irish.
He married, in 1863, the eldest daughter of Thomas
Drummond, whose administration of Ireland during
the Melbourne Government (1835-40) has given him
an abiding place in the affections of the people. As
X. said, Kay was in favour of an ' inquiry ' pure and
simple ; he wished to see what would come of it. He
was not sure that it would lead to Home Rule ; but he
did think that it might lead to an examination and
a removal of Irish grievances which might obviate the
necessity of Home Rule. However, his supporters in
Salford and in London thought chiefly of the Irish
vote. With them the question was to get the Liberal
candidate in.

Some extracts from letters written by influential
Liberals at the time anent the Salford election will
make this very clear. Thus, one writes from the
House of Commons on April 4 : ' I have had a conversation this evening about the Home Rulers. It is
most essential that the promise to vote for Mr. Butt's
motion should be given cheerfully [by Mr. Kay] and at
once, as both Mr. Butt and Lord Francis Cunningham

assure me that such a promise will secure the cordial
and thorough support of the Irish voters, and without
such promise, whatever else is said, many will abstain,
and may possibly, under Bishop Vaughan's influence,
go to the other side.'

Another Liberal wrote, on April 6 :

'I have had a long talk with S—— and J——
to-day. They are both against any promise to the
Irish faction, but I feel a promise will be necessary if
you are to win.' Ultimately S—— and J—— agreed
that it was 'necessary' for Kay to make the 'promise,'
in order 'to win.'

J—— himself wrote, oddly enough, on this very
6th of April, saying : 'I understand that the Irish
vote is so large that it would be necessary for the
Liberal candidate to support Mr. Butt's motion for an
inquiry on the subject of Home Rule. Of course I do
not know Mr. Kay's views, but I have no doubt that
this difficulty can be overcome.'

On April 12 another Liberal wrote : 'I think Mr.
Kay should go in for the inquiry into Home Rule. I
got that up with Mr. Butt at the Manchester election,
and the Tory, Mr. Powell, swallowed it. If it will get
the Catholic vote I think Mr. Kay should swallow it
too. It means nothing, and I got it up with Mr. Butt
for that very reason.'

Mr. Kay did promise to vote for an inquiry, with
the approbation of the party managers. But he lost
the election. Then the Liberals were, forsooth,
scandalised, and ascribed his defeat to 'Home Rule
crotchets.' 'London and other newspapers at a distance,' wrote a Salford Liberal, 'may attribute the
defeat to the concession to Home Rule. . . . How is
it that this burning zeal for putting down Home Rule

crotchets on the part of Liberal newspapers did not
manifest itself when a Liberal Home Ruler was
elected for Manchester?   Verily nothing succeeds like
success.'

'Kay lost the seat,' says X., 'by a small majority,
and then there was a great howl among the Liberals
against Home Rule.   They never howled when Liberals
got in on the Home Rule ticket; but the moment
they lost, then it was the " d——d Irish."   But we
stuck to our guns.   When Waddy stood for Sheffield
some time later we made him take the pledge, and put
him in.   Then there was no howl against the Irish.
We showed them our power.   We had to be conciliated,
and the only way to conciliate us—the only way to get
the Irish vote—was to take the Home Rule pledge.
That was the root of the matter.'

In 1877 the Home Rule Confederation of Great
Britain was, then, a formidable body, and to it Parnell
came when his struggle with Butt had reached a crisis.
X. and the Fenians within the Confederation,
though warmly attached to Butt, were thoroughly out
of sympathy with his conciliatory tactics.   They
believed not in soft words, but in hard blows.   I have
already said that the Irishman who carries out a
fighting policy against England in any shape or form
is bound to command the sympathy of the rank and file
of the Fenian organisation.

Throughout 1877 X. saw Parnell frequently in
London.   Parnell said that in order to keep up the fight
in Parliament he should be supported in the country.
'You must get me a platform,' he said to X. in the
summer of 1877.   'You must organise meetings in
England.   I must show that I have something at
my back.   A few men in the House of Commons

cannot carry on the struggle alone. We must have
encouragement outside.' X. organised the meetings.
' In a very short time,' he said, ' I organised thirteen
meetings. I came to the House of Commons and told
Parnell. I expected to find him very much pleased.
But suddenly he looked quite melancholy. " Oh,"
said he, " that will never do." " What will never
do ? " said I. " Thirteen meetings," said he, with a most
lugubrious look ; " you will have to knock one off or put
on one. Don't you know thirteen is a most unlucky
number ? " '

On May 29 Parnell addressed what was practically
a Fenian gathering at Glasgow. Speaking on obstruction he said :

' I am satisfied to abide by the decision of the Irish
people. Are they for peace, and conciliation, or for
hostility and war ? (Cries of " War.") Are you for
making things convenient for England, and for advancing English interests ? If so I will bow to your
decision, but my constituents will have to get someone
else to represent them.'

On July 2 he was in his place in Parliament, again
carrying on the war with renewed vigour. The second of
July was a famous night in the obstruction campaign.
The House was in Committee of Supply. About midnight Mr. O'Connor Power moved to report progress.
' He declined to vote away the public money at such a
late hour.' This was not quite the mode of obstruction
Parnell favoured. It was too transparent, and gave no
opportunity of amending some particular measure so as
to show useful results if the charge of obstruction were
made. Nevertheless, he stood by his colleague. The
motion was defeated by 128 votes to 8. But the fight
was kept up. Mr. O'Donnell next moved ' that the

chairman do now leave the chair.' This motion was defeated by 127 to 6. Then Major O'Gorman came to the front amid 'strong expressions of disapprobation,' and moved to 'report progress,' and so the battle went on. Obstructive motion succeeded obstructive motion, until the House was thrown into a fever of excitement and anger. At three o'clock in the morning, when the obstructives were reduced to five, Parnell, with characteristic coolness, asked the Chancellor of the Exchequer what he wanted. 'Does the right hon. gentleman want a victory over five Irishmen? What is the principle for which he is contending?'

The Chancellor of the Exchequer answered: 'That a small minority shall give way to a large majority.'

But Mr. O'Connor Power, who led the fight, would not give way, and the struggle continued. At half-past three Mr. Whalley protested that the business of the House ought to be carried on 'in the light of day.' The House was weary and angry; but the unconscious humour of this appeal was too much. It was a brilliant July morning, and the 'light of day' was streaming in through the open windows. The House roared, and Whalley succumbed. Mr. O'Donnell rose nearly an hour later to protest once more 'against the shame of this midnight legislation.' The House, however, sat on steadily voting down the irrepressible five, who kept alternately moving that 'the chairman do report progress' and that 'the chairman do now leave the chair' until 7 A.M., when the Government threw up the sponge and left the obstructives triumphant.

On July 15 Parnell addressed a great meeting at Manchester, one of X.'s thirteen, or rather fourteen meetings. He said: 'For my part, I must tell you that I do not believe in a policy of conciliation of English feeling or English prejudices. I believe that you may go on trying to conciliate English prejudice until the day of judgment, and that you will not get the breadth of my nail from them. What did we ever get in the past by trying to conciliate them?'

A Voice. 'Nothing except the sword.' (Applause.)

Parnell. 'Did we get the abolition of tithes by the conciliation of our English taskmasters? No; it was because we adopted different measures. (Applause.) Did O'Connell gain emancipation for Ireland by conciliation? (Cries of " No.") I rather think that O'Connell in his time was not of a very conciliatory disposition, and that at least during a part of his career he was about the best-abused Irishman living. (Laughter and loud applause.) Catholic emancipation was gained because an English king and his Minister feared revolution. (Applause.) Why was the English Church in Ireland disestablished and disendowed? Why was some measure of protection given to the Irish tenant? It was because there was an explosion at Clerkenwell and because a lock was shot off a prison van at Manchester. (Great applause.) We will never gain anything from England unless we tread upon her toes; we will never gain a single sixpennyworth from her by conciliation.' (Great cheering.)

On July 25 there was another encounter between the Irishmen and the Government. The South Africa Bill—the Bill for the annexation of the Transvaal—was in committee. It was opposed, not only by Parnell and his little band, but by some British members as well, notably by Mr. Courtney and Mr. Jenkins. On this particular night Mr. Jenkins and 'other hon. members' were charged by Mr. Monk with 'abusing the forms of the House.' Mr. Jenkins individually repudiated the imputation, and moved that Mr. Monk's words 'be taken down.'

Parnell. 'I second that motion. I think the limits of forbearance have been passed in regard to the language which hon. members opposite have thought proper to address to me and to those who act with me.' Here the Chancellor of the Exchequer somewhat precipitately pounced on Mr. Parnell, and moved that his words 'be taken down.' The House expected Parnell to withdraw or explain. He would do neither. On the contrary, he delivered, amidst constant interruption, a series of short, cutting speeches which irritated the House, and expressed his own utter contempt of the whole proceedings. Sir Stafford Northcote watched him carefully to see if, under the excitement of the moment, he might slip into some incautious phrase which would deliver him into the hands of his enemies. At last the moment for which the Chancellor had anxiously watched arrived. Parnell, concluding his remarks with apparent warmth and raising his voice almost to a shriek, while the assembly, wild with passion, surged around him, said: 'As it was with Ireland, so it was with the South African Colonies; yet Irish members were asked to assist the Government in carrying out their selfish and inconsiderate policy. Therefore, as an Irishman, coming from a country that had experienced to its fullest extent the results of English interference in its affairs and the consequences of English cruelty and tyranny, I feel a special satisfaction in preventing and thwarting the intentions of the Government in respect of this Bill.'

There was a roar of indignation from all parts of the House as the member for Meath resumed his seat. Sir Stafford at once arose, amid a salvo of cheers,

which were repeated again and again as he moved
'that the words of the hon. member be taken down.'
The Speaker was sent for.   Parnell's words were
taken down: 'I feel a special satisfaction in preventing and thwarting the intentions of the Government.' The wily rebel had at length been caught
napping, his coolness had for once deserted him.
So thought the House, as Sir Stafford moved, amid
general applause : ' That the hon. member for Meath
be suspended from his functions of speaking and
taking part in the debates of the House until
Friday next.'   The Speaker at once called on
Parnell to 'explain.'   Parnell rose, and in his iciest
manner said that his words had been accurately taken
down ; though he rather thought that he had used the
word ' interest ' instead of ' satisfaction.'   He regretted
that the whole of his speech was not taken down, as he
wished to emphasise his condemnation of the Government policy.   ' I need not refer to history to support
the accusation that successive Governments of this
country have always treated those whom they thought
they could bully and oppress without reference to their
interest.'

This was not 'explanation,' it was 'defiance,' and
the Speaker called Parnell to order.   Parnell's whole
answer was that he condemned the policy of the
Government, and would persevere in his efforts to
thwart it.   He then withdrew, and taking up a position
in the gallery looked down on the scene below.   He
soon witnessed the complete discomfiture of the Chancellor of the Exchequer and his own absolute triumph.
It was the Chancellor, not Parnell, who had been
carried away by the excitement of the moment.   Parnell
had said that he would ' thwart,' not the business of

the *House of Commons* (which was the meaning attached to his words in the general confusion), but the intentions of the *Government*—a very different thing.

Mr. Knatchbull-Hugessen, who had not a particle of sympathy with Parnell, put the case clearly before the House after Parnell had withdrawn. 'I am sure,' said he, 'that the Chancellor of the Exchequer would not contend that the member for Meath should be punished because he wished to thwart the intentions of the Government.' 'Certainly not,' said Sir Stafford with emphasis. The House soon saw the situation. Sir Stafford had blundered. Mr. Gathorne-Hardy rose immediately to move that the 'debate (on the motion to suspend Parnell) be adjourned until Friday.'[1] The motion was carried, and Parnell, escorted by Biggar, returned to the House, and resumed his speech on the South African Bill just at the point where he had been interrupted, as if nothing unusual had occurred.

On Friday, July 27, Sir Stafford Northcote proposed two new rules for dealing with obstruction, the effect of which was (1) that a member twice declared out of order might be suspended; (2) that the motion 'to report progress,' and kindred motions, could only be moved once by the same member in the same debate. Parnell offered no serious opposition to these rules. He knew it would be useless. But he made a short speech in defence of his own conduct, which may be taken as a fair specimen of his concentrated style of argument and general mode of repelling obstructive accusations.

'I suppose every newspaper in England contained charges of obstruction against me on account of my action on the Prisons Bill. But what was the result

---

[1] The debate was never resumed.

of my action? Why, it was that more of the clauses
of the present Bill have been proposed and carried by
me than by all the Conservative members put together.
Those clauses were admittedly useful and good ones;
and I was told afterwards that if I confined myself to
moving such amendments or to discussing measures
in that way, instead of obstructing them, I would be
filling a good and useful part in the House.   Then
came the discussions on the Mutiny Bill. I ventured
to propose some amendments in those time-honoured
institutions, which I suppose have not been interfered
with for a quarter of a century, and again I was told I
was obstructing. I moved some amendments in committee, but, owing to the paucity of attendance, I did
not get many members to support them—not more
than 40 or 50. There was also the disadvantage that
they had been prepared hastily, and that I had not had
time to get them on paper. I determined therefore to
move them again on report. This also was obstruction.
What right had an Irish member to move amendments
on report which had already been rejected? Again
I was justified by the results; for I was supported by
140 or 150 members, including the whole of the front
Opposition bench, and including gentlemen who had
since been loud in charging me with obstruction.'

Four days after the adoption of the new rules obstruction was carried to an extent hitherto unparalleled
in the history of the House of Commons. On Tuesday,
July 31, the House was again in committee on the
South African Bill. The Government wished to push
the measure through the committee stage that night.
The Irishmen were determined to prevent them. About
5 P.M. Mr. O'Donnell began operations by moving 'to
report progress.' Parnell supported the motion, saying

that there was much information that the House yet needed on the whóle question, and protesting against rash legislation. Sir William Harcourt quickly joined in the fray, interrupting Parnell, charging him with deliberate obstruction, and appealing to the House to put down the small minority who sought to destroy its utility. When Sir William sat down, Parnell said, in the most unruffled manner, ' Sir, I will now continue my observations.' He was greeted with a perfect storm of yells from every part of the House. He paused, waited patiently until there was a lull, and then went on with his remarks. The chairman called him to order, but still he persevered with excellent temper and great courtesy, complimenting the chairman on the fairness of his ruling, but nevertheless showing no intention of giving way. Finally the motion ' to report progress ' was withdrawn. But other obstructive motions rapidly followed, and the House was soon thrown into a ferment of disorder. At one stage of the proceedings the din was so great that Parnell, finding it impossible to command the attention of the chairman, walked very coolly from his place below the gangway to the table, and there, amid a lull caused by his supreme audacity, resumed his observations.

Upon another occasion he warned hon. members that they were wasting the time of the House in entering into personal quarrels, instead of sticking to the Bill. 'As for the threats of physical endurance held out to me, I can assure the House if hon. members divide themselves into relays, my friends [1] and I can divide ourselves into relays too.'

At three o'clock in the morning Butt burst in upon

---

[1] Parnell's force ' all told ' numbered five men—Biggar, O'Donnell, O'Connor Power, Kirk, and Parnell.

the scene, denounced the obstructives, and then disappeared. But the fight went on. At 7 A.M. the
Chancellor of the Exchequer asked the minority to
yield. 'They were suffering considerable physical inconvenience,' he said, and he recognised the gallantry
with which the struggle had been carried on. But
Parnell would not yield. 'The Government are
bringing up reserve forces,' he said, 'the first mail-
boat will bring them from Ireland; and even in
London the member for Cavan (Biggar), though now
peacefully asleep, will soon return like a giant re-
freshed.' At 7.40 A.M. Biggar re-appeared and informed
the House that he had had 'a long sleep and a good
breakfast,' and was ready to carry on the fight à
outrance. Parnell retired at 8 A.M., but was back again
at twelve noon, Mr. O'Donnell, Mr. Kirk, Captain
Nolan, Mr. Gray, and Biggar, having meanwhile
kept the obstructive flag flying. At twelve Parnell
pressed the Government to allow progress to be
reported; but the Government refused. The fight
then went on for two hours longer, when at 2 P.M.
the Bill was passed through committee and the House
adjourned, having sat continuously for twenty-six
hours. Through that long sitting there was one
occupant of the Ladies' Gallery who never deserted
her post—Miss Fanny Parnell.

Parnell was now one of the most universally
detested men in England. In Ireland and among
the Irish in Great Britain he was a hero. He had
flouted the House of Commons, he had harassed the
Government, he had defied English public opinion.
These were his claims to Irish popularity. 'The
Fenians,' said X., 'did not wish public attention
to be fixed on Parliament. But Parnell fixed it on

Parliament by fixing it on himself. Yet many of our people thought that he was simply wasting his time. He was a man of energy and resource, that was clear. But were not his powers lost in Parliament? Could not his abilities be turned to infinitely better account in the Fenian organisation? So many of our people thought. And in fact I was, about this time, deputed to ask Parnell to join us. I did ask him. He said "No" without a moment's hesitation. He had the fullest sympathy with us. He wished our organisation to remain intact. He had no desire to interfere with us in any way. But he said we ought not to interfere with him. He felt that he could turn the parliamentary machine to good account. He had no doubt on the point. He was not disposed to argue the question. All he would say was that he saw his way quite clear. "Have patience with me," he said; "give me a trial for three or four years. Then, if I cannot do anything, I will step aside. But give me a trial and have patience with me!" That was a favourite phrase of his, "have patience."'

'What was it about Parnell that struck you most?'

X. 'His silence. It was extraordinary. One was not accustomed to it. All Irish agitators talked. He didn't. He listened with wonderful patience. His reserve was a revelation. We used to say: "If ever there was a man for a secret society, this is the man—he can hold his tongue!" But I could never discover that Parnell had the least notion at any time of joining us. That was just what was so remarkable about him. He never led any of us to believe that he would become a Fenian, and nevertheless he gained a complete ascendency over us. Why he gained this ascendency nobody could very well tell, but that he gained it everyone felt.

Then he was delightful to do business with : so quick, so ready, so clear-headed, and never in doubt about anything which ought to be done. He was a great man of action.'

' Was he at this time pleasant, genial, sociable ? '

X. ' Pleasant, certainly, but genial, sociable— scarcely. All the pleasure was in doing business with him. He was always at his best when dealing with practical questions. In general conversation he drooped. I think he hated talking. However, I have seen Parnell " at play." One evening coming from the House of Commons, in April 1877, I said : " Mr. Parnell, do you ever go to places of amusement ? " " Oh, yes, sometimes," he said ; " would you like to go to any place now ? " I said, " Yes ; let us go to the theatre." " Oh, no," said he, " let us go and see Dan O'Leary walk." [1] And we went to the Agricultural Hall to see the walking match between O'Leary and Weston. Parnell took a keen interest in the match, but the interest was centred entirely in O'Leary. O'Leary won and Parnell was highly pleased. The band struck up " God save the Queen " as soon as the match was over. " What nonsense ! " said Parnell, " why, it ought to be ' God save Ireland ' in honour of Dan O'Leary —the man who won. Make them play ' God save Ireland.' " I said that was impossible ; that it was the custom of the country to play " God save the Queen " at the end of these entertainments. " Oh, nonsense ! " said he, " they must compliment the man who won, that's only fair. Tell them to play ' God save Ireland ' ; explain the reason. Here, give them

---

[1] Dan O'Leary was a native of Cork and a naturalised citizen of the United States. In April 1877 there was a great walking match between him and Weston (an American), at the Agricultural Hall, Islington, for 1000*l*., or 500*l*. aside. The match lasted six days and O'Leary won.

these two sovereigns." Well, I laughed at the notion;
but he was so earnest that I went off to the band.
The bandmaster was a German. I did not ask him
to play " God save Ireland," for I knew he would not
understand it. But I asked him to play " Tramp,
tramp, tramp, the boys are marching," which is the
same tune. He said : " Oh, now we have played ' God
save the Queen ' it is all over." I explained to him that
"Tramp, tramp, tramp, the boys are marching " was
very appropriate, and that O'Leary, who had won, was
anxious to hear it. The German smiled at this, and
seemed to think there was something in it. At the
same time I slipped four sovereigns into his hand (two
from myself as well as Parnell's two), and the band
immediately struck up "Tramp, tramp," &c., to the
delight of Parnell and to the bewilderment of everybody
else. I remember Sir John Astley was there, and he
was very vexed.'

'Had Parnell any sense of humour?'

X. 'Oh, yes, he had, but it was very peculiar.
He would never laugh at the ordinary good story. In
fact, you never could tell what would exactly amuse
him. Certain things used to tickle him very much,
though other people used not to see much fun in them.
For instance, John Barry and Garrett Byrne, two of
the stoutest men of the Irish party, were " paid off "
on one occasion to " schedule " the distressed districts.
Parnell used to smile immoderately at this (he never
laughed outright). " Look," he would say, " at the
tellers for the _distressed_ districts," and he would enjoy
the joke very quietly to himself. His face used quite
to beam at the idea when he would see Barry or
Byrne, fat and well favoured, walking across the lobby.
There was a farmer in County Wicklow named Codd—

Nicholas Codd ; he was popularly called Nicky Codd.
He had a dispute with his landlord. He offered the
landlord a reduced rent, which the landlord would not
accept. An ambassador was sent to Nicky to see if a
compromise could be arranged. " But suppose, Mr.
Codd," said the ambassador, "that the landlord insists
on not accepting your offer, is there not some alternative." " Yes," said Nicky, " there is." The ambassador
was satisfied. He thought that they would at length
arrive at a *modus vivendi.* " What is the alternative,
Mr. Codd ? " said he. " He may go to hell," said
Nicky. I told this story to Parnell and it tickled him
greatly. Afterwards, whenever he was engaged in
negotiations himself, and whenever he made an offer
which was refused, he would say, " Very well ; they
can take Nicky Codd's alternative." Nicky Codd's
alternative became quite a saying of his.'

Another informant, one of Parnell's obstructive
colleagues in the House of Commons, corroborates,
more or less, X.'s statement about Parnell's 'social
qualities.' This gentleman also said that Parnell was
rather 'pleasant than genial, or sociable, though he
always had a charm of manner which made him a
most agreeable companion. We [the obstructives] used
to dine together at Gatti's in the Strand. He certainly
did not contribute much to the " fun " of the meeting.
He never told a good story, he was not a good con-
versationalist in any sense, but he was appreciative
and a splendid listener. We all talked around him,
and he seemed to enjoy the conversation while taking
little part in it. He was only " on the spot " when
something had to be done. One evening he and I
were walking along Oxford Street (I think). We passed
a music-hall. He looked at the people going in and

said : " Let us go in to this place," and we went in.
But he took little interest in the performance. He sat
down in a dreamy state and seemed to me to be half
asleep most of the time. But an acrobat soon appeared,.
and Parnell suddenly woke up. He watched this man
all the while, then said to me, " Now, why should that
man be tumbling about on the stage and I sitting here ?
Why shouldn't I be on the stage and he here ? Chance,
just that. You see everything is chance."

'This seemed to show the democratic strain which
ran through the Parnells' character. Aristocratic and
autocratic as he was, he couldn't recognise anything
but chance in the arrangement of things. The accident
of birth was everything.'

Parliament was prorogued on August 14. No
measure of any importance had been passed for Ireland.
Another year of failure had been added to the record
of the Parliamentarians.

Land, education, franchise, all questions great and
small were left unsettled ; while, as for Home Rule,
the ' Times '[1] well expressed English public opinion on
the subject in the following contemptuous sentences :

'Parliament will not, cannot grant Home Rule.
The mere demand for it lies beyond the range of
practical discussion. The utmost favour which the
House of Commons can show to its advocates is to
listen to them with patience and courtesy once a year.'[2]
England would not legislate for Ireland, nor allow
Ireland to legislate for herself ; that was the situation.

---

[1] *Times*, April 20, 1877.

[2] Butt's annual motion for an inquiry into the nature, extent, and
grounds of the demand for Home Rule was rejected in 1877 (April 24)
by 417 to 67 votes. The following English members voted for the
motion : Barran (Leeds), Jacob Bright (Manchester), Gourley (Sunderland), Hibbert (Oldham), Lawson (Carlisle), Macdonald (Stafford).
Philips (Bury), Cowen (Newcastle).

The Irish people were steadily losing faith in parliamentary agitation; but they watched the career of Parnell with interest and curiosity. What would become of him? Would he remain in Parliament or would he glide into revolution? That was the question which many men in Ireland asked themselves in 1877.

On August 25 Parnell and Biggar attended a great meeting at the Rotunda, Dublin. 'About this time,' says one who was present, 'it was a question among advanced men whether Parnell or Biggar would take foremost place. The Rotunda meeting settled it. The gathering was practically got up by the Fenians. Biggar and Parnell both spoke. Biggar made a very long speech and produced no effect.

'Parnell then came forward. He made a short, quiet speech, badly delivered; but it produced great effect. We said, talking the matter over afterwards: "Biggar has said all he had to say, but Parnell has barely opened his mind to us; there is a lot behind."'

Nevertheless, Parnell stated his views with characteristic clearness, and in the language best suited to the audience he addressed. 'I care nothing,' he said, 'for this English Parliament and its outcries. I care nothing for its existence, if that existence is to continue a source of tyranny and destruction to my country.'

On September 1 the most remarkable event which had yet taken place in the life of Parnell occurred. On that day the Home Rule Confederation of Great Britain held their annual meeting at Liverpool. I must again fall back on X. for an account of what happened: 'Butt was at this time our president, but many of our people had lost confidence in him. We all were warmly attached to him; for he was one of the most

genial and affectionate of men.   Then he had defended
the Fenian prisoners, and had afterwards thrown
himself heart and soul into the amnesty movement.
But his conciliatory tactics in the House of Commons,
his submission to the House of Commons, his deference
to English opinion and feeling, made us distrust him;
not his earnestness, not his anxiety to do the best for
Ireland, but his power to effect anything.   He was
courting English opinion, instead of leaning on us.   We
thought his policy hopeless.   We believed all the time
that you could get nothing out of England but by
fighting her, by showing her we were a power, and
that if she did not grant our demands we could and
would do her harm.   The Irish voters in England had
forced English candidates to take the Home Rule
pledge.   It was not love of us; it was not belief in
Home Rule; it was simply the knowledge that they
could not do without us.   Well, Butt was really
ignoring all that.   He talked in the House of Commons
as if he could, by mere reason and eloquence, persuade
the English to give a Parliament to Ireland.   Why, it
was nonsense.   Parnell's tactics were very different.
He did not believe in talk.   He did not waste time in
argument.   He thought only of one thing (as the
Yankees say), twisting the tail of the British lion.
That was the true policy.   But it was not the policy
of Isaac Butt.

'Well, as the time for holding the meetings of the
Confederation came round I saw Parnell, and discussed
the situation with him.   He said to me one night: "I
think there must be quite a new departure in our
party.   We are only at the beginning of an active
forward policy; but it must be pushed to extremes.   A
few men in the House of Commons can do nothing

unless they are well supported in the country. Something striking must be done. Your organisation must do something striking. You must show plainly you mean to stand by the active men in the House of Commons." That was all he said, but it was enough. "Something striking must be done." I well remember how he said these words; what suppressed energy there was in the voice and manner of the man, and what a strange voice. And how the words used to be forced, as if they were too precious to be parted with— "Something striking must be done"—with outstretched hands and clenched fists, and eyes that went through you all the time. Well, I left Parnell, determined that Butt should be deposed, and that Parnell should become president of the Confederation. That was the most "striking thing" I could think of. It was very painful. I was very fond of Butt. He was himself the kindest-hearted man in the world, and here was I going to do the unkindest thing to him. I had brought him into the association, I had made him president, and here was I now going to depose him. But Parnell's words, "Something striking must be done," rang in my ears, and I felt he was right. But it was a sad business all the same. The meeting took place in September. There was a great gathering. Of course the Fenians bossed the show, and they were determined to a man to make Parnell president. Butt was there, Parnell was there, everyone was there. And what a contrast between Butt and Parnell! Butt with his leonine head, his beaming face, his sparkling eyes, and the merry laugh which used to ring out so cheerily and musically. Parnell, cold and reserved, dignified and almost austere. "My dear fellow, delighted to see you," Butt would say, and he would almost take you into his arms. How

different Parnell's "How do you do, Mr. —— ?" with
a handshake which was warm though hard, and a smile
which was sweet and gracious; you felt there was a
gulf between you and him.   It was different with Butt.
You felt he brought himself down to your level.   You
forgot his genius in his pleasant homely ways.   But
Parnell never descended.   No matter how familiar he
might be, he kept the distance always between himself
and you.   He was always encased in steel.   Well, the
hour of business came.   One of the first items on the
agenda was the election of president.   Parnell was
proposed and seconded, and elected by acclamation.
There was no competitor.   The whole thing was done
in a quiet business-like way, as if it were a mere matter
of form.   I looked at Butt.   There was no mistaking
his feelings.   He felt the blow keenly.   He rose, after
a little time, and said that he was obliged to go to
Dublin on urgent matters of business, and hoped that
the meeting would excuse his absence.   He then
retired.   I followed him from the hall.   There was no
blinking the fact—he was greatly pained by what had
happened.   I determined to tell him frankly the reason
why we had chosen Parnell—that we wanted an advanced policy, and that Parnell was the man to carry
it out.   I came up with Butt near the door.   "Mr.
Butt," I said, "I am very sorry for what has happened,
but it could not be helped."   He turned round; his
eyes were filled with tears, as he said in the most
touching way, "Ah! I never thought the Irish in
England would do this to me."   Well, my voice stuck
in my throat.   I couldn't say anything.   Butt took my
hand in both his, pressed it, and rushed off.   There
was not a bit of malice in the man.   He was full of
sorrow, but I do not think he was angry with anyone.

I went back to the meeting.   Parnell was there, looking like a bit of granite.   But no one could help
thinking he was the man to fight the English ; he was
so like themselves, cool, callous, inexorable, always
going straight to the point, and not caring much how
he got there, so long as he did get there.   There was
one thing about Parnell on which the Fenians believed
they could rely, his hatred of England.   They felt that
that would last for ever.'

The election of Parnell as president of the Home
Rule Confederation of Great Britain was the turning-
point in his career.   The Irish in England and Scotland
had practically passed a vote of censure on Butt, had
practically endorsed the policy of Parnell.   'The Irish
in Great Britain,' Parnell said to X., 'must take the lead.
It is easier for the advanced men to push forward
here than in Ireland.   Ireland will follow.'

'How did he come to rely on the Fenians ?   How
did he know anything about them ? '

X.   'How did he know anything?   By instinct.
He knew nothing of the details of Fenianism.   He
hated details—all details.   But he knew that Fenians
were men who had run risks, and were ready to run
risks again.

'A Constitutionalist was a man who was ready to
go into Parliament for Ireland.   A Fenian was a man
who was ready to go into penal servitude for Ireland.
Parnell grasped that fact.   He felt the Fenians were
the men to drive the ship, but he wanted to steer her
himself.   That was about the state of the case.   Of
course many of the Fenian leaders did not want to
drive the ship for Parnell, but the rank and file of the
Fenians did.   They believed that Parnell would not
steer the ship into an English port, and that he would

steer her into an Irish port, and perhaps a port not far
from the one of their choice.'

The following incident, related to me by an official
of the Home Rule Confederation of Great Britain, shows
how from the beginning Parnell kept in touch with the
advanced men. 'The first time I saw Parnell was
in 1875—the time of the O'Connell centenary. The
members of the Confederation resolved to attend the
Dublin demonstration in honour of O'Connell. We
came in great force from Liverpool, Manchester, and
other northern towns. On arriving in Dublin, I was
deputed to call on the Dublin organisers and to arrange
for the place which our men should take up in the procession. I waited on a gentleman whose name I now
forget. He met me very bluntly and said, " Oh, we are
not going to give a place in the procession to Fenians."
I replied : " We are not Fenians. We represent the
Home Rule Confederation of Great Britain, and surely
we ought to have a place." But he would not give way.
Of course there were Fenians amongst us, and there were
a good many Fenian sympathisers ; we appreciated
the earnestness and grit of the Fenians, and we
sympathised with the men who had suffered for Ireland. But the majority of the men who came from
England were not, so far as I know, sworn Fenians.
I came back and told our people what had happened,
how we had been refused a place in the procession.
" Oh ! " said they, " very well ; if they do not give us a
place, we will take one ourselves." Accordingly, when
the day came we formed in order with our cars and
banners, and took up a position in advance of everybody else—in fact, we headed the procession—and
marched forward. Some of the Dublin organisers
were much annoyed, and very foolishly told the coal-

porters to dislodge us.   The coal-porters generally had
the place of honour in these processions since O'Connell's
time.   In fact they used to be called "O'Connell's
bodyguard."   Well, so far as we were concerned we
did not want a front place ; we dropped into the place
as much by accident as anything else.   The coal-
porters came forward in great numbers.   When they
saw us with our banners flying, "Liverpool Home
Rule Branch," "Manchester Home Rule Branch,"
and so forth, and at the head of all an amnesty car
with the words "Freedom for the Political Prisoners,"
they simply cheered us and fell in, in the rear.
Then P. J. Smyth—as a protest, I suppose, against
our insubordination—swooped down on us with a
number of men, and cut the traces of the amnesty car,
and drove off the horses.   Then I saw Parnell for the
first time.   He dashed to the front with a number
of others—O'Connor Power was there and a lot
more—and they seized the traces and dragged the car
forward themselves, while we all cheered heartily.
We then got to the place in Sackville Street where
the centenary address was to be delivered.   Lord
O'Hagan had written the address.   But we objected
to his reading it.   We said O'Hagan was a Whig,
and the proper person to address us was Butt, the
Home Rule leader.   Butt could not be found, whereupon [X.] went off and discovered Butt at the Imperial
Hotel, brought him along at once, and then he
addressed us from the platform.   So altogether the
Irish in England asserted themselves pretty firmly.
But we had plenty of sympathisers in Dublin.   The
Dublin Fenians and the Fenians from the country
of course stuck by our Fenians.   Afterwards we
adjourned to the Imperial Hotel, where we all talked

over the day's doings. Parnell was at the Imperial
Hotel too, but he did not talk. Everybody talked but
him. He seemed to be a shy, diffident, gentlemanly
young fellow. Looking at him in the room at the
Imperial you would never think that he would have
flung himself into the work at the amnesty car as
he did.'

During September Parnell addressed several meetings in Great Britain and Ireland, dealing chiefly with
the question of obstruction. In these speeches he never
failed to impress on his hearers the necessity for
parliamentary action—vigorous parliamentary action.
He never hesitated to tell the Fenians that there must
be parliamentary agitation. He never hesitated to
tell the Constitutionalists that outside Parliament
there must be forces to co-operate with the men
within. ' The followers of Mr. Butt,' he said at Burs-
lem in Staffordshire on September 8, ' say we must
behave as the English members behave; in fact, we
must be Englishmen. We must go into English
society and make ourselves agreeable, and not cause a
ruffle on the smooth sea of parliamentary life, lest we
forget our position as gentlemen and as members of
the British House of Commons. Mr. Biggar and
myself, however, think that that is a wrong view to
take, and that it is better for us always to remember
that we are Irish representatives.' At Kilmallock, on
September 17, he sounded another note : ' We none of
us can do any good unless the Irish people stand
behind us ; but if the people stand behind us I care
nothing for the threats of the Chancellor of the
Exchequer—these funny old womanish threats ; I care
not for the threats of any Englishman. We shall
show them that with the Irish people at our backs we

shall meet their threats with deeds.' At Greenock, on September 22, where the Fenians were in force, he declared : ' We must carry out a vigorous and energetic policy in the House of Commons. If that be done, then I believe we have a power in Parliament of which few men have any notion.' Addressing a meeting of his own constituents, where Fenians were not strongly represented, on September 24, he said : ' I think that opposition to English rule is best which is most felt. . . . O'Connell gained Catholic emancipation outside the House of Commons. . . . No amount of eloquence could achieve what the fear of an impending insurrection, what the Clerkenwell explosion and the shot into the police van, had achieved.'

In October there was a conference of Irish members in the City Hall, Dublin. Here Butt denounced obstruction with impassioned eloquence, and singled out Parnell for special animadversion.

Parnell replied briefly and quietly. He said he did not care whether his policy was called a policy of obstruction or not. There was no value in a name ; it was a policy of energy and earnestness, and that was what the Irish people wanted. Mr. O'Connor Power and Mr. A. M. Sullivan, two eloquent speakers, defended the ' forward ' policy at greater length. Indeed, Parnell left the talking to them.

Parnell now felt he had many of the rank and file of the Fenians at his back, and he believed that the future was with them. Butt's policy of conciliation only helped to estrange Fenian sympathisers and to undermine the influence of the Home Rule leader.

In December an event fraught with important results in the development of Parnell's relations with the Fenians occurred. Michael Davitt, a Fenian convict, was released from Dartmoor Prison. Davitt was born near Straide, in the County Mayo, in 1846. When he was quite a child his parents emigrated to England, settling at Haslingden, near Manchester. There Davitt grew up. He attended a Wesleyan school in the town, entered a factory (where he lost his right arm, which was caught accidentally in the machinery), became in turn an assistant letter-carrier, a bookkeeper in the post office, a commercial traveller, and finally joined the Fenian organisation in 1870. He was tried at Newgate for treason-felony, found guilty, and sentenced to fifteen years' penal servitude. Seven years and seven months of this sentence he endured. He was then, on December 19, 1877, released on ticket-of-leave.[1] He immediately rejoined the organisation, and ultimately became a member of

[1] Davitt had been engaged in collecting arms, and some 14,000 rounds of revolver cartridges and 400 Snider rifles were traced to him. Apropos of Davitt's release, the official of the Home Rule Confederation whom I have already quoted told me the following incident: 'There was a local Home Rule association called the "Westminster Home Rule Union." It was an association for the "respectable" members of the organisation who did not like to rub shoulders with Fenians and Fenian sympathisers. Of course, at the central office we were glad of the association; every association in league with us helped. One night I was at a meeting of the Westminster Union. Suddenly a Fenian named C—— popped in his head rather mysteriously, and popped it out again without saying anything. He returned in about ten minutes, and brought in a dark, delicate-looking young fellow of about thirty with him. "Here," he said, without any ceremony, "is Michael Davitt, who has just been released from Dartmoor." Well, the "respectables" were in a fix. They couldn't turn Davitt out, so they asked him to sit down. He and C—— stopped for about twenty minutes, and then went away. When they were gone some of the members of the Union said: "What the devil does that fellow C—— mean by coming in here and bringing this Davitt with him?" I said: "You need not turn up your nose at a man who has suffered seven years' penal servitude for Ireland whether you agree with him or not." They simply sneered. However, before many weeks these gentlemen were on the same platform with Davitt, and were loud in their praises of the man who had "suffered for Ireland." You see that is the way Fenianism colours our political movements and influences the most constitutional of us.'

the supreme council. Three other Fenians were released about the same time as Davitt—Sergeant McCarthy, Corporal Chambers, and John P. O'Brien. On January 5, 1878, all three returned to Ireland. They were met on their arrival at Kingstown by Parnell, O'Connor Power, and others.

The men received a great ovation on reaching Westland Row, and with the cheers for the 'political prisoners' were mingled cheers for 'Parnell.'

Parnell invited the four men to breakfast at Morrison's Hotel, where a tragic scene occurred. As Sergeant McCarthy, who had suffered much in prison, entered the room he was seen to grow faint and stagger. He was immediately helped to a sofa, where, in a few minutes, he died. Parnell was much shocked, but the tragedy served to increase the respect and sympathy which he always felt for those who did and dared for Ireland. McCarthy, like many another Fenian, had risked all, and lost all, for the faith that was in him.

CHAPTER VIII

THE NEW DEPARTURE

On January 14 and 15, 1878, another Home Rule conference was held in Dublin, in the hope of closing the widening breach between Butt and Parnell.

Butt once more condemned the policy of obstruction, and Parnell once more defended it. An extract from the speech of each will suffice.

Mr. Butt. 'I took the liberty some time ago at Limerick to lay down what I believed was the policy to pursue, and that was to make an assault all along the whole line of English misgovernment, and to bring forward every grievance of Ireland, and to press the English House of Commons for their redress; and I believed, and believe it still, that if once we got liberal-minded Englishmen fairly to consider how they would redress the grievance of Irish misgovernment, they would come in the end to the conclusion that they had but one way of giving us good government, and that was by allowing us to govern ourselves.'

Parnell. 'If I refrain from asking the country to-day, by the voice of this conference, to adopt any particular line of action, or any particular policy, or to put any definite issue in reference to it before this conference, I do so solely because I am young, and can wait——'

Butt. ' Hear, hear.'

Parnell. ' And because I believe the country can also wait, and that the country which has waited so long can wait a little longer. Mr. Butt has very fairly explained the policy that he has carried out during the three or four years that this Parliament has lasted, and he has pointed to his speech at Limerick, in which he described his policy as one which was designed to make an attack on the whole line of English misgovernment in Ireland by laying bare the grievances under which Ireland suffers. He has also told us his belief that if he made it clear to Englishmen that we did really suffer under many unjust laws, that he would be able to induce fair-minded Englishmen to direct their attention to the redress of these grievances, and that he would be able to persuade them that the best way to redress our grievances would be to leave us to redress them ourselves. Now I gladly agree with Mr. Butt that it is very possible, and very probable, that he would be able to persuade a fair-minded Englishman in the direction that he has indicated ; but still I do not think that the House of Commons is mainly composed of fair-minded Englishmen. If we had to deal with men who were capable of listening to fair arguments there would be every hope of success for the policy of Mr. Butt as carried out in past sessions ; but we are dealing with political parties who really consider the interests of their political organisations as paramount, beyond every other consideration.'

This conference led to no practical results. Parnell, backed by the advanced men, stood to his guns, and Butt, ill-supported by the Moderates and broken in health, gradually gave up the struggle. Indeed, before the end of the year 1878 the young member for Meath

was virtually master of the situation. Almost immediately on the meeting of Parliament the Government took up the question of obstruction, and appointed
a select committee to inquire into the subject of public
business.   Humorously enough, Parnell was placed
on this committee. The chief criminal was not put
into the dock ; he took his seat among the judges, and
from that vantage ground he cross-examined with
much shrewdness and skill the Speaker, the Chairman
of Committees, and other high authorities on parliamentary procedure.   The sittings of the committee
lasted from March until July, when a report was
prepared on which the Government took action early
in 1879.

Parnell drafted a report of his own, which, however,
the committee refused to accept.   In this report the
member for Meath (*inter alia*) said : ' The Committee
cannot shut their eyes to the fact that the House is composed of several different nationalities who sympathise
little with the aspirations, and who understand less of
the affairs, of each other.   Considerable friction, heat,
and ill-feeling is frequently engendered by the interference of members belonging to one nationality in
the affairs of the others, with the result of delay, loss
of time, and obstruction to the general progress of
business.   In addition, the affairs of Ireland and India
are neglected, and the representatives of these two
countries, if they attend the sittings of the House, find
themselves in a position of enforced idleness, unless they
occupy themselves with English affairs and so incur
the risk of the ill-will of the majority of the House.'

Leaving the question of obstruction, I must now
turn to Parnell's relation with Fenians during the year
1878.   We have seen how X. formed the Home Rule

Confederation of Great Britain, drew some of the Fenians into it, and made Parnell president. The difficulties which X. had to encounter from the beginning in reconciling Fenianism with Parliamentarianism in any shape or form much increased in 1878. I shall, however, let him tell his story in his own way :

'I was always opposed by a party on the supreme council who wished to have nothing whatever to do with the Parliamentarians. They wished the Fenians to remain within their own lines, to go on collecting arms, drilling, keeping alive the separatist spirit, watching, waiting, preparing. They believed in a policy of open warfare. Parliamentarianism, they said, was bound, sooner or later, to undermine the secret movement. I had no objection to the policy of open warfare, but open warfare seemed a long way off, and here was a new field of activity, which ought not to be neglected. Our great idea was to keep the spirit of nationality alive. This could always be done by fighting England. In Parnell we had a man who hated England, and who was ready and able to fight her at every available point. I thought that such a man ought to be given his head. He had asked for a fair trial, and I felt he was entitled to it. However, in the spring of 1878 there was a crisis.

'The supreme council—which was the governing body of the Fenians on this side of the Atlantic— consisted of eleven members. It is an open secret that Kickham was a member of the supreme council, and the most important man among us. Well, Kickham was dead against any alliance with the Parliamentarians. He believed that contact with them was demoralising, and that Parliamentarianism was nothing more nor less than an Anglicising influence. In fact he did not think that the question was arguable. It is also an open secret that Biggar and Egan were members of the supreme council. The other names have not transpired, and accordingly cannot be published. In 1878 Kickham and those who thought with him determined to take action. They brought forward a resolution pledging the council to sever all connection with the parliamentary party. This resolution was carried by a majority of one. I immediately resigned. I said that I did not agree with the decision of the council, and as I wished to have a free hand I would retire. Biggar agreed with me, but refused to resign. Parnell advised him to resign. He said, "No, sir, I never withdraw from anything. Let them expel me." They did expel him. They also expelled Egan, and others who voted with me. I saw Parnell and told him what I had done. He said I acted quite rightly; that I could not very well remain a member of a body from which I had differed on a cardinal point.'

'Which would be the more accurate thing to say : that the Fenians helped, or did not help, the Parnell movement, so called, in the years following 1878?'

X. 'Oh, helped, certainly. The heads of the I. R. B. were against Parnell, but many of the rank and file went with him. That was just the cleverness of the man. He appreciated the energy and earnestness of the Fenians, but turned these qualities to the account of his own movement. He did not try to weaken the force of Fenianism, but he diverted it into a channel of his own choosing. Had he attempted to break up Fenianism he would have gone to pieces. He therefore leant on it ; he walked on the verge of treason-felony, and so won the hearts of many of the rank and file.

He was always the master of himself, and ultimately became the master of us.

'In the spring of 1878, about the time I left the supreme council, the American Fenians sent an agent to London to discuss the question of united action with Parnell. But that part of the story belongs to the Clan-na-Gael. I can only speak of what happened between Parnell and the Clan by hearsay.'

The Clan-na-Gael, be it said, was the American branch of the Fenian organisation. The Clan had watched Parnell closely, and was interested in his operations. The question was what could be done with him. In the Clan-na-Gael, as in the I. R. B., there was a difference of opinion about the advisability of co-operating with the constitutional party. Some of the American leaders were heartily in sympathy with the supreme council of the I. R. B., and believed that it would be a mistake to come into touch with the Parliamentarians in any way. Parliamentarianism, they said, would fizzle out, as it had always fizzled out; and then, if Fenianism were not kept intact, the people would be left without any political organisation. Let Fenianism—which was based on Nationality, and on nothing but Nationality—keep itself to itself. That, briefly, was the position of the no-alliance party in the Clan-na-Gael. But there was another party, led mainly by Mr. John Devoy, who favoured combined action between the parliamentary and the revolutionary forces. Fenianism, they said, had kept itself to itself far too much all the time. It ought now to mingle with the public life of the country, to interest itself in everything which interested any section of the population. In the old days the farmers had held aloof from Fenianism. Why?

Because Fenianism had held aloof from them. The
land question was a vital question ; the Fenians should
not leave it wholly in the hands of the Constitutionalists.
Every man would not become a Nationalist, because
nationality was a high ideal. Most people were not
influenced by high ideals. They were influenced by
selfish considerations, and these considerations had,
unfortunately, to be worked upon. If the Fenians
helped the farmers, the farmers would help the Fenians.
By co-operating, then, with the ' open movement,' by
mingling in the public life of the country, by directing
the current of agitation into channels favourable to
Fenian expansion, the cause of nationality would best
be served. Let the Fenians go into the constitutional
movement and keep it on national lines. That was the
true policy to follow.

'In the spring of 1878 one of the heads of the
Clan-na-Gael, being in London, desired to bring about
a meeting between Parnell and some of the Parliamentarians, and himself and some of the most influential
among the Fenians. The meeting took place at the
Clan-na-Gael man's lodgings in Craven Street, Strand.
There were present Parnell, an Irish member (who, it
may as well be said, was selected by the Fenians
because he had never been a Fenian and was not open
to the fatal fault in their eyes of having taken two
conflicting oaths), the chief official of the supreme
council, one of the three most prominent Fenians then
living, and, of course, the Irish-American gentleman
himself. What occurred that night was shortly this.
Parnell was mostly silent, but certainly impressively so.
The Fenian official scarcely spoke at all, and the Clan-
na-Gael man said but little. All the talking, roughly
speaking, was done by Parnell's colleague and the

prominent Fenian, with the result that after much
argument things remained very much as they had been
at the beginning, the M.P. producing little or no effect
upon the possibly too uncompromising Fenian, and the
Fenian probably producing no effect whatever on the
M.P. In fact the chasm between them was too wide
to be overleaped. What effect either, or anything that
occurred, produced upon Parnell it would be hard to
say ; but most certainly Parnell, silent as he was, and
possibly somewhat because of his silence, produced a
very great effect upon everyone present. The Clan-na-
Gael man met the M.P. some days after, and, no doubt,
Parnell more than once. The prominent Fenian also had
a long talk with Parnell some short time afterwards,
without their coming any nearer to each other in policy,
though then, as before and even after, this Fenian
was strongly impressed by the striking personality of
Parnell.' [1]

Parnell had, as we have seen, the strongest
sympathies with Fenianism, but he was resolved not to
be managed by the Fenians—nor, indeed, by any force
whatever. He believed profoundly in Fenian help,
but saw the danger of Fenianism swamping the constitutional movement. His policy was to keep Parliamentarianism well in front, and to mass the Revolutionists behind it. The Fenians were to be his reserves.
He certainly had no objection to an alliance between
Fenianism and Constitutionalism, but he was determined that he should be master of the alliance. ' A
true revolutionary movement in Ireland,' he said
publicly, ' should, in my opinion, partake both of a
constitutional and illegal character. It should be both
an open and a secret organisation, using the constitu-

---

[1] This account has been given to me by one who was present. Mr.
" Martin " (*ante*, p. 65) was at this Craven Street meeting.

tion for its own purposes, but also taking advantage of its secret combination.'[1]

At this time another attempt was made to draw him into the ranks of the I. R. B. A Fenian agent was once more deputed to call on him, and ask him to join the organisation. He again refused firmly. ' I think,' he said, ' I can do good with the parliamentary machine. I mean to try it, at all events. Purely physical-force movements have always failed in Ireland.' The Fenian reminded him that purely constitutional movements had always failed too. Parnell agreed, saying : ' But I do not want to break up your movement. On the contrary, I wish it to go on. Collect arms, do everything that you are doing, but let the open movement have a chance too. We can both help each other, but I am sure I can be of more use in the open movement.' On another occasion he said to another Fenian : ' I am sure I can do something with the parliamentary machine. I cannot explain how I am going to do it, but I am quite satisfied I can do it. I see my way clearly.'

Despite the attitude of the leaders of the I. R. B., Parnell was gaining some influence over the rank and file of the society. I asked the official of the Home Rule Confederation of Great Britain from whom I have already quoted[2] how far the Fenians were helping the Home Rule movement in England in 1878 and 1879. He said : ' The leaders opposed us, but the rank and file were divided. Some supported us, others did nothing. When there was nothing particular doing, very few of the Fenians troubled themselves about us. But when there was something special afoot—a parliamentary election, a municipal

[1] *New York Herald*, January 2, 1880.　　[2] *Ante*, p. 145.

election, anything of that kind—then certainly many
Fenians came in and helped us. They were full of
energy; they were about the best workers we had. It
always seemed to me that they could not help having
a "go" at England whenever an opportunity of any
kind offered; and they certainly felt that in fighting
for a Home Rule candidate against a Unionist they
were striking in some way against English authority in
Ireland. I had rather a curious experience myself of
the Fenians about this time. There was a working
men's club composed entirely of Irish. I came in
contact with the members, as I was always knocking up
against Irishmen in London and other parts of England.
These working men asked me to do some secretarial
business for them—to keep their books, &c. I agreed,
and used to attend their meetings occasionally. Looking through their books I found there was a fine lot of
names, and they were a fine lot of fellows too, and I
did not see why they should not join the Confederation.
So one day I sent a circular to all the members of the
club inviting them to join. Some time afterwards I
went to the club as usual, but I was met with scowls.
As every man dropped in he looked at me askance and
suspiciously. I could see that I was in some sort of
disgrace, but I could not make out what it was all
about. At last one of them got up and said : "What
I suspected has happened. I was against Mr. ——
coming in here and doing anything for us. He is
a Home Rule agent, and I knew he would be interfering with us. I am as thankful to him as anyone
here for the work he has done for our club. But we
are not Home Rulers. We are Fenians, and we do
not want to be interfered with, that's all." The circular was the cause of the whole row. I expressed

regret for sending it, said I thought there was no harm, and so forth. The upshot of the whole business was that, after mutual explanations, they asked me still to come and help in the business of the club, but to leave Home Rule alone. This I did. But whenever there was an election on, or whenever there was fighting to be done, I used to ask these men to give me a hand, and they always did. They did not join the Confederation, but they gave us outside help, and we got lots of assistance from Fenians in that way.'

An ex-Fenian who had suffered in the cause also throws some light on the effect produced by Parnell's vigorous parliamentary action. He says: 'When I came out of prison I went back at once to the organisation. I began to collect arms, to conceal them, to organise. Then my attention was turned to what was going on in Parliament, and to Parnell chiefly. This was something new. Here was a handful of men fighting the British Government on its own ground. People do not become Revolutionists for the fun of the thing. Every Fenian carried his life in his hand. There is not much fun in that. Why were we Fenians? Because in Fenianism was the only hope for Ireland. Parliamentarianism had always been contemptible. It was worse, it was mischievous. The London Parliament was simply a school for Anglicising Irishmen. We hated the thing. But if there were the slightest chance of getting an Irish Parliament by constitutional means, the vast majority of Fenians would be Constitutionalists. A real Irish Parliament, not a sham, would have satisfied the great majority of our people all the time. But we saw no chance of getting an Irish Parliament or anything else by constitutional

means, and we became Revolutionists. But here was
a new departure. Here was a new man with new
methods. There was no chance of English society
seizing him, for he was making himself detestable to
all Englishmen. Ought he not to get a trial, ought not
his methods to get a trial? That is what I thought,
and as the years passed Parnell impressed me more and
more with his power, and ultimately I left the Fenian
organisation and joined him.'

While, then, the Fenian mind in Ireland and America
was much exercised by Parnell's manœuvres, Michael
Davitt landed in New York in August 1878. Why
had he gone? First, to visit his mother at Philadelphia; secondly, to meet the members of the Clan-
na-Gael, and to discuss the political situation generally.
Davitt was still a Fenian; but there can be no doubt
that he was gradually, perhaps unconsciously, drifting
away from the movement. He took a keen interest
in the land question.[1] He had come from the peasant

[1] I have elsewhere given some account of the relation between landlord and tenant in Ireland, and may here repeat what I have written.
'The tenant, "scrambling for the potato " and left without any resource
but the land, offered an exorbitant rent, which the landlord accepted
and exacted to the uttermost farthing. Freedom of contract between
landlord and tenant there was none. The tenant came into the market
under circumstances which left him entirely at the mercy of the landlord. The "bit of land" meant life to him, the want of it death; for
in the absence of commercial industries the people were thrown upon
the land mainly for existence. "The treaty between landlord and
tenant [in Ireland]," says Mr. Nassau Senior, " is not a calm bargain, in
which the tenant, having offered what he thinks the land worth, cares
little whether his offer is accepted or not; it is a struggle, like the
struggle to buy bread in a besieged town, or to buy water in an African
caravan." In truth, the landlord had a monopoly of the means of
existence, and he used it for his own aggrandisement, regardless of the
tenant's fate or the public weal. " The landlords in Ireland," said
Lord Donoughmore in 1854, "have been in the habit of letting land, not
farms." Never has a happier description of the Irish land system been
given than this. The landlord let "land "—a strip of bog, barren, wild,
dreary. The tenant reclaimed it, drained, fenced, reduced the waste to
a cultivated state, made the "land " a "farm." Then the landlord

class; he felt their wrongs acutely, and longed to right them. He has sometimes been credited with the invention of what came to be called the 'new departure,' the combined action of Constitutionalists and Revolutionists for the common purpose of national independence. But the fact is the 'new departure' was in the air before Davitt arrived in America. James O'Kelly, John Devoy, and others had been thinking it out while Davitt was in jail. 'Had Davitt come to America in the beginning of 1877,' said a member of the Clan-na-Gael to me, ' he would have found a few men ready to discuss the new departure and to favour it. But neither he nor we could have dared broach it at a public meeting of the clan. But a change had taken place in a twelvemonth. Parnell's action in Parliament had made people think that something might be done with the Parliamentarians after all. Parliamentarianism was apparently becoming a respectable thing. It might be possible to touch it without becoming contaminated. Parnell had, in fact, made the running for Davitt, and Davitt arrived in New York just in the nick of time. Many influential members of the Clan were full of the notion of an alliance with the Constitutional party, and were now ready to co-operate with Davitt in bringing it about.' Davitt had, of course,

---

pounced upon him for an increased rent. The tenant could not pay; his resources had been exhausted in bringing the bog into a state of cultivation, he had not yet recouped himself for his outlay and labour. He was evicted, flung on the roadside to starve, without receiving one shilling compensation for his outlay on the land, and the "farm" which he had made was given to another at an enhanced rental. What did the evicted tenant do? He entered a Ribbon Lodge, told the story of his wrong, and demanded vengeance on the man whom he called a tyrant and an oppressor. Only too often his story was listened to and vengeance was wreaked on the landlord, or the new tenant; and sometimes on both. This is briefly the dismal story of the land trouble in Ireland.'—*Thomas Drummond, Life and Letters.*

seen Parnell before he started for America, and Parnell knew that he would see the leaders of the Clan-na-Gael. But the cautious member for Meath gave him no code of instructions, and sent no message to the Clan, as has sometimes been suggested. That was not Parnell's way of doing business. He never wished to know too much, and was at all events careful not to let others into the secret of his knowledge, whatever it might be. On arriving at New York one of the first men whom Davitt met was John Devoy—the champion of the new departure in the Clan-na-Gael. Devoy was a Revolutionist. He wished to draw the farmers into the revolutionary movement; and believed this could be done by making agrarian reform a plank in the national platform. Devoy and Davitt agreed at once on a common programme and worked together as one man to carry it out; 'the land of Ireland,' to use the words of Davitt, 'was to be made the basis of Irish nationality.'

In September both men attended a large public meeting, composed chiefly of members of the Clan-na-Gael, in New York, when the following resolutions, proposed by Devoy, were carried:

' 1. That we deem the present a fitting opportunity to proclaim our conviction of Ireland's right to an independent national existence. That as Ireland has never forfeited her right to independence, and as no action on the part of England has given any justification for the acceptance of the Union, we hereby protest against all attempts at compromise, and renew our resolve to work for the complete overthrow of British domination.

' 2. That the landlord system forced on the Irish people by English legislation is a disgrace to humanity and to the civilisation of the present century. It is the direct cause of the expatriation of millions of the Irish race, and of the miserable condition of the Irish peasantry. That as the land of Ireland belongs to the people of Ireland, the abolition of the foreign landlord system and the substitution of one by which the tiller of the soil will be fixed permanently upon it, and holding directly of the State, is the only true solution of the Irish land question, which an Irish Republic can alone effect.'

A month later Devoy and Davitt attended another public meeting in New York, when the former advocated the policy of the new departure in a vigorous speech. He said : 'I claim that by the adoption of a proper public policy and a vigorous propaganda the Nationalists can sweep away the men who misrepresent us [the followers of Butt chiefly] and obtain control of the public voice of the country. Every public body in the country, from the little boards of poor-law guardians and land commissioners to the city corporations and members of Parliament, should be controlled by the National [the Fenian] party, and until it is able to control them it will be looked upon by foreigners as a powerless and insignificant faction. . . . Now I believe in Irish independence, but I don't believe it would be worth while to free Ireland if that foreign landlord system were left standing. I am in favour of sweeping away every vestige of the English connection, and this accursed landlord system above all and before all. But while I think it is right to proclaim this, and that the national party should proclaim that nothing less than this would satisfy it, I know it is a solution that cannot be reached in a day, and therefore I think we should in the meantime accept all measures tending to the prevention of arbitrary eviction, and the creation of a peasant proprietary as a step in the right direction.'

This was the policy of John Devoy. This was the policy of the New Departure. The Fenians were to have a hand in everything that was going on, and ' above and before all' they were to have a hand in the land question. Agrarian reform or agrarian revolution was to be made the stepping-stone to separation from England. Devoy did not believe in Home Rule. But he did not wish to raise the separatist flag publicly. He suggested that the limits of national independence should not be defined. Let 'self-government' and ' self-government' only be demanded. Then the Fenians could co-operate cordially with the Constitutionalists. Each section could put its own construction on the meaning of the words.

Devoy succeeded in carrying many of the leaders of the Clan-na-gael with him on these lines, and in October 1878 he despatched a cablegram to Parnell, setting out the terms of alliance between the Revolutionists and the Constitutionalists; the cablegram ran as follows : ' The Nationalists here will support you on the following conditions :

' First. Abandonment of the Federal demand and substitution of a general declaration in favour of self-government.

' Second. Vigorous agitation of the land question on the basis of a peasant proprietary, while accepting concessions tending to abolition of arbitrary eviction.

' Third. Exclusion of all sectarian issues from the platform.

' Fourth. Irish members to vote together on all Imperial and Home Rule questions, adopt an aggressive policy, and energetically resist coercive legislation.

' Fifth.   Advocacy of all struggling nationalities in
the British Empire and elsewhere.' [1]

These were the terms offered by the Clan-na-gael
to Parnell in October 1878.

What did Parnell do?   He never answered the
cablegram.   The Clan had shown its hand.   Parnell
declined to show his.   Devoy, a man of remarkable
energy and grit, was not, however, discouraged.   In
December he addressed a letter to the ' Freeman's
Journal '—the Home Rule organ in Dublin—still
further expounding his policy, and practically urging
the union of Constitutionalists and Revolutionists for
the common purpose, however veiled, of undermining
English authority in Ireland.   Towards the end of the
year he sailed for Europe, resolved to deal with the
Irish situation on the spot.

But to return to Parnell.   He had now an established position in Parliament.   He was a power in the
House.   The skill and ability which he displayed on
the committee appointed to inquire into the subject of
obstruction won the admiration of his most inveterate
enemies, and even English publicists wrote that if
Parnell would only apply himself seriously to public
affairs he would soon become a valuable citizen.   Of
course there was obstruction during the session of 1878,
but there were fewer of those ' scenes ' which had
characterised the manœuvres of 1877.   Butt had said
that the policy of obstruction would prevent useful
legislation for Ireland.   This prophecy, however, was
destined to be falsified, for in 1878 an important Irish
measure became law—the Intermediate Education Bill.[2]

---

[1] The cablegram was signed by Devoy, Dr. Carroll, Breslin, General
Millin, and Patrick Mahon.

[2] A Board, called the ' Intermediate Education Board of Ireland,' was

Parnell also scored a success by causing the Mutiny Bill—which he again obstructed—to be referred to a select committee, a step which was followed by important reforms in the ensuing session. Altogether he had already proved to the House and to the country that he was a man with a future.

Outside Parliament he devoted himself industriously to the cause of Home Rule. As President of the Home Rule Confederation of Great Britain he attended regularly at the meetings of the executive body, and took a leading part in the transaction of its business.

'Parnell was an excellent chairman,' says the official of the Confederation on whose information I have already drawn. 'He used to rattle through the business with great speed. Faith, he allowed no obstruction in our work.'

'Was he as pleasant a man to do business with as Butt?'

Official. 'There was a great difference between them. Butt was genial and lovable. You did not feel you were doing business with him at all. I used often to go to his lodgings in London. He always received you with open arms; sat you down to a cup of tea, or a glass of whisky punch, and chatted away as if you had only called to spend a social evening. He was a delightful companion, so friendly, and so homely. He would crack a joke, tell a good story, and gossip away in the happiest style. I quite loved the old man. But Parnell was altogether different. He was certainly a very pleasant man to do business with, very quick at

formed for the purpose of holding examinations and granting exhibitions and prizes to students who passed in subjects of secondary education. A sum of 1,000,000*l.*, taken from the Irish Church surplus, was devoted to the objects of the Board.

seeing a thing, very ready to show the way out of a
difficulty, courteous, agreeable, making the most of
what you did and the least of what he did himself.   If
he differed from you it was in the mildest way, and he
always put his points as if it were for you and not for
him to decide.   " Don't you think it would be better ? "
" Suppose we say so-and-so," that was his formula.
But, pleasant and even charming as he could be, you
always felt that there was a piece of ice between you
and him.   I used to go to his apartment as I went to
Butt's, but we never had a glass of punch together or
even a cup of tea.   It was business all the time.   Occasionally he would take a strong line, but very seldom.
However, when he said "That cannot be done," one
knew there was an end of the discussion.   I remember
on one occasion reading a report for the executive
when Parnell was in the chair.   I stated in the report
that the Catholic clergy in England gave the Confederation a good deal of trouble, because they tried to
make the Irish vote Tory.   The English priests did
did not care about Home Rule, they only cared about
education, and as the Tories were more with them on
that subject than the Liberals, they went Tory, and
wanted to bring our people with them.   As soon as I
had read the paragraph he said, " I'm not going to fight
the Church."   There was some dissent, but Parnell
was very firm, though smiling and rather chaffing us
all the time.   But the paragraph went out.   That was
Parnell's policy.   He would not fight with any Irish
force.   His aim was to bring all Irish forces into line.
He would no more fight with the Church than he
would with the Fenians.   Parnell never talked freely
with me or with anyone, so far as I could make out.
The only time I ever heard him make any attempt at

conversation was when someone introduced the subject
of mechanics.   Then he started off, greatly to my surprise, talking in a lively way, and giving us a lot of
information about mechanics.   Then someone referred
to politics, and he stopped in an instant.   He would
never talk politics unless something had to be done.'

I asked an Irish member, who had been a Fenian,.
on one occasion, if Parnell had been forced to quarrel
either with the Fenians or the Church, which it
would be ?   He said : ' The Church, for Parnell liked
the Fenians, but he did not like the Church.   He
knew, however, the power of the Church, and he wished
unquestionably to have a great conserving force like it
at his back.   Parnell would never quarrel with the
Church unless the Church forced the quarrel, there can
be no doubt of that.'

Butt was now breaking fast.   One remembers how
in the session of 1878 he moved about the House careworn and dejected.   He felt that the ground was slipping beneath his feet.   He knew the time was gone
when he could hope to lead a united Irish party to
victory.   The dissensions among the Parliamentarians
were fatal to his command, if they were not, in truth,.
fatal to the triumph of the Home Rule cause itself..
All these things he saw clearly, and he was bowed
down with sorrow and despair.   In April he addressed
a manifesto to the electors of Limerick, condemning
the policy of obstruction, pointing out the disasters.
which he believed it would bring on the Home Rule
cause, pleading ill-health as a reason for retirement, and
formally announcing his resignation of the leadership.
But his followers urged him to reconsider his decision,.
and ultimately he withdrew his resignation.   The
breach, however, between him and Parnell remained.

as wide as ever.   In October the Home Rule Confederation of Great Britain held its annual meeting
in Dublin.   Butt objected to this proceeding.   The
organisation, he felt, ought to confine its operations to
the other side of the channel.   But the Confederation
had come to Dublin for a special reason.   By the Convention Act of 1793 no meeting attended by delegates
could be held in Ireland.   'But,' the leaders of the
Confederation argued, 'we shall hold our meeting in
Dublin, and we shall summon delegates from England,
and then we shall present to the Irish and the English
public the extraordinary spectacle of an Irish organisation with its headquarters in England summoning delegates from England to sit in the Irish capital, while no
organisation in Ireland can summon delegates from
Ireland for the same purpose ; and if that does not kill
the Convention Act we don't know what will.'   I cannot
say whether this manœuvre did kill the Convention
Act, but, as a matter of fact, it was repealed the next
year.

Efforts were still made to bring about a *modus
vivendi* between Butt and Parnell, but in vain.   'You
are in rebellion,' said Professor Galbraith to Parnell.
'Yes,' was the answer; 'but in justifiable rebellion.'
'I do not want *you* to become an obstructive,' he said
to Butt; 'I do not want anyone to become an obstructive; but there must be a vigorous policy.   I am
young and active, and I cannot be kicking my heels
about the English House of Commons doing nothing.
Englishmen will not give me an opportunity of con-
cerning myself about the affairs of my own country,
and I mean to concern myself about the affairs of their
country.'

'Butt,' he said on another occasion, 'is hopeless.

He is too much under the English influence. He
wants to please the English. But you may be sure
that when we are pleasing the English we are not
winning. We must not care for English opinion.
We must go right on in the way Ireland wants.'
'There is a great force in England,' he said, addressing
the Confederation in Dublin. 'A British force,' cried
a voice in the crowd. 'No,' retorted Parnell, amid
tremendous cheers, 'an Irish force. We must,' he
urged, 'see that the Irish in England think only of
Ireland and vote only for Ireland, and that they
make English candidates vote for Ireland too. I
said when I was last on this platform that I
would not promise anything by parliamentary action,
nor any particular line of policy; but I said we could
help you to punish the English, and I predicted that
the English would very soon get afraid of the policy of
punishment.'

It was at this time suggested to Parnell that he
ought to address more meetings in Ireland. 'Ah,' he
said; 'but I have not an independent platform.'

'If I get up a meeting for you, will you come to
it?' said a friend. 'Certainly,' answered Parnell.
A great meeting—a land meeting—was organised in
Tralee. Parnell addressed it in November. He made
a vigorous speech, saying plainly enough that nothing
short of a revolution would bring about a change in
the land laws, and urging the establishment of a
tribunal for fixing rents, and the creation of a peasant
proprietary. 'It will take an earthquake to settle
the land question, Mr. Parnell,' someone said to him.
'Then we must have an earthquake' was the reply.

CHAPTER IX

THE LAND LEAGUE

DEVOY arrived in Ireland about January 1879. He was soon joined by Davitt, who had preceded him across the Atlantic. No one played a more important part in Irish politics at this crisis than Michael Davitt. He was still a Fenian. He was even yet a member of the supreme council of the I. R. B. He possessed the confidence of the Fenians in America. He was in touch with Parnell. In a word, he was the connecting-link between the American Revolutionists and the extreme wing of the constitutional party; the very pivot on which the 'new departure' turned.

The time was ripe for the plans of the Neo-Fenians. The land agitation had already commenced, ' Tenants' Defence Associations ' had been formed in various parts of the country, and public attention was fixed on the subject. Distress accompanied discontent, and both causes combined to excite and influence the peasantry. Rents could not be paid, and non-payment of rent was followed by eviction. Landlords were unreasonable, tenants were exasperated, and soon the flame of agitation was fanned in every part of the country. I have already said that the Land Act of 1870 had proved a failure. It had been passed to prevent arbitrary evic-

tions and to secure to industrious tenants compensation
for improvements, and in certain cases for disturbance.
But it neither effected the one purpose nor the other.
The power of the landlords remained practically
unchecked. Between 1876 and 1879 Bills had been
introduced to make the legislation of 1870 a reality.
But they were rejected in the House of Commons.
The Irish tenants saw at last that the Irish members
could not help them, and they resolved to help them-·
selves.

Devoy had come to Ireland with the view of
bringing about an alliance between Revolutionists and
Constitutionalists for the common purpose of undermining English authority in the island. The land
question, he felt, was the basis on which that authority
rested. The overthrow of the land system was accordingly, from his standpoint, a matter of paramount
importance. Davitt was also in favour of separation, but nevertheless looked upon landlordism as an
evil in itself, which ought, apart from all other considerations, to be swept utterly away. Both men now
saw that a *bonâ-fide* land agitation had, without any
reference whatever to their aims, commenced ; and the
question was, how could it be turned to the account of
the separatist movement ?

Devoy had two interviews with Parnell in the
presence of Davitt. The member for Meath was as
usual cautious, and took good care not to give himself
away. He entered into no compact with Devoy, but
listened to all that Devoy had to tell him about the
Clan-na-Gael. The furthermost extent to which he
went was to ask, as he had on previous occasions
asked, for time to work the parliamentary machine.
He did not mind letting Devoy see his antipathy to

England and his sympathy with the Fenians. But he entered into no understanding with the Clan.

At a meeting of the supreme council of the I. R. B. in Paris, when the question of the 'new departure' was fully discussed, Kickham was present, and offered a vehement opposition to it. He regarded it as dishonest and immoral, and denounced Devoy in vigorous language. Kickham, it should be said, was very deaf, and could only be approached through a speaking-trumpet. As he proceeded in his condemnation of Devoy's scheme, Devoy and Davitt tried now and again to get at the trumpet and to put in a word in reply ; but Kickham waved them off. He carried the council with him; in fact Devoy and Davitt found only one supporter in that body. One point, however, Devoy gained. It was agreed that, while no alliance should be entered into between the supreme council and the Parliamentarians, 'the officers of the organisation should be left free to take part in the open movement if they felt so disposed—such officers to be held responsible for acts or words deemed to be injurious to the revolutionary cause.' [1]

Devoy now sailed for America, where, in defiance of the supreme council of the I. R. B., he threw himself heart and soul into the work of the 'new departure'; and Davitt stayed in Ireland to co-operate cordially and vigorously at his end with the American Fenians.

Meanwhile the land agitation grew apace. In Connaught, Davitt's province, the pinch of poverty was most sorely felt, and Connaught became the centre of disturbance.

On April 20 a great land meeting was held in

---

[1] This permission was withdrawn in 1880. Davitt attended no more meetings of the supreme council.

Irishtown, County Mayo. Three Fenians besides Davitt attended, and they were unquestionably the ablest and most energetic men present. There is little use in mincing words over these transactions now. Official Fenianism in Ireland held aloof from the land agitation. But that agitation would probably have never reached the formidable proportions it assumed had not individual Fenians flung themselves into it with characteristic earnestness and daring.[1] The ' Land League Fenians ' were, no doubt, ultimately expelled from their own body; but they carried into the new movement the fire and energy of the old, unchastened and unrestrained, however, by that purer spirit of nationality which animated the founders of the Fenian organisation.

At the Irishtown meeting was struck the spark which soon set Ireland in a blaze. But before the conflagration had yet spread throughout the land Isaac Butt, perhaps fittingly, passed away. In July 1878 he felt seriously alarmed about his health, and wrote to his medical adviser and friend, Dr. O'Leary :

' United Hotel, Charles Street, St. James's,
' July 4, 1878.

' MY DEAR O'LEARY,—You have always shown such kindness and care to me that I would like you to know every little thing that happens to me. I am not happy about myself. Yesterday I crossed over in a good passage. I laid down the latter half of the way. Before getting up I felt an uneasy sensation at my heart, with something like palpitation. Getting up I

---

[1] The freedom given to the Fenian officers at the Paris meeting was of course, very useful to Devoy and Davitt; the reason, no doubt, why it was taken away in 1880.

had difficulty in breathing, nearly as great as I used to
have at Buxton on the night I came over with you.
It has continued more or less ever since.   My journey
to the sitting-room here—you know the length—has
been a series of relays and pantings, and all this is
accompanied by vagueness in my trains of thought.
Now surely, my dear friend, it is useless to say that
this is of no consequence.   Is it not better to accept
the truth that it is the knell of the curfew telling
us the hour is come when the fire must be put out
and the light quenched?   If not, is it not at least
something that requires more care than you or I
or Butcher have given it?   In other respects I am
improving.   You will see in this letter that my hand
is steadier, but does not this give to these symptoms
a worse character?   I have observed latterly that in
writing I very frequently omit a word, far oftener
the syllables or letters of a word.   When half-an-hour
in bed last night I had lost all recollection of where I
was, or how I came to be where I was.   I had great
difficulty in settling to myself whether the change from
Irish to English time made my watch fast or slow.
Is it not through the want of blood to feed the action
of the brain, or is it only congestion of the ganglionic
nerves?   Do not laugh at this, tell me honestly, and as
a true, because a candid, friend what you think.   I will
go to Quain to-morrow, but I fear this is of no use.   I
have taken a strange notion in my head.   I would like
to consult a perfect stranger who does not know me,
and see what he would say.   If I were to carry out this
perverse notion, who would be the best man to select?
Can I depend on you to tell me the truth?   I will
write to you to-morrow what Quain says.   I am afraid
I must stay here until the Education Bill passes.   If I

go over I must come back again. I will know to-morrow what I will do.

'Yours ever sincerely,

'ISAAC BUTT.'

Parnell and Butt came into conflict for the last time on February 5, 1879. It was at a public meeting in the Leinster Lecture Hall, Molesworth Street, Dublin. The old question of obstruction was again discussed. Butt again condemned the tactics of the forward party, and Parnell spoke once more of the inaction of Butt. Issue was joined on the following resolution, proposed by Mr. T. D. Sullivan and seconded by Mr. Biggar:

'That this meeting highly approves of the declarations made by Mr. Butt at the National Conference of November 1873, to the following effect: that "the more every Irish member keeps aloof from all private communications with English ministers or English parties the better;" that "there is enmity between the English Government and the Irish nation;" and that "the representatives of the people must accept this position;" that "they should hold no private parley with the power which is at war with the Irish people, and with which, therefore, the Irish members should be at war." That this meeting respectfully but earnestly recommends all the Home Rule representatives to act in the spirit of the foregoing declarations, and re-affirms (as specially applicable to the present time) the following resolution adopted by the National Conference held in the Rotunda on January 15, 1878: "That, in view of the present circumstances, we think it desirable in the interests of the Home Rule cause that more energetic action should be taken in Parliament, and we therefore impress upon the Home Rule members the necessity of increased activity and more regular attendance during the ensuing session." '

Butt defended his policy with much of the old fire and eloquence, and succeeded in defeating the resolution by eight votes.[1]

He was gratified with the result and left the hall in his usual genial pleasant way, leaning on the arm of a member of the 'forward' party. He never appeared on the political stage again. A short time afterwards he fell seriously ill, and on May 13 sank peacefully to rest.

The founder of the Home Rule movement has to some extent been overshadowed by the remarkable man who was so near bringing that movement to a successful issue. Nevertheless, Isaac Butt will always stand in the front rank of the Irish political leaders of the nineteenth century.

On the collapse of Fenianism there was every danger that Ireland would sink into the slough of Whiggery. From any danger of such a calamity he saved her. He created a great national movement, and led it with conspicuous ability and in a true spirit of chivalry. Under his command Ireland sent sixty Home Rule members to the House of Commons, the Irish vote in England was organised, and many English parliamentary candidates were constrained to take the Home Rule pledge. He had, however, the defects of his qualities. He was a scrupulous constitutional leader,

---

[1] Technically, the division was taken on an amendment, proposed by Mr. D. B. Sullivan, to the effect that all reference to Mr. Butt should be omitted, and that merely the resolution passed at the conference of 1878 should be re-affirmed.

and instinctively shrank from revolutionary methods.
He revered representative institutions, and revolted
against all proceedings calculated to bring them into
contempt.   No Englishman respected the House of
Commons more than Isaac Butt, and he fought the
advanced section of his own party in defence of that
venerable institution.

'No man,' he said, addressing a meeting in Dublin
in January 1879, 'can damage the authority of the
House of Commons without damaging the cause of
representative government and of freedom all over the
world.'

It was a misfortune for which he certainly was not
to blame that, while the House of Commons influenced
him, he did not influence the House of Commons.   He
appealed to the reason and justice of Englishmen, but
the English did not respond to the appeal.   He was
a loyal citizen of the empire, but his loyalty did not
get him a hearing.   He kept the agitation within the
limits of the law, respected the opinions and feelings of
opponents, the conventions of society.   But no Englishman took him seriously.   'Do you really mean Home
Rule?' an old Whig said to him one day in the Four
Courts, Dublin.   'Indeed I do,' he answered, with
genial earnestness.   The old Whig smiled and walked
away.   No one ever asked Parnell if he meant Home
Rule.   There were those who thought that he meant
a great deal more.

And what was Parnell?   A Revolutionist working
with constitutional weapons.   We have seen what Butt
said of the House of Commons.   What said Parnell?
'I said when I was last here [in Dublin] that I would
not promise anything by parliamentary action, nor by
any particular line of policy; but I said we could

punish the English, and I predicted that the English
would very soon get afraid of punishment.'

Nothing can better show the chasm which separated
the two men in thought and feeling than these two
sentences. Yet the House of Commons despised Butt;
and Parnell became the greatest figure in it, in his day,
with a single exception.

I have said that Butt was a constitutional agitator.
He was also a great advocate. And if pure advocacy
—able, earnest, courteous—could have won the Irish
cause he would have succeeded. It could not, and he
failed hopelessly.

Constitutional agitation, strictly speaking, disappeared
with Butt. Revolutionary agitation followed. Davitt
preached the new departure in public and in private,
visited the most distressed and disaffected districts, and
swept all the Fenians he could into the new movement.
On June 7 another great land meeting, organised by
Davitt and the local Fenians, though of course attended
by thousands of tenant farmers who were not Fenians,
was held at Westport, County Mayo. Parnell was invited. He hesitated, for he had not yet gauged the force
of the agrarian agitation. His attention was probably
first seriously directed to the subject in the course of
a conversation with Kickham, the date of which I
cannot give. 'Do you think, Mr. Kickham,' he asked,
'that the people feel very keenly on the land question?'
'Feel keenly on the land question?' answered Kickham. 'I am only sorry to say that I think they would
go to hell for it.' Finally Parnell resolved to accept
the invitation of the Westport men. The Archbishop
of Tuam, who saw something besides land in the new
movement, condemned the meeting, and indirectly

warned Parnell not to come. But he came, and delivered a stirring speech, which was long remembered
by friends and foes.

' A fair rent is a rent a tenant can reasonably pay
according to the times ; but in bad times the tenant cannot be expected to pay as much as he did in good times,
three or four years ago. If such rents are insisted upon
a repetition of the scenes of 1847 and 1848 will be witnessed. Now, what must we do in order to induce the
landlords to see the position? You must show the
landlords that you intend to hold a firm grip on your
homesteads and lands. You must not allow yourselves
to be dispossessed as you were dispossessed in 1847.
You must not allow your small holdings to be turned
into large ones. I am not supposing that the landlords
will remain deaf to the voice of reason, but I hope they
may not, and that on those properties on which the
rents are out of all proportion to the times that a reduction may be made, and that immediately. If not, you
must help yourselves, and the public opinion of the
world will stand by you and support you in your
struggle to defend your homesteads. I should be
deceiving you if I told you that there was any use in
relying upon the exertions of the Irish members of
Parliament on your behalf. I think that if your members were determined and resolute they could help you,
but I am afraid they won't. I hope that I may be
wrong, and that you may rely upon the constitutional
action of your parliamentary representatives in this the
sore time of your need and trial ; but above all things
remember that God helps him who helps himself, and
that by showing such a public spirit as you have shown
here to-day, by coming in your thousands in the face
of every difficulty, you will do more to show the land-

lords the necessity of dealing justly with you than if you had 150 Irish members in the House of Commons.'

Davitt also made a rattling speech, full of defiance and rebellion.

The fire spread, and the Government did nothing to put it out. They did not concede, they did not coerce. They listened neither to tenants nor to landlords. They unwittingly gave Davitt his head. With a little wisdom and foresight the fire might have been quenched at the outset. But the Irish Secretary—Mr. James Lowther—was ignorant, indifferent, incapable, and he faithfully represented English statesmanship in Ireland. On June 26 the question of agricultural distress in Ireland was brought before the House of Commons by Mr. O'Connor Power. He was treated with disdain by Mr. Lowther, and literally howled down by the Tories. Here is the official account of the scene.

'From the time when the hon. member stated his intention to move the adjournment of the House, and it appeared probable that a debate was about to be raised, hon. members ceased to pay any attention to the hon. member's remarks, and conversation became so general and so loud that the hon. member could with difficulty be heard.' [1]

So disgraceful were these interruptions that Mr. John Bright felt himself constrained to intervene and to sharply rebuke the Irish Secretary and his unmannerly followers. Nothing, of course, was done. The Government had not the most remote notion of what was brewing in Ireland ; not the faintest conception that by neglecting the demands of the farmers

---

[1] *Hansard*, 3rd series, vol. ccxlvii. p. 696.

they were throwing the country into the hands of the Revolutionists.

Other work now lay ready to Parnell's hands in the House of Commons. I have said that in 1878 a committee was appointed to consider the subject of obstruction. Early in 1879 Sir Stafford Northcote gave notice of six resolutions for dealing with the question; but he had to abandon them all except one, which proved of little use. The object of this resolution was to prevent members from discussing various miscellaneous grievances before the House went into Committee of Supply. The House was kept for three nights discussing this single resolution, and in the end amendments were added which much weakened its force.

So far all attempts to deal with obstruction had failed, as Parnell showed when the Army Discipline Bill came up for consideration. Over this Bill—or rather over one subject included in it, flogging in the army—the fight of the session took place.

We have seen that Parnell had opposed and obstructed the Mutiny Bills in 1877 because the Government would not abolish flogging. In 1878 he returned to the charge, succeeded in getting the Bills referred to a select committee, and wrung from the Government a pledge that before they were brought in again an amended Army Bill would be introduced. In 1879 this pledge was redeemed, and the Army Discipline and Regulation Bill was introduced. The new measure contained a clause retaining the punishment of flogging. Parnell opposed the clause. In 1877 and 1878 he and his band of obstructives stood almost alone in their opposition to the 'cat.' Now they were supported by a crowd of English Radicals. Parnell wisely allowed

these Radicals to take the lead. On May 20 Mr.
Hopwood opened operations by moving an amendment
abolishing flogging altogether. He was supported by
Parnell and the Irish, opposed by Sir William Harcourt
(who asked what punishment could be substituted for
flogging), and beaten by fifty-six votes. On June 10
Parnell stepped to the front, moving an amendment
which was technically in order, but which practically
raised the question which had, in fact, been settled by
vote on May 20. 'I was asked the other night,' he
said, ' by the hon. member for Oxford (Sir William
Harcourt) what punishment could be substituted for
flogging. I could not answer the question at the time.
I have since consulted military authorities, and I
can answer it now.' He then suggested alternative
punishments; but his amendment was defeated by forty-
three votes. Mr. Hopwood next came forward once
more, moving that the number of lashes should be
reduced from twenty to six. Parnell and the obstructives supported. The amendment was still under
consideration when the House met on June 17—in
some respects the most eventful night of the debate.
Mr. Chamberlain now interposed, condemning flogging
as ' unnecessary and immoral,' and calling upon the
Government to put in a schedule specifying the offences
for which it was to be inflicted. Sir William Harcourt
supported this demand. Then John Bright, in a short
but powerful speech, urged the Minister of War,
Colonel Stanley, to show a spirit of conciliation, and
to reduce the number of lashes from fifty to twenty-
five at the least. This suggestion[1] was accepted,
Hopwood withdrawing his amendment in favour of

[1] Bright's suggestion later on moved as an amendment by Mr.
Brown.

it. Nevertheless the battle of the 'cat' was not yet
over. Mr. Hopwood immediately moved that the
punishment should be inflicted by a 'cat' with one
tail, instead of a 'cat' with nine tails. Lord Hartington opposed this amendment, which was defeated by
110 votes. An Irish member, Mr. Callan, next proposed that a specimen of the 'cat' should be exhibited
in the Library. 'Yes,' said Parnell, fastening upon
this suggestion, 'I should like to see what sort of
an instrument is to be used, for I understand there
are several kinds.' The Government would not, however, gratify the curiosity either of Mr. Callan or
Parnell. Other amendments were now proposed, and
on June 19 Parnell once more appealed to the Government to abolish the cat. 'Let us,' he said, 'as this
day's work abolish flogging. If you do that I will
wash my hands of the Bill and give you no further
trouble.'

'No,' said Sir William Harcourt, supported by
Ministers ; 'as the Bill now stands (with Bright's
amendment) it is satisfactory, and when the schedule
asked for by the hon. member for Birmingham
(Chamberlain) is put in we may feel content.'

'I will not accept the advice of the hon. member for
Oxford,' said Mr. Chamberlain with much warmth ;
'he is far too favourable to this Bill. Nothing can
be done without obstruction,' he added, and then
wound up with this compliment to Parnell : 'I will
only add before I sit down that the friends of humanity
and the friends of the British army owe a debt of
gratitude to my hon. friend the member for Meath for
standing up alone against this system of flogging when
I myself, and other members, had not the courage
of our convictions. The hon. member had opposed

flogging in the Mutiny Bill, but unsuccessfully; he had opposed it unsuccessfully in the Prisons Bill; but now he raises the question again, and I hope his efforts will be crowned with success.'[1]

Parnell, with characteristic tenacity, had never lost sight of Mr. Callan's suggestion that specimens of the 'cat' should be exhibited in the Library. 'I should like to know,' he said, 'what the Government knows about these "cats." I have a shrewd suspicion that they know very little. Let the "cats" be produced.' But the Government were obdurate. They had given way on Bright's amendment. They now meant to stand firm. Parnell, however, kept pegging away. He moved that when a man received more than twelve lashes he should be expelled from the army with ignominy, but the amendment was defeated by 109 votes.

Obstruction, of which there had been very little up to about June 20, now began, and the Irish pushed to the front, 'Mr. Parnell,' as the 'Annual Register' put it, 'providing them with opportunities by moving a succession of minute amendments relative to the provisions for enlisting and billeting.'

On July 3 Mr. Callan, in an amusing speech, informed the House that he had paid a visit to the Library, and had seen the 'cat'—in fact, several 'cats'—which he graphically described. The Ministers questioned the accuracy of Mr. Callan's description of the 'instruments of torture.' 'Produce the "cats,"' said Parnell; 'then we shall know who is right.' Ultimately the 'cats' were produced on July 5. Mr. Callan's description

---

[1] 'Chamberlain,' said Mr. Justin McCarthy, 'spoke to me with great admiration of Parnell, and said that his obstructive tactics were the only tactics to succeed.'

was accurate, and the sight of the 'instruments of torture' proved fatal to the position of the Government. 'Abolish flogging,' urged Mr. Chamberlain on this same day (July 5), ' and your Bill will be passed at once; otherwise it will be systematically opposed and obstructed.'

Colonel Stanley asked Mr. Chamberlain to suspend further opposition until the schedule was put in. 'Agreed,' said Chamberlain, and he appealed to Parnell to let the clauses then under consideration go through. ' No,' cried Parnell, and he moved to report progress on the instant, showing a relentless front and keeping the committee sitting for three hours longer.

On July 7 Colonel Stanley announced that the Government had resolved to abolish flogging in all cases except when death was the alternative.

Mr. Chamberlain expressed his dissatisfaction with this arrangement, and urged that flogging should be wholly and unconditionally abolished. Lord Hartington supported the Government, when Mr. Chamberlain denounced him in a bitter speech as : ' The noble lord, lately the leader of the Opposition, now the leader of a section of the Opposition.' Bright stood by Chamberlain, and Parnell and the Irish took the same side.

On July 15 Parnell and Mr. Chamberlain still showed fight, when Lord Hartington promised that if they allowed the Bill to pass through committee he would move a resolution on the report to give effect to their wishes. They agreed, and on July 17 Lord Hartington, on behalf of the whole Liberal party, moved : ' That no Bill for the discipline and regulation of the army will be satisfactory to this House which provides for the retention of corporal punishment for military offences.' This was the final struggle. The Government stood

by their concession of July 7, and defeated Lord
Hartington's resolution by 291 to 185 votes.   So ended
the campaign against the 'cat' in 1879—flogging was
abolished in all cases except when the alternative
punishment was death.   In 1881 it was abolished
altogether.   In the end other men became as anxious
for the abolition of the 'cat' as Parnell; but it was
he who began the fight, and who carried it on with a
skill and tenacity which made victory secure.

From Westminster Parnell hastened to Ireland to
take part in the Ennis election in July.   There were two
candidates in the field : Mr. William O'Brien (Whig),
a Catholic barrister and Crown prosecutor, and Mr.
Finnigan (Home Ruler), Parnell's nominee.   The bishops
and the priests supported Mr. O'Brien, the advanced
men stood by Mr. Finnigan.   It was the Ennis election
that tested Parnell's strength in the country.   'If Ennis
had been lost,' he said afterwards, ' I would have retired
from public life, for it would have satisfied me that the
priests were supreme in Irish politics.'   Ennis was
not lost.   Mr. Finnigan was returned.

Some days later an incident occurred which caused
a good deal of commotion at the time, and gave Parnell
not a little trouble.   The Irish University Bill (which
afterwards became law)[1] was before the House of
Commons.   Parnell took an advanced position in the
discussion.   He was, in fact, in favour of the extreme
Catholic demand—namely, a Catholic university.   Mr.
Gray, the proprietor of the 'Freeman's Journal,' and
other moderate Catholic members were in favour of a

---

[1] The Bill establishing a Royal university—practically an examining
board.   Curiously enough, the Government said they would not deal
with the subject at the beginning of the session ; but, to buy off Parnell's
opposition to their measures generally, they introduced and passed it at
the end.

compromise such as the Government proposed. There was a meeting of the Irish members to consider the subject. Some hot words passed between the extreme and the moderate men, and Parnell was reported to have referred contemptuously to the moderates as 'Papist rats.' Currency was given to this report in the 'Freeman's Journal.' Parnell said the statement was 'absolutely false,' and several of the extreme Catholics corroborated his assertion. Still, there was a good deal of unpleasantness over the matter, and many people believed that Parnell used the words. As a matter of fact he did not use them. They were used by an extreme Catholic just as the meeting had broken up and when there was a good deal of confusion in the room. 'The first time I ever had a talk with Parnell about politics,' Mr. Corbett, the present member for Wicklow, said to me, 'was about the "Papist rats" incident. Gray and Parnell had differed on the education question. Gray was in favour of a compromise; Parnell wanted the extreme Catholic demand. Gray succeeded in carrying the party with him, and Parnell was reported to have said, on leaving the room, "these Papist rats." I asked Parnell if he had used the words. He said: "No. The words were used, but not by me. Why, Corbett, should I offend the Catholics of Ireland by speaking insultingly of them? Certainly it would be very foolish, to put the matter on no other ground. An Irish Protestant politician can least of all afford to offend the Catholic priests or laity. No; I would not insult the priests."'

The condition of Ireland was now alarming. Distress was increasing; evictions were imminent; agitation, fed by the poverty of the tenants and the follies of the landlords, spread like wildfire. Towards the end of

April a great land meeting was held in Limerick. Parnell attended. The chairman—a parish priest—made a moderate speech, but the meeting was in no temper for moderation. 'The farmers of Ireland,' said the priest, 'if there are to be peace and loyalty, ought to have free land, as the farmers of Belgium, France, and Holland.' 'We want physical force,' shouted the crowd. 'We must not have Fenianism,' said the priest. 'Three cheers for the Irish republic,' was the response.

Parnell sat calm and impassive while the vast mass before him surged with discontent. When his time for speaking came he made one of those cold-blooded, businesslike speeches which fired the people more than the wild rhetoric of some of his more inflammable colleagues. Repeating the advice he had given at Westport, he told the farmers to keep a 'firm grip on their homesteads,' and to show 'a firm and determined attitude' to the landlords. 'Stand to your guns,' he said, 'and there is no power on earth which can prevail against the hundreds of thousands of tenant farmers of this country.' On September 21 he attended another land meeting in Tipperary. There he once more told the people to rely upon themselves, and themselves alone.

'It is no use relying upon the Government, it is no use relying upon the Irish members, it is no use relying upon the House of Commons. (Groans.) You must rely upon your own determination, that determination which has enabled you to survive the famine years and to be present here to-day—(cheers)—and if you are determined, I tell you, you have the game in your own hands.' (Prolonged cheers.)

Davitt, who was the soul of this land agitation,

now resolved to sweep the various tenant defence
societies scattered over the country into one great
organisation, and to call it the Land League. His
plan was to have a central committee in Dublin, and
local branches in the rural districts. He put his views
before Parnell. Parnell for a moment hesitated. He
had often heard Butt say that organisations of this
kind were attended with a good deal of danger. The
central authority could not always control the local
branches, yet it was responsible for every act of a
local branch. The moderate members of the parliamentary party, while sympathising thoroughly with
the cause of the tenants, shrank from Davitt's proposal.
Parnell, however, with the clearness of vision which
always characterised him, saw that the promotion of
the League was inevitable. The question was, should
it go on without him?

After the conversation with Kickham, if not before,
he fully realised that the tenant farmers could never be
left out of account; therefore, to hold himself apart
from a great land movement would be political suicide.
Farmers, Fenians, Home Rulers, bishops, priests—
all should be brought into line, and he should lead all.
That was the policy, that was the faith, of Parnell.

'Unless we unite all shades of political opinion in
the country,' he had said at a meeting of the Home
Rule League on September 11, 'I fail to see how we
can expect ever to attain national independence.' To
have a Land League standing by itself and out of touch
with the Home Rule League seemed to him, after a
little reflection, the height of folly. His principle all
the time was 'unity,' and assuredly it would not make
for unity to have Davitt at the head of one league and
himself, or somebody else, at the head of another.

He saw all the risks of the situation, and he resolved to face them. A united Ireland was the paramount consideration.

On October 21 there was a conference of Nationalists and Land Reformers at the Imperial Hotel, Dublin, and there and then the 'Irish National Land League' was formed, for the purpose of 'bringing about a reduction of rack rents' and facilitating the creation of a peasant proprietary. 'The objects of the League,' so ran one of the resolutions, 'can best be attained by defending those who may be threatened with eviction for refusing to pay unjust rents ; and by obtaining such reforms in the laws relating to land as will enable every tenant to become the owner of his holding by paying a fair rent for a limited number of years. Parnell was elected president of the League ; Mr. Biggar, Mr. O'Sullivan, Mr. Patrick Egan, hon. treasurers ; Mr. Davitt, Mr. Kettle, Mr. Brennan, hon. secretaries. Thus of the seven first chosen officers four were Fenians or ex-Fenians—Biggar, Egan, Brennan, Davitt—and all were in sympathy with Fenianism. The Land League was, in fact, the organisation of the New Departure. Within twelve months of his return from America Davitt had established a formidable association, well fitted in every respect to carry out the policy which he and Devoy had planned. Davitt and his colleagues might be in rebellion against England. They were also in rebellion against the governing body of the Fenian society. Land League meetings were now held constantly throughout the country, and speeches of extreme violence were delivered. The fight between the League and the Government had commenced in earnest.

The agitators acted with vigour and ability ; the Government with supineness and stupidity. Disbe-

lieving in the reality of the land movement, they had
allowed it to grow ; then, suddenly alarmed at the out-
look, they struck at it in the moment of its strength, and
finally recoiled from the impetus of their own blow.
Davitt, Daly (a Mayo journalist), and Killen (a barrister)
addressed a meeting at Gurteen, in the county of Sligo,
on November 2. They made violent speeches, not, however, exceeding in ' lawlessness ' of tone the calm incite-
ments to ' rebellion ' which had characterised the
unrhetorical utterances of Parnell at Westport, Limerick,
and Tipperary. Yet the Government resolved to punish
them while letting the wily Parliamentarian go free.
On November 19 the three Land Leaguers were
arrested. Parnell showed his appreciation of this move
by attending a meeting at Balla, County Mayo, a few
days later, summoned to protest against evictions and
to denounce the Government. Brennan, one of the
secretaries of the League, was the orator of the day.
He delivered a furious oration, defying the authorities,
and appealing to the Royal Irish Constabulary who
were present to stand by ' their kith and kin,' and not
to play the base part of the ' destroyers of their own
people ' by helping on the work of eviction. While the
meeting wildly cheered the fiery sentences of Brennan,
Parnell sat unmoved. Then he rose, congratulated
Brennan on the ' magnificent speech ' to which they
had listened, and added, with imperturbable gravity : ' I
fear very much that the result of the lead which Mr.
Brennan has taken in the movement will be that he
will be sent to share the fate of Mr. Davitt, Mr. Daly,
and Mr. Killen.' This proved a true prediction. On
December 5 Brennan was arrested. What happened ?
In a few days the Government flinched, dropped the
prosecution, and discharged the prisoners. They had

realised, though rather late in the day for their own dignity, that no jury could be got to convict the Leaguers, and they did not wish to risk a verdict of 'not guilty.' All Ireland laughed at this performance; and landlords and tenants, who had so little in common, joined in regarding the action or non-action of the Administration with contempt and ridicule. As winter approached famine threatened the west, and committees were formed by the Duchess of Marlborough (the wife of the Lord-Lieutenant) and by the Lord Mayors to collect food and clothing for the starving peasantry. At the Land League Conference of October 21 a resolution had been passed requesting Parnell to visit America 'for the purpose of obtaining assistance from our exiled fellow-countrymen.' This resolution was now put into effect, and on December 21 Parnell set out for New York (accompanied by Mr. Dillon) on the twofold mission of appealing for funds to save the tenant farmers from immediate ruin, and of consolidating the union between the Irish at home and the Irish abroad.

CHAPTER X

THE CLAN-NA-GAEL—THE GENERAL ELECTION

' WELL, Parnell has his work cut out for him now, at
all events. If he can hold his ground with the
Clan-na-Gael, and afterwards hold it in the House of
Commons, he will win Home Rule. The Clan-na-Gael
are the open and avowed enemies of England. Their
policy is to strike her anywhere and anyhow. What
is Parnell going to say to them? If he speaks with
an eye to the House of Commons his speeches won't
go down with the Clan. If he speaks with an eye to
the Clan his speeches will be used with tremendous
effect against him in the House. It is all very well
for men who are not members of Parliament to go
among Revolutionists. But the member of Parliament
has to face the music at St. Stephen's; and how
Parnell is going to face it after his visit to the Clan-
na-Gael I don't know.'

So said an Irish Home Rule member to me on the
eve of Parnell's departure for the United States.

Parnell himself set out on his mission with a light
heart. What the House of Commons would think, or
would not think, gave him little trouble. He was not
in the habit of forecasting the future to an extent which
would interfere with the operations of the present.

' Sufficient for the day is the work thereof ' ; that was practically his motto. He saw his way clearly to a given point; he went straight to that point, and then surveyed the situation afresh. ' The critical side of his character is too strongly developed. He can only see difficulties.' This has been said of an English Liberal statesman of our own day. It could not be said of Parnell. No man certainly was so quick in seeing, or rather in judging, difficulties; but neither was any man so adroit, so ready, so resourceful in over-coming them. Difficulties paralyse the mere man of thought; they nerve the man of action. Parnell had the eye of a general. He took in the whole situation at a glance. He knew when to advance, when to retreat. He divined with the instinct of genius when a position had to be stormed, and when it could be turned with safety.

When the time for action came he made up his mind quickly; he did not hesitate, he did not flinch. His objective now was the union of all Irishmen, not only in Ireland but all over the world, against England. This was a vital point, and he was prepared to do anything, to risk anything, for it. The opinion of the House of Commons was nothing to him. The House, he felt, would give way quickly enough before a united Ireland; and of a united Ireland he thought alone. The Irish in America were a great force. It was essential to bring them into line with the Irish at home. The Clan-na-Gael was probably not an im-maculate organisation. But was the English Govern-ment in Ireland immaculate? He would avail himself of every power within his reach to attack that Government; and would show exactly the same amount of ' scruple ' in dealing with England that England had habitually shown in dealing with his own nation. If he could he would have preferred to settle the Anglo-Irish question by open warfare. That was not possible. He would, therefore, use whatever means were ready to his hand for out-manœuvring the 'common enemy.' He had no more intention of giving himself away to the Clan-na-Gael than he had of giving himself away to the British Minister. But, after all, there was something in common between him and the Clan, however much they might differ about the *modus operandi*. They both hated England. Between him and the British Minister there was nothing in common. He would accordingly use the Clan, as he would use every Irish organisation, to fight the Britisher. For the rest he would trust to the fortunes of war.

Parnell arrived in New York early in 1880. His work was indeed cut out for him. The Clan-na-Gael were not united in favour of the 'new departure.' There were many important members of the organisation opposed to the parliamentary movement and anxious to make war against it. These men had to be won over, or their hostility, at least, disarmed. Success in this respect was, however, only half the battle. There were thousands of Irishmen who were not Fenians, yet they had to be brought into line with the Fenians. Lastly, the sympathy of the Americans themselves had to be enlisted in the cause of Ireland. How were these things to be accomplished? Most Irish agitators believe in talking. Parnell believed in listening, and by listening, chiefly, he got into the good graces of the Clan-na-Gael. He saw the leaders. He heard what they had to say. He held his tongue. He made no compact ; he entered into no undertaking. He asked only for fair play for the parliamentary

movement. 'I believe in it,' he said; 'give it a chance.'
His path was not a smooth one in America. There
were those in the Clan who said: 'Do not trust
Parnell; he will use you for his own purposes, he will
make our movement subservient to his.' This was
particularly the opinion of the Fenian agent who had
been sent to Europe in 1878. Then he was more or less
favourably disposed to the 'new departure.' Now he was
vehemently against it. He quarrelled with Parnell.
'Mr. Parnell,' he said one day with much warmth,
'you are always making inquiries about the Clan-na-
Gael. We don't like it. It shows you suspect us. I
cannot work with a man who suspects me. The fact
is, Mr. Parnell, you want to become the master of the
Clan-na-Gael, to use it for the constitutional movement. That is your aim. Well, I won't work on
that basis.' It was Parnell's luck—if luck it is to be
called—that he almost always succeeded in neu-
tralising the hostility of the men who opposed him;
and this particular Fenian soon found himself in a
minority.

The public platform is the breath of the nostrils of
the ordinary Irish agitator. He loves it. Parnell
detested it. 'I hate public assemblies,' he once said
to a friend; 'it is always an effort for me to attend
them. I am always nervous. I dislike crowds.'
The public platform had, however, to be used, and,
despite his aversion to it, Parnell used it with effect in
America.

At Brooklyn, on January 24, 1880, he said: 'We
do not ask you to send armed expeditions over to
Ireland (a voice, "That's what we would like." Applause.) I know that you would like to do that very
much. (Applause, "Right.") I think I know what

you are going to say, and what you would like to do, and what you are willing to do, and how willing you will be to help us all. But we ask you to help us in preventing the people who have taken our advice, and who are exhibiting an attitude of devotion which has never been surpassed—what we ask you to do is to help us in preventing these people from being starved to death. This is not a new enterprise; this struggle has gone on for many centuries, and it is bound to go on to the bitter end, and in one way or another the Irish people will insist upon having the land of Ireland for themselves, and the end of it will be that these men who till the soil will also own it. The high heart of our country remains unquelled, the will and courage of our race unquenched, and they are strengthened by the great power of our people in this free land. I feel very confident that the day is very near at hand when we shall have struck the first blow, the first vital blow, at the land system as it now exists in Ireland, and then we shall have taken the first step to obtain for Ireland that right to nationhood for which she has struggled so long and so well.'

At Cleveland, on January 26, 1880, he said : ' I have said that we are fighting this battle against heavy odds. I have also said that we feel confident of winning it. It has given me great pleasure during my visit to the cities of this country to see the armed regiments of Irishmen who have frequently turned out to escort us ; and when I saw some of these gallant men to-day, who are even now in this hall, I thought that each one of them must wish, with Sarsfield of old, when dying upon a foreign battlefield, " Oh ! that I could carry these arms for Ireland." Well, it may come to that some day or other.'

At Cincinnati, on February 23, 1880, he said: ' I feel confident that we shall kill the Irish landlord system, and when we have given Ireland to the people of Ireland we shall have laid the foundation upon which to build up our Irish nation. The feudal tenure and the rule of the minority have been the corner-stone of English misrule. Pull out that corner-stone, break it up, destroy it, and you undermine English mis-government. When we have undermined English mis-government we have paved the way for Ireland to take her place among the nations of the earth. And let us not forget that that is the ultimate goal at which all we Irishmen aim. None of us, whether we be in America or in Ireland, or wherever we may be, will be satisfied until we have destroyed the last link which keeps Ireland bound to England.'

At Rochester, in February 1880, he said : ' I am bound to admit that it is the duty of every Irishman to shed the last drop of his blood in order to obtain his rights, if there were a probable chance of success, yet at the same time we all recognise the great responsibility of hurling our unarmed people on the points of British bayonets. We must act with prudence when the contest would be hopeless, and not rush upon destruction.'

It would be doing scant justice to Parnell to suggest for an instant that these speeches were made merely for the purpose of conciliating the Clan-na-Gael. Far from it. In what he said he spoke the faith that was in him. Other speeches he made to Irishmen who were not Fenians, and then he dealt with the land question alone. But he did not take off his coat to reform the land laws of Ireland. He took off his coat to loosen the English grip on the island. Therefore at

Brooklyn, Cleveland, and Cincinnati he spoke from his heart.

His progress in America was a triumphal procession. He went everywhere, and everywhere he was received with open arms. Large towns and small vied with each other in showing honour to him, and sympathy for the cause he represented. Public bodies presented addresses to him. Irish soldiers lined the streets of the cities through which he passed. Governors of States waited on him. Congress itself threw open its doors to let him plead the cause of his country before the Parliament of the republic. 'In spite, and partly perhaps because, of the attacks directed at us by a portion of the Eastern Press,' he wrote to P. Egan on March 1, ' the enthusiasm increases in volume as we proceed from place to place, military guards and salvoes of artillery salute our coming, and the meetings which we address, although high admission charge is made, are packed from floor to roof. State Governors, members of Congress, local representatives, judges, clergymen, continually appear upon the platform.'

' In two months,' he said subsequently, ' we visited sixty-two different cities—that is, little more than one city a night. Between two of these cities we on one occasion travelled 1,400 miles. During the two months we remained in America we travelled together something like 10,000 or 11,000 by land. This, joined to the 6,000 miles of ocean there and back, amounts roughly to 16,000 miles in three months, which is not bad for a man. The net result of these sixty-two cities was 200,000 dollars actually in the hands of our committee in America.' [1]

---

[1] The honour extended to Parnell of addressing the House of Representatives was shared only by three other individuals. Curiously enough O'Meara Condon, one of the men tried and convicted in con-

From the United States Parnell went to Canada, whither he was accompanied by Mr. Healy, who had joined him in America. 'I was with him,' says Mr. Healy, 'for about three weeks, but I have not much to tell beyond what appears in the newspapers. We went to Canada together. Before starting the Bishop of Toronto wrote to Parnell to warn him against coming, suggesting that he would probably be attacked by the Orangemen. Parnell sent a dignified reply, saying he had promised to come, that he would keep his word, and that he had no apprehensions of disturbance. We came. There was no row, nor sign of a row. "Perhaps," said Parnell with an enigmatical smile, "the Orangemen do not wish to attack a Protestant." On arriving at Toronto Parnell went straight to a telegraph station, and told me to "come along." He took up a telegram form, wrote out a message with great pains, and then tore up the form. He tried again, and went on boggling over his message until I thought he would never get done. At length he apparently satisfied himself, and then handed the message to me, saying, 'Is that all right?' It was simply a wire to his mother in New York saying that he had arrived safely, and that she need have no fears about him as all was quiet and peaceful. But *it was written in French*. That was the cause of the boggling. I thought it was very odd that he should (to secure secrecy) send a telegram in French from Toronto, where they speak French as well as they do in Paris. I felt inclined to tell him so; but thought on reflection that it was no business of mine. Moreover, it struck me

nection with the Manchester rescue, and who had cried from the dock, 'God save Ireland,' was a prominent member of the committee which organised Parnell's reception by Congress.

that perhaps he wanted to keep someone in the dark in New York. Another thing struck me about this incident. There was this cold, callous man, who seemed not to care for anyone, rushing off to a telegraph office to wire his mother not to be uneasy about him. He was a man of surprises, and certainly very fond of his own family.

'We had a great meeting at Toronto. But the biggest meeting I ever attended was at Montreal. It was here he was first called the "uncrowned king." A high charge was made for admission. The hall, the biggest in the city, could not hold all the people who wanted to come. The enthusiasm was tremendous. Parnell sat like a sphinx the whole time. He seemed not to be a bit touched by the demonstration. The whole town went mad about him. Everyone was affected but himself.

'Next day, as we steamed out of the railway station, returning to New York, I repeated some humorous lines which I had recently read about Montreal. I wanted to see if Parnell could see the fun of them. He listened in a dreamy way until I was done, and then said: "I have been thinking if anyone will ever pay to come and hear me lecture again." The poem was thrown away on him.

'We left New York for Ireland on a bitterly cold March morning. The 69th Regiment [1] saw us off. As soon as I got on board the tender I turned towards the cabin to get under shelter from the driving sleet. Parnell stood on the bridge the whole time until the tender left with head uncovered; and it was a fine sight to see the 69th salute as we sailed off, and Parnell wave his hand in response, looking like a king.'

[1] This regiment was at one time composed entirely of Fenians.

Parnell's last act before starting for Ireland was to form an American Land League. A hurried meeting was held in New York. The Fenians dominated it, though Constitutionalists also attended at Parnell's special request. A committee of seven was appointed to frame a constitution for the new association, and out of these seven four were members of the Clan-na-Gael. We have seen that Davitt was one of the secretaries of the Irish Land League. John Devoy was now appointed one of the treasurers of the American Land League. Thus the joint authors of the policy of the new departure held important posts in the joint organisations founded (*inter alia*) to carry out that policy. What then, briefly, was the situation in the spring of 1880? Within the American Land League there were Constitutionalists, between whom and the Revolutionists much friction existed; but the Revolutionists were always in a majority. In the Irish Land League the overwhelming majority were Constitutionalists, but the most active spirits were Fenians or ex-Fenians. The supreme council of the I. R. B. fought to the last against the Leaguers—without, however, producing any permanent effect on the course of events. Parnell all the time concentrated the whole of his energies in uniting the discordant elements of which the whole movement against England was composed. He was the centre of unity.

Meanwhile the agitation in Ireland went steadily on. The distress of the people in the western districts grew appalling. Evictions increased. No reductions in rent were made. The landlords, with the madness of the old French *régime*, foresaw nothing, and unconsciously fanned the flames which were to consume them. On the meeting of Parliament Mr. Shaw moved

an amendment to the Address affirming that, ' although
in possession of timely warning and informátion, the
Government had not taken adequate steps to alleviate
the distress,' and adding that ' it was essential to the
peace and prosperity of Ireland to legislate at once in
a comprehensive manner on those questions which
affect the tenure of land in Ireland, the neglect of
which by Parliament had been the true cause of the
constantly recurring disaffection and distress in Ireland.'
In the debate which followed Sir Stafford Northcote
made a statement on the subject of that distress which
we are told ' startled ' the House.   ' The statistics,' says
the 'Annual Register,' 'given by Sir S. Northcote
from the report of the Registrar-General on the agricultural condition of Ireland were startling.   It was
estimated that there had been a falling off in the principal crops from the yield of the previous year to the
value of 10,000,000l.   The value of the potato crop
was more than 6,000,000l. below the average. . . .
Figures of such an enormous deficiency startled many
who had been previously disposed to believe that the
Irish distress had no serious foundation except in the
imaginations of the Home Rulers and anti-rent agitators.'   The British Parliament, with characteristic
indifference, had turned a deaf ear to the remonstrances
of the Irish representatives until famine was upon the
land and the fires of agitation were blazing in every
district.   Even then Ministers pottered with the situation.   Of course Mr. Shaw's amendment was defeated
by an overwhelming majority—216 against 66—the
notion of reforming the land laws of Ireland was
scouted, and an inadequate Relief Bill passed.[1]

[1] This Relief Bill was thus described by the present Lord Chief
Justice of England before the Parnell Commission : ' The form it took

Then, to the astonishment of everyone, the Dissolution was sprung upon the country.[1]   The Government tried to make Home Rule the issue of the conflict, and to stir up English passion and prejudice against Ireland. 'My Lord Duke,' said Lord Beaconsfield in his letter to the Irish Viceroy, the Duke of Marlborough, 'A danger in its ultimate results scarcely less disastrous than pestilence and famine, and which now engages your Excellency's anxious attention, distracts Ireland.

was advancing to Irish landlords 1,100,000*l*. of the surplus funds of the disestablished Church in Ireland, to lend that money to Irish landlords without interest for two years, and at the end of two years at the rate of one per cent. ; and, unless numbers of landlords are gravely maligned, when they employed their tenants and paid them wages out of this fund for working upon their own farms (which wages went towards payment of rent), those tenants were charged in some cases four and five and even more per cent., and that in perpetuity, on the very money advanced by the State for their relief, thus getting the relief filtered through the hands of the landlords in this indirect and very ineffective fashion ' (Speech of Sir Charles Russell, p. 159).

[1] The Government made another attempt in February to deal with obstruction, and passed the following resolution : ' That whenever any member shall have been named by the Speaker or by the chairman of a committee of the whole House as disregarding the authority of the chair, or abusing the rules of the House by persistently and wilfully obstructing the business of the House or otherwise, then, if the offence has been committed in the House, the Speaker shall forthwith put the question or motion being made, no amendment, adjournment, or debate being allowed : "That such member be suspended from the service of the House during the remainder of that day's sitting ;" and if the offence has been committed in a committee of the whole House, the chairman shall, on motion being made, put the same question in a similar way, and if the motion is carried shall forthwith suspend the proceedings of the committee and report the circumstance to the House, and the Speaker shall thereupon put the same question, without amendment, adjournment, or debate, as if the offence had been committed in the House itself.   If any member be suspended three times in one session under this order, this suspension on the third occasion shall continue for one week and until a motion has been made, upon which it shall be decided at one sitting by the House whether the suspension shall then cease or for what longer period it shall continue, and on the occasion of such motion the member may, if he desires it, be heard in his place. Provided always that nothing in this resolution shall be taken to deprive the House of the power of proceeding against any member according to ancient usages.'

A portion of its population is attempting to sever the
constitutional tie which unites it to Great Britain in
that bond which has favoured the power and prosperity
of both.'[1] Mr. Gladstone refused to accept the issue
as stated by Lord Beaconsfield, and resolved to fight
the Government upon the whole line of their policy ;
but chiefly on the question of foreign affairs. To the
paragraph in the Prime Minister's letter dealing with
Ireland Mr. Gladstone replied in his address to the
electors of Midlothian : ' Gentlemen, those who endan-
gered the Union with Ireland were the party that maintained there an alien Church, an unjust land law, and
franchises inferior to our own ; and the true supporters
of the Union are those who uphold the supreme
authority of Parliament, but exercise that authority
to bind the three nations by the indissoluble tie of
liberal and equal laws. Let me say that in my
opinion these two great subjects of local government
and the land laws ought now to occupy a foremost
place in the thoughts of every man who aspires to be a
legislator. In the matter of local government there
may lie a solution of some national and even Imperial
difficulties. It will not be in my power to enter
largely [now] upon the important question of the
condition of Ireland ; but you know well how unhappily the action of Parliament has been impeded
and disorganised, from considerations, no doubt, conscientiously entertained by a part of the Irish repre-

---

[1] A month before the Dissolution an election took place at Liverpool
which once more showed the power of the Irish vote in the English
constituencies. Lord Ramsay, the Liberal candidate, was obliged to take
the Home Rule pledge (*i.e.* to vote for an inquiry).   He was beaten by a
majority of 2,000, but the fact that the Liberal wire-pullers felt that the
Home Rulers had to be won over in a great constituency like Liverpool
produced a strong impression in political circles throughout the whole
country.

sentatives, and from their desire to establish what they term Home Rule. If you ask me what I think of Home Rule, I must tell you that I will only answer you when you tell me how Home Rule is related to local government. I am friendly to large local privileges and powers. I desire, I may almost say I intensely desire, to see Parliament relieved of some portion of its duties. I see the efficiency of Parliament interfered with, not only by obstruction from Irish members, but even more gravely by the enormous weight that is placed upon the time and the minds of those whom you send to represent you. We have got an over-weighted Parliament, and if Ireland or any other portion of the country is desirous and able so to arrange its affairs that by taking the local part or some local part of its transactions off the hands of Parliament it can liberate and strengthen Parliament for Imperial concerns, I say I will not only accord a reluctant assent, but I will give a zealous support to any such scheme. One limit, gentlemen, one limit only, I know to the extension of local government. It is this ; nothing can be done, in my opinion, by any wise statesman or right-minded Briton to weaken or compromise the authority of the Imperial Parliament, because the Imperial Parliament must be supreme in these three kingdoms. And nothing that creates a doubt upon that supremacy can be tolerated by an intelligent and patriotic man. But, subject to that limitation, if we can make arrangements under which Ireland, Scotland, Wales, portions of England, can deal with questions of local and special interest to themselves more efficiently than Parliament now can, that, I say, will be the attainment of a great national good.'

It was the sudden Dissolution that forced Parnell
to bring his American tour to an abrupt termination,
and to hasten back to Ireland, where he arrived on
March 21.

Parnell thought much of the Clan-na-Gael as a
powerful political organisation. In his evidence before
the Special Commission he said : ' I believe that so far
as any active interest was taken at the time of my
going to America by Irishmen in the Irish question, it
was by the men of revolutionary physical-force ideas.
I believe that the great bulk of the Irish people in
America, until I went there, did not take any interest
at all in Irish politics.' Nevertheless, he disliked the
Clan, because he feared it would give him much
trouble. Even at this early date he foresaw that some
of its members might run into excesses, which would
compromise him and bring discredit on the national
movement. He knew, too, that as three thousand
miles of ocean separated him from the organisation, he
could exercise little restraining influence over its
operations.

But he could not ignore the Clan ; he could not
ignore any important Irish political association. His
central idea was to attack England. He took the help
of all allies for that purpose, and faced the consequences. On landing at Queenstown he was met by
some members of the I. R. B., who presented him with
an address which contained these words :

' We must take the opportunity to express our clear
conviction of the hopelessness of looking for justice to
Ireland from the English Parliament, and the firm
belief of the intelligent manhood of the country that
it is utterly futile to seek for any practical national
good through the means of parliamentary representation.

Impelled by such convictions, the Nationalists of the
country have determined, as a political party, they will
take no part in the coming elections, and consequently
no part in the adoption, rejection, or support of the
parliamentary candidates.'

We have seen that in 1879 the supreme council of
the I. R. B. passed a resolution to the effect that the
members of the rank and file might take part in the
parliamentary movement at their own risk.　In 1880
this resolution was rescinded, and it was declared that
no Fenian, under any circumstances, should co-operate
with the constitutional party.　The Queenstown address
simply gave expression to this determination.　Some
days later Parnell received further proof that all the
Fenians had not acquiesced in the new departure.
The platform from which he addressed a meeting in
Enniscorthy in support of the parliamentary candidature of his nominees, Mr. Barry and Mr. Byrne, was
attacked, and he himself almost dragged from it to
the ground.　Mr. John Redmond, who stood by his
side on the platform, has thus described the scene
to me :

'I met Parnell in 1880 after his return from
America.　I was at Enniscorthy with him.　It was an
awful scene.　There were about 4,000 to 5,000 people
there.　They all seemed to be against him.　I remember one man shouting, though what he meant I
could not tell : " We will show Parnell that the blood
of Vinegar Hill is still green."　The priests were
against Parnell.　Parnell stood on the platform calm
and self-possessed.　There was no use in trying to
talk.　He faced the crowd, looking sad and sorrowful,
but not at all angry ; it was an awful picture of patience.
A rotten egg was flung at him.　It struck him on the

beard and trickled down. He took no notice of it, never wiped it off, and was not apparently conscious of it; he faced the crowd steadfastly, and held his ground. One man rushed at him, seized him by the leg, and tore his trouser right up from bottom to top. There was no chance of a hearing, and we got away from the platform and went to the hotel to lunch. Parnell ate a hearty lunch while a waiter was busy stitching his trousers all the time. It was a comical sight. Afterwards we went for a walk. We were met by a hostile mob, and I was knocked down and cut in the face. I got up as quickly as I could and made my way to the railway station. When Parnell saw me he said: "Why, you are bleeding. What is the matter?" I told him what had happened, and he said, smiling: "Well, you have shed your blood for me at all events."'

Into the General Election Parnell flung himself with ardour and vigour, working literally day and night, selecting candidates, superintending all details, flying from constituency to constituency, and inspiring everyone with his energy and determination. Three constituencies vied with each other for the honour of electing him—Meath, Mayo, and Cork City. The circumstances under which he was nominated for Cork were curious, and even remarkable. Here is the story as told to me by his election agent and faithful friend, Mr. Horgan :

'The nomination for Cork City was fixed for March 31, the candidates being H. D. Murphy (Whig), William Goulding (Conservative), and John Daly (Home Ruler). Up to the day of the nomination the advanced Nationalists of Cork took no interest in the election. Of course, they cared nothing for the

Whig nor the Tory, and the Home Ruler was far too
moderate.

' On the day of the nomination, however, a politician
of supposed Nationalist leanings (whom we shall
call Y.) came into my office, accompanied by some
genuine Nationalists. He handed me a nomination
paper bearing Parnell's name. The paper was signed
by the Rev. John O'Mahony, C.C., and another
priest, the Rev. Denis McCarthy, and by several other
electors. Y. asked me to sign as nominator, and
to hand the paper to the Sheriff. Before signing I
asked him if he had Mr. Parnell's sanction. He replied
that he had, and produced 250*l.* in bank-notes, which
he said Mr. Parnell had sent him from Dublin that
morning.

' I was at once convinced by the production of the
money that the matter was all right. I signed the
nomination paper, and had only time to rush from my
office across the street to the Sheriff's office and hand
it in. Y. gave me 50*l.* to pay the Sheriff's fees.
There were a few thousand people on the South Mall,
opposite the Sheriff's office, and when they heard that
Parnell had been nominated they cheered vigorously
and became intensely excited.

' The friends of Daly and Murphy were both greatly
annoyed, and as I was returning to my office I was
jostled about by some of them, and the late Sir
D. V. O'Sullivan shouted into my face : " Parnell will
not poll the 511 given to John Mitchell at the last
election."

' Of course it was the advanced Nationalists who
had supported Mitchell at the last election, and the
same men were supporting Parnell now. The result
of bringing Mitchell forward then was to split the

Liberal vote and to let the Tory Goulding slip in.
O'Sullivan feared a similar result now, though in any
case he would not like to see an "Extremist" like
Parnell returned.

' Murphy was a strong candidate, having immense
local influence, and the Catholic Bishop, Dr. Delaney,
was at his back. In the evening I had a wire from
Parnell from Morrison's Hotel, Dublin, thanking me
for nominating him, and saying he would come down
by the night mail on Friday, April 2.

' During Friday afternoon a rumour was freely
circulated that Parnell was the Tory nominee. On
Saturday morning he arrived at 2 A.M. I met him at
the railway station. He surprised me by asking how
he came to be nominated. "Why," I said, "did you
not authorise Y. to nominate you, and send him
250*l*. to pay expenses?" "I did not send him a
farthing," said Parnell, "and I know nothing whatever
about him; never heard of him. There is something
that wants looking into here." "Well," I said, "let
us come to the hotel, at all events; have a rest, and I
will send for Father O'Mahony." Accordingly, we
went to the hotel. Parnell had some hours' rest, and
came down to breakfast looking as fresh as paint.
Father O'Mahony had also come, and was much
excited about the rumour that Parnell was being
run by the Tories. Tim Healy was present too. I
told the whole story of how Y. came to me over
again.

' When I was done Parnell said, as quick as light-
ning : "Send for Y." We despatched a messenger for
Y., who soon appeared upon the scene. Parnell at
once took Y. in hand, and went straight to the point
without a moment's delay. "Where did you get the

250*l*. you showed Mr. Horgan on Wednesday last?"
he asked, with a keen, determined look. Y. shuffled
for a bit, but soon collapsed and made a clean breast
of it. He had gone one evening into Goulding's committee rooms, where they were freely discussing the
chances of the Nationalists putting forward O'Donovan
Rossa or some other impossible candidate, who, like
Mitchell, might draw away five or six hundred votes
from Daly and Murphy. In such case, they said,
Goulding would once more slip in between the broken
Liberal ranks.

'Y. was personally known to some of the Tory
wire-pullers, and looked upon as an "Extremist" who
cared neither for Whig nor Tory, and would not in
the least object to spoil the Whig game. He was
sounded there and then, and told that if he could get
an extreme Nationalist candidate the Tories would
pay the Sheriff's fees and give him (Y.) 200*l*. for
himself.

'Y. undertook to bring forward such a candidate,
but said he would not disclose the name until the
day of nomination. He stipulated, however, that the
250*l*. should be given to him at once. This was agreed
to, and Mr. B —— handed Y. the money (250*l*.).

'That was Y.'s plain unvarnished tale. When
he had finished Parnell said : "You gave 50*l*. to
Mr. Horgan on the day of the nomination. Where is
the remaining 200*l*.?" Y. refused to tell. Parnell
pressed him ; he still held out. "Y.," said Parnell
at last, with a determined look, "if you do not tell
me at once where the money is I will raise that
window and denounce you to the citizens of Cork."
An immense crowd had by this time gathered outside.
Y. looked at the crowd and then at Parnell, and

finally put his hand into his breeches pocket and pulled out a bundle of bank-notes. " There is the 200*l*.," said he. Healy, who was nearest to him, seized the notes at once. " Now," said Parnell, " the question is what shall we do with the money." " Return it to the Tories at once," said Father O'Mahony. " Nonsense," said Healy. " We'll fight the election with it. It will be all the sweeter to win the seat with Tory money." Tim relished the fun of the thing immensely. " I think the best thing to do at present," said Parnell, " is to hand the money to Mr. Horgan until we have time to consider the matter." Tim then handed me the notes. Well, we kept the money. It was barely enough, although we ran the contest on the most economical lines.

' Parnell addressed the citizens (an enormous crowd) from the hotel windows that night, and was cheered with wild delight. I remember that the " Cork Examiner " (Whig), which attacked Parnell, was publicly burned outside the window. On Sunday, April 4, we started after breakfast with Parnell and a large body of supporters on cars for Douglas, a village three miles from Cork, where Parnell addressed the rural voters after Mass, and then we drove to Blackrock, another rural parish, where he also addressed another meeting. Then we drove to the other side of the city to Glanmire, where the people took the horses from his car and drew him back to Cork.

' Next we proceeded to the city park, where he addressed thirty thousand people wild with excitement. His horses again were unyoked, and he was drawn back to the hotel. That night at eight o'clock he addressed the people from the hotel window. The crowd was enormous, and occupied the whole of

Patrick Street. I never will forget his opening words.
They acted like an electric shock on the excited
people. He said, in slow and measured language, with
a deep pause after each word : " Citizens of Cork. This
is the night before the battle. To your guns then."
It was quite evident that we had all Cork with us, and
that there was no fear of Parnell at the election next
day.

'At breakfast on Monday morning Parnell decided
to nominate Mr. Kettle for the county [1]; the nomination
was to be on that day from ten to twelve o'clock at the
Court House. The difficulty was to get a nomination
paper without disclosing what we were about. So I
wrote out the form of nomination on an ordinary sheet
of notepaper. Then the difficulty was to get ten
county electors to sign it, as the city liberties extend
seven or eight miles around the city. As twelve o'clock
was the latest hour fixed for receiving nominations, we
were hard pressed for time. I suggested that I should
get a county list of voters, and with it proceed to the
corn and butter markets, where numbers of county
farmers usually were. Accordingly we drove off to the
corn market, and every man we saw with a frieze coat
we asked his name and where he was from, and then
looked out for the name in the list of voters, and, on
finding it, got the man to sign the nomination paper.
At the corn market we only got a few names ; we then
drove to the butter market, where we got some farmers
from Castletown Bearhaven, and some from Chorle-
velly, and different other parts of the county. Then
we drove to the Court House, where Kettle and Parnell
missed each other, and as the last moment for lodging the

[1] The Home Rule candidates already nominated were Shaw and
Colonel Colthurst.

paper was at hand great excitement prevailed. Kettle
—who, as the candidate, had to hand in the nomination paper—could not be found ; none of his nominators
were on the spot either.   Parnell was very anxious,
and kept dashing up and down the stairs and about the
court doors, seeking for Kettle.   At the last moment
Kettle arrived and handed Mr. Johnson, the sub-sheriff,
the nomination paper.   John George McCarthy, the
agent for Shaw and Colthurst, objected, first on the
ground that we were late ; but the Sheriff said the time
by his watch wanted half a minute to twelve o'clock,
and accordingly ruled that we were in time.   Then
McCarthy objected to the paper because it was in-
formal, being on a sheet of notepaper instead of the
Sheriff's printed form.   That was also overruled, and
then the names of the nominators were questioned ;
but they were found to be all right, and so Kettle was
nominated.   There was a great commotion as soon as
it was known that Parnell had put up Kettle against
Shaw and Colthurst.   The local Press were dead
against him.   Next day the county was placarded with
a letter signed by the four Catholic bishops of Cork,
Cloyne, Ross, and Kerry (the latter has jurisdiction
over several parishes, Millstreet, Glengariff, and Castletown Bere, which, though in the County Cork, are
in the Kerry diocese), strongly advocating Shaw and
Colthurst.   I managed the election all over the county.
The priests attended the polling booths, ranged on
the side of Shaw and Colthurst, and did all they
could against Kettle.   Parnell went off immediately
after nominating Kettle to Mayo and Meath, being
also candidate for each of these counties.   On April 6
the poll for the city was declared, and Parnell and Daly
were elected.   From this until the county polling on

April 14 Parnell kept flying around the counties of Cork, Mayo, and Meath. He was nights and days travelling between the three counties and addressing meetings. James O'Kelly, with Healy and Kettle, remained with me in Cork, and also Lysath Finnigan. These gentlemen scattered themselves about parts of the county, but they were unable to visit one-fifteenth part of the constituency. One day Parnell was in Mayo, next day in Cork, and next in Meath, and so on, eternally flying from one county to the other. I do not believe Parnell slept in a bed for ten days. He was also much engaged with looking after his other various candidates all over Ireland. The county election took place on April 14. Reports came in that the priests were working hard at every polling centre on behalf of Shaw and Colthurst. On April 15 the scrutiny took place. It was very exciting. The voting was very even for some hours. Colthurst was so sure of defeat by Kettle that he retired from the room; but towards the end it was found that Colthurst was ahead of Kettle by 151. Shaw polled 5,354, Colthurst 3,581, and Kettle 3,430, which was a splendid result considering the opposition of the four bishops and all the priests, and the short time we had for preparation.

'About a month after the election Y. brought me a letter from Mr. Harvey, solicitor, demanding payment on behalf of Mr. B—— of the 250l. which B—— had given Y., and threatening an action at law if it was not paid. I took Mr. Harvey's letter, and told Y. I would see *him* harmless over the matter and attend to it myself. I wrote to Harvey saying I would accept service of the writ on behalf of Y. I was never served with the writ, so that we had the satisfaction of returning Parnell at the expense of the Tories.'

Parnell was returned for all three constituencies— Meath, Mayo, and Cork City. He elected ultimately to sit for Cork. It may be asked, What was the attitude of the Catholic Church towards him at this crisis? The majority of the priests were certainly for him, the majority of the bishops were against him. Cardinal McCabe, the late Archbishop of Dublin, was indeed a vehement opponent both of Parnell and of the League.

'The schemes of amelioration proposed by the League,' his Eminence said, 'are of such an order that no Government laying claim to statesmanship can for a moment entertain them.' The Archbishop of Tuam was in sympathy with the Archbishop of Dublin. We have seen how the Bishops of Cork, Cloyne, Ross, and Kerry opposed him at the Cork election. Dr. Croke, the Archbishop of Cashel, was, however, then as later, in favour of a forward policy, and not hostile to the man who was the embodiment of that policy. Of the National Press, the 'Nation' supported Parnell, the 'Freeman's Journal' opposed him. He himself made light of his opponents, feeling that the masses of the people were at his back, and that the dissensionists would soon fall into line.

'But is the movement not opposed by the Nationalists (Fenians) and the priests?' he was asked by an interviewer. 'Indeed it is not,' he answered. 'I should despair of Ireland if the most active forces in the country arrayed themselves against a movement like this. Individual priests may have condemned chance indiscretions; individual Nationalists have protested that we should lie by while preparations are being made to cope with England by physical force, but that is all.

Everyone is welcome to his opinion about this movement, and to express it.'

In Great Britain the Liberals swept the constituencies. In Ireland the Nationalists more than held their ground. Out of 105 seats they won 60, against 44 Unionists. Thus the general result of the election in Great Britain and Ireland (all told) was—Liberals, 349; Tories, 243; Home Rulers, 60.

On April 26 the Irish parliamentary party met in Dublin to elect a leader and to consider other business. The election of leader was postponed until the adjourned meeting in May. 'If Parnell,' an experienced Nationalist said to me at the time, 'allows himself to be nominated as leader of the party he will commit a great mistake. He will do infinitely better, for the present, at all events, by remaining leader of the extreme left, and by keeping the moderates up to the collar. As leader of the whole party his relations with the advanced men would make his position very embarrassing. What we want is a moderate man like Shaw to command the whole party, and an extreme man like Parnell to lead the van.' This was not Parnell's view of the situation. He believed that he was able to lead the Irish party, and that no other man could. The election of leader came off in May. Shaw was nominated by Morris Brooke and Richard Power; Parnell by the O'Gorman Mahon and Biggar.

Result

Parnell	23 votes
Shaw	18 „
Majority for Parnell . .	5 [1] „

---

[1] For Parnell: Sexton, Arthur O'Connor, O'Kelly, Byrne, Barry, McCarthy, Biggar, T. P. O'Connor, Lalor, T. D. Sullivan, Dr. Comyns,

On April 30 there was a great Nationalist meeting
at the Rotunda, and it was upon that occasion that
Parnell made what has been called the 'bread and
lead speech.' He said : ' The Americans sent me
back with this message—that for the future you must
not expect one cent for charity, but millions to break
the land system. And now before I go I will tell you
a little incident that happened at one of our meetings
in America. A gentleman came on the platform and
handed me $25, and said : " Here is $5 for bread and
$20 for lead." '

Parnell was now in the saddle, where for eleven
years he sat firmly without a competitor or an equal.
' How came Parnell,' I asked Mr. Justin McCarthy, ' to
acquire his great ascendency ? ' He answered : ' He
owed his ascendency to his strength of will and his
readiness to see what was the right thing to do at a
given moment. He was not liked by the party as a
whole. S. never liked him. H. very soon began to
dislike him. D. was loyal to him, but did not like
him. O. liked him. I liked him. But, like or
dislike, all bowed to him, because all felt that he was
the one man who knew what to do in moments of
difficulty, and that he was always right. He had the
genius of a Commander-in-Chief. It was that which
gave him his power. Others of us might be useful in
fixing lines of policy in advance. But when a crisis
arose, when something had to be done on the instant
which might have a serious effect in the future, we
were no good. We were paralysed. Parnell made

Gill, Dawson, Leamy, Corbet, McCoan, Finnigan, Daly, Marum, W. H.
O'Sullivan, J. Leahy, O'Gorman Mahon, O'Shea—23.
    For Shaw : McFarlane, Brooke, Colthurst, Synan, Sir P. O'Brien,
Foley, Smithwick, Fay, Errington, Gabbett, Smyth, R. Power, Blake,
McKenna, P. Martin, Meldon, Callan, Gray—18.

up his mind in an instant, and did the thing without doubting or flinching.'

'As a parliamentary strategist,' says Mr. Healy, Parnell was simply perfect. No one was like him for seeing the difficulties of a situation and for getting out of them.'

'To what do you ascribe Parnell's success?' I asked Sir Charles Dilke.

He answered : 'To his aloofness. He hated England, English ways, English modes of thought. He would have nothing to do with us. He acted like a foreigner. We could not get at him as at any other man in English public life. He was not one of us in any sense. Dealing with him was like dealing with a foreign Power. This gave him immense advantage, and, coupled with his iron will, explains his ascendency and success.' Inexorable tenacity, sound judgment, knowledge of his own mind at all times, dauntless courage, an iron will, and the faculty of controlling himself and others—these were the qualities which made Parnell leader of the Irish people and arbiter of English parties.

CHAPTER XI

LEADER

MR. GLADSTONE was now Prime Minister, Lord Cowper Irish Viceroy, Mr. Forster Chief Secretary. The new Parliament met on April 29. The Queen's Speech dealt with every subject of public importance except the Irish land question. The Government, in truth, did not realise the gravity of the Irish situation. Mr. Gladstone has said with perfect frankness that he thought the Irish question was settled by the Church Act of 1869 and the Land Act of 1870. It troubled him no more. Mr. Bright, however, still felt keenly interested in one branch of the Irish question—the land; but he did not see his way to do anything. On January 9, 1880, he wrote: 'On this question of the land the difficulty would not be great. All might be done which is not of a revolutionary character, and the present time seems favourable for such changes as are possible without violence and by consent of the Imperial Parliament.'[1]

On January 12 he returned to the subject, expressing his doubt as to the practicability of establishing any satisfactory tribunal for fixing 'fair rents.' He said: 'I do not see how what is called a " fair rent " is to be

---

[1] Private letter.

determined. A " fair rent " to one man would be much
more than another could pay, and less than a third man
could without imprudence agree to give.' [1]

Lord Hartington also showed some interest in the
land question, though, like Mr. Bright, he did not see
his way to action. On January 22 he wrote : 'I think
that the failure of the Land Act [1870] is not established
by the figures which you give. The difference between
rentals and the Government valuation in some cases, as
well as the increase in the number of notices of ejectment, may be, and I think probably are, capable of
some explanation, and so far as I am aware all the
cases of cruel evictions on a large scale which are
related by you took place before the passing of the Act.
I am not opposed to any reasonable or practical proposals for improving the working of the Bright clauses
[the purchase clauses] of the Act, but I am of opinion
that the difficulties of inducing Parliament to legislate
in this direction have been greatly increased by the
recent anti-rent agitation. The advice which has been
given, and which has to some extent been acted upon,
to disregard the contract now existing between landlord
and tenant, is not calculated to give Parliament any
confident expectation that greater respect will be shown
to the contract which it is proposed to create between
the State and the tenant purchaser.' [2]

I think it but just to Mr. Bright and Lord Hartington
to set out the views which they privately expressed in
January 1880. Nevertheless, in April the Liberal
Government as a whole thought not of Ireland. 'The
Government,' said Lord Cowper, 'were not thinking
of the land question when I came to Ireland.'   'The

[1] *Ibid.*   [2] *Ibid.*

present Government,' said the Duke of Argyll in 1881,
' was formed with no express intention of bringing in
another great Irish Land Bill . . . it formed no part
of the programme upon which the Government was
formed.'

It is strange that this should have been so. The
land question had been kept constantly before Parliament since 1876. Mr. Butt's Bill, based on the
three F.'s, was then introduced. It was rejected by
290 against 56 votes.

In 1877 Mr. Crawford, an Ulster Liberal, introduced
a Bill to extend the Ulster custom—the right of free
sale—through the rest of Ireland. It was talked out.
In 1878 Mr. Crawford again introduced the Bill. It
was defeated by 85 against 66 votes. Mr. Butt's Bill
of 1876 was also re-introduced. It was defeated by 286
against 86 votes. In 1879 Mr. Butt's Bill was again
brought in. It was again defeated by 263 to 61 votes ;
and Mr. Crawford's Bill was again talked out. The
land agitation had been growing in intensity since
1877.[1] Sir Stafford Northcote's statement in the House
in February 1880 demonstrated the reality of Irish
distress. Everything that was happening showed the
discontent and the misery of the people. Yet on the
meeting of Parliament in April Mr. Gladstone's Government gave no sign that Ireland filled any place in the
thoughts of Ministers.

The first appearance of the Irish members in the
House of Commons showed that there was still a
division in their ranks. Mr. Shaw, with those who
had supported him at the public meeting, sat upon one

---

[1] I have dealt fully with the land controversy in *The Irish Land
Question and English Public Opinion* and in the *Parliamentary
History of the Irish Land Question*. See also Sir Gavan Duffy, *League
of North and South*.

side of the House ; Parnell and his party, reviving the practice of the Independent Opposition party of 1852, sat on the other. He said that the Irish Nationalists should always sit in Opposition until the full measure of their demands was conceded. In the last Parliament they had sat in Opposition with the English Liberals. They would now, since the Liberals had succeeded to office, sit in Opposition with the Tories. Thus they would emphasise their position as an independent party, and show that Whigs and Tories were all alike to them.

Mr. Shaw took a different view. The Liberals, he said, were the friends of Ireland. It was, therefore, the duty of the Irish members to support the Liberal Government. He would accordingly adhere to the old custom, and sit on the Liberal side of the House.

This idea of an independent Irish party Parnell constantly said he had got from Gavan Duffy and the Tenant Leaguers of 1852. 'I had some knowledge, not very deep, of Irish history,' he said before the Special Commission, 'and had read about the independent opposition movement of Sir Charles Gavan Duffy and the late Mr. Frederick Lucas in 1852, and whenever I thought about politics I always thought that that would be an ideal movement for the benefit of Ireland. Their idea was an independent party reflecting the opinions of the masses of the people ; acting independently in the House of Commons, free from the influence of either English political party ; pledged not to take office or form any combination with any English political party until the wants of Ireland had been attended to. The passing of the Ballot Act rendered this possible in my judgment, because for the first time it enabled the Irish electors to vote free from the coercion of the Irish landlords.'

In the last Parliament Parnell had to fight Butt as well as the British Minister. Now he had to fight Shaw and the 'moderate' Home Rulers. But his task was comparatively easy. In the struggle against Butt he began by having only a handful of Fenians at his back. Now he was supported by a section of the Clan-na-gael, by many of the rank and file of the I. R. B., by the farmers, by the priests, and by the 'Nation' itself, partly a clerical organ. Shaw and the 'moderates' were supported by the bishops and the 'Freeman's Journal.' A new, perhaps unexpected, ally came also to his side—her Majesty's Government. Timely concessions from Ministers would have strengthened the hands of Shaw and the 'moderates,' and might have broken up the union between Fenians, farmers, and priests. The refusal of concession in time consolidated this union, discredited the policy of the 'moderates,' and threw the game into Parnell's hands.

The Parnellite members lost no time in calling the attention of Parliament to Ireland. Mr. O'Connor Power brought in a Bill practically to 'stay evictions.' Under the Land Act of 1870, compensation for disturbance could not be awarded if the 'disturbed' tenant owed a year's rent. Mr. O'Connor Power now proposed that compensation should (under existing circumstances) be awarded in any case of disturbance.

The Government—who, at the beginning of the session, had refused to deal with the land question—were now undecided what to do. They would not support the Parnellite Bill; but, said Mr. Forster, 'I am not prepared to vote against the principle.' A few days later the Government gave way, and on June 18 Mr. Forster himself, taking up the question, introduced the famous 'Compensation for Disturbance Bill.' This measure proposed that an evicted tenant should be entitled to compensation when he could prove to the satisfaction of the Court—

1. That he was unable to pay the rent.

2. That he was unable to pay it, not from thriftlessness or idleness, but on account of the bad harvest of the current year, or of the two preceding years.

3. That he was willing to continue the tenancy on just and reasonable terms as to rent and otherwise.

4. That these terms were unreasonably refused by the landlord.

Lord Hartington justified this measure in an effective speech.

The Bill, he said, was the logical outcome of the Act of 1870, and had been framed simply with a view of preventing the objects of that Act from being defeated by exceptional circumstances which could not be foreseen. 'In some parts of Ireland the impoverished circumstances of the tenant have placed in the hands of the landlord a weapon which the Government never contemplated, and which enables the landlord, at a sacrifice of half or a quarter of a year's rent, to clear his estate of hundreds of tenants, whom in ordinary circumstances he would not have been able to remove, except at a heavy pecuniary fine.

'I ask whether that is not a weapon calculated to enable landlords absolutely to defeat the main purposes of the Act.

'Supposing a landlord wished to clear the estate of a number of small tenants; he knows that this is the

time to do it, and if he should lose this opportunity
he can never have it again, without great pecuniary
sacrifice.'   But, despite the weight which Lord
Hartington carried with all moderate men, many
Liberals opposed the Bill.   It was, however, read a
second time, on July 5, by 295 against 217 votes ;
20 Liberals voting against it, and 20 walking out.

The Irish Nationalists to a man supported the
Government.   Harried by the dissentient members of
their own party, Ministers proposed in committee to
introduce an amendment, which aroused the hostility
of Parnell.   The purpose of the amendment was to
disallow the tenant's claim to compensation, provided
the landlord gave him permission to sell his interest
in the holding.   'This is impossible,' said Parnell.   'In
the present state of affairs in Ireland no one will buy
the tenantlright, and,' he added, turning to Mr. Forster,
" unstable as water thou shalt not excel." '   Parnell was
supported by Mr. Charles Russell (now Lord Russell of
Killowen, the Lord Chief Justice of England), who
denounced the amendment as a 'mockery' and begged
the Government to withdraw it.   The Government,
still wavering, did finally withdraw it, substituting in
its place an alteration proposed by Mr. Gladstone (and
carried), to the effect that the tenant 'should be entitled
to compensation if the landlord had refused the terms
set out in the Bill without the offer of any reasonable alternative.'   The next crisis in the fate of the
Bill was the acceptance by Ministers of a proposal
from the Opposition to the effect that the application
of the measure should be limited to tenancies not
exceeding 15*l.* a year.   Parnell protested against this
limit, which, under his pressure, was abandoned, a
new limit of 30*l.* valuation, equivalent to 42*l.* rent,

being agreed to. The third reading was carried on
July 26 by 304 to 237 votes; 16 Liberals voting
against the measure, and Parnell and his followers
(dissatisfied with the alterations and the 'weakness'
of the Government) walking out. The Bill had been
under the consideration of the Commons for over a
month. The Lords disposed of it in two nights. It
was rejected by 282 to 51 votes.

The rejection of this Compensation for Disturbance
Bill was the signal for extreme agitation in Ireland.

'Soon after the rejection of the Bill,' says the
'Annual Register,' 'there came most disquieting reports
from Ireland. There were riots at evictions; tenants
who had ventured to take the place of the evicted
occupiers were assaulted, their property damaged,
their ricks burned, their cattle maimed; there was a
mysterious robbery of arms from a ship lying in
Queenstown Harbour; and it was said that a plot had
been discovered for the blowing up of Cork Barracks.'

The story of the 'robbery of arms' throws a curious
light on the relations between the Fenians and the
Land League. In August a party of Fenians attacked
a vessel called the 'Juno' in Cork Harbour, and carried
off forty cases of firearms. The Constitutionalists in
the local branch of the League were much exercised by
this act. They were anxious, fearing that some suspicion might rest on their organisation, to vindicate
themselves and to show their loyalty. Accordingly, a
resolution was proposed by Mr. Cronin and seconded
by Mr. J. O'Brien declaring that 'we deeply regret
that a robbery of useless old firearms has taken place,
that we condemn lawlessness in any shape, and we
believe the occurrence must have been effected by
those who desire to see a renewal of the Coercion Acts

inflicted upon this country, and who wish to give the Government good value for their secret service money.'

An amendment was moved by an 'advanced man,' Mr. O'Sullivan, who protested against the right of the League to interfere with any other organisation. Mr. O'Sullivan was, however, in a hopeless minority on that day, and the resolution was triumphantly carried. But the Fenians were resolved to teach the Constitutionalists in the League a lesson which should not be forgotten. The matter was at once brought under the notice of the central body in Dublin, when, on August 17, Mr. Brennan, himself a Fenian, condemned the action of the Cork branch, saying that they had no more right to consider the subject of the 'Juno' raid than they had to discuss the relative merits of the candidates for the presidency of the United States. Mr. Dillon, who was the chairman on the occasion, agreed with Mr. Brennan, and said that 'the meeting entirely disclaimed the resolution passed by the Cork branch.' On August 21 there was another meeting of the Cork branch. Mr. John O'Connor attended. Mr. O'Sullivan was again in evidence. He proposed that the resolution of August 13 should be expunged, and it was expunged *nem. con.* However, the incident was not yet closed. On October 3 Parnell visited Cork. As he approached the city an armed party of Fenians stopped the procession, seized Mr. Cronin and Mr. O'Brien, who were in the carriage by his side, carried them off, and detained them for the day. They were resolved that no man who had struck at Fenianism should join in the welcome to Parnell. Soon afterwards the Cork branch of the League was 'reconstructed.'

Meanwhile Parnell had made up his mind to wage

relentless war against the Government. He did not
throw all the blame for the rejection of the Compensation Bill on the House of Lords. 'If the Government,' he would say, 'had the people of England
behind them the Lords dare not do this. Well, we
will stiffen the back of the Government. Then we
shall see what the Lords will do.' He told the Ministers that they were half-hearted, that they did not
believe in their own measures, that they wanted grit.
He called upon them to give assurances of legislation
for the next session, else they would receive little help
from him. Lord Hartington—who was leading the
House in the absence of Mr. Gladstone through serious
illness—refused to give assurances, and said the Government had no further concessions to make. Parnell
had thrown down the gauntlet. Lord Hartington
picked it up. 'War to the knife, sir—war to the
knife,' said Biggar. 'The next thing will be a State
trial. The Whigs always start with a State trial.
Something for the lawyers, you know. Whigs—rogues,
sir.'

Returning to Ireland, Parnell flung himself heart
and soul into the land agitation. The Government
had failed to protect the tenants. The tenants
should now protect themselves. The scenes of 1847
should not be re-enacted. No more peasants should
be cast on the roadside to die. What the Government had failed to do the Land League would do.
But the tenants must rally to the League; they must
band themselves together; they must cast aside the
weak and cowardly in their ranks, and fight sturdily for
their homes and country against the destroying landlords and their ally, the Government of England.
This was the doctrine which Parnell and the Leaguers

preached from the hilltops, and which the masses of the people willingly obeyed.

On September 19 Parnell attended a mass meeting at Ennis. There, in a speech which rang throughout the land, he struck the keynote of the agitation ; he laid down the lines on which the League should work. Slowly, calmly, deliberately, without a quiver of passion, a note of rhetoric, or an exclamation of anger, but in a tone that penetrated his audience like the touch of cold steel, he proclaimed war against all who should resist the mandates of the League.

'Depend upon it that the measure of the Land Bill next session will be the measure of your activity and energy this winter. It will be the measure of your determination not to pay unjust rents ; it will be the measure of your determination to keep a firm grip on your homesteads. It will be the measure of your determination not to bid for farms from which others have been evicted, and to use the strong force of public opinion to deter any unjust men amongst yourselves—and there are many such—from bidding for such farms. Now what are you to do to a tenant who bids for a farm from which his neighbour has been evicted ? '

Here there was much excitement, and cries of ' Kill him ! ' ' Shoot him ! ' Parnell waited, with his hands clasped behind his back, looking quietly out upon the crowd until the tumult subsided, and then softly re-- sumed : ' Now I think I heard somebody say " Shoot him ! "—(A voice : " Yes, quite right ")—but I wish to point out to you a very much better way—a more Christian and a more charitable way, which will give the lost sinner an opportunity of repenting.'

Here there were inquiring glances, and a lull, and a

silence, which was scarcely broken until Parnell finished
the next sentence—a long sentence, but every word of
which was heard, as the voice of the speaker hardened
and his face wore an expression of remorseless determination. 'When a man takes a farm from which
another has been evicted, you must show him on the
roadside when you meet him, you must show him in
the streets of the town—(A voice: "Shun him!")—
you must show him at the shop counter, you must
show him in the fair and in the market-place, and
even in the house of worship, by leaving him severely
alone, by putting him into a moral Coventry, by
isolating him from his kind as if he was a leper of old
—you must show him your detestation of the crime he
has committed, and you may depend upon it that there
will be no man so full of avarice, so lost to shame, as
to dare the public opinion of all right-thinking men and
to transgress your unwritten code of laws.'

The closing sentence was received with a shout of
applause ; the doctrine of boycotting, as it afterwards
came to be called, was accepted with popular enthusiasm.

Three days afterwards the peasants of Connaught
showed how ready they were to practise as Parnell had
preached. Captain Boycott, the agent of Lord Erne,
had been offered by the tenants on the estate what they
conceived to be a just rent. He refused to take it, and
the tenants refused to give more ; whereupon ejectment processes were issued against them.

On September 22 the process server went forth to
serve the ejectments. He was met by a number of
peasants, who forced him to abandon the work and
retreat precipitately to the agent's house. Next day
the peasants visited the house and adjoining farm, and
ordered the servants in Captain Boycott's employ to

depart—a mandate which was promptly obeyed ; the
result being that the unfortunate gentleman was left
without farm labourers or stablemen, while his crops
remained ungathered and unsaved.   Nor did the
peasants stop here.   They forbade the local shop-
keepers to serve him, told the blacksmith and laun-
dress not to work for him, threatened the post-boy
who carried his letters, and upon one occasion stopped
and 'cautioned' the bearer of a telegram.

Captain Boycott was left 'severely alone,' 'put
into moral Coventry.'   As days wore on it became
a matter of pressing importance to him to have his
crops saved, but no one in the neighbourhood could
be got to do the work.   In these circumstances an
opportunity, gladly seized, for ' demonstrating in force '
was given to the Ulster Orangemen.   One hundred of
them offered to 'invade' Connaught to save Captain
Boycott's crops.   The Captain informed the authorities
of Dublin Castle that fifty men would be quite sufficient
for agricultural purposes ; and being himself a man of
peace, he did not feel at all disposed to see a hundred
Orangemen marching in battle array over his farm,
shouting 'to hell with the Pope,' and drinking the
memory of the glorious, pious, and immortal William
at his expense.   Fifty Orangemen were accordingly despatched to Connaught under the protection of a large
force of military and police (with two field pieces) to
save Captain Boycott's crops.   The work done the
Orangemen, accompanied by Captain Boycott, departed
in peace, and the Connaught peasants were left masters
of the situation.

The 'isolation' of Captain Boycott was followed by
another famous case.   Mr. Bence Jones, of Clonakilty,
in the County Cork, had incurred the popular dis-

pleasure, and was, in the phraseology of the day, boy-
cotted. He tried to sell his cattle in Cork market, but no
one could be got to buy. He then sent them to Dublin
to be shipped off to the Liverpool markets, but the men
in the service of the Dublin Steam Packet Company
refused to put them on board. Finally, after a great
deal of difficulty, the cattle were taken in small batches
across the Channel and sold.

After these cases boycotting became a great weapon
in the armoury of the League, and was, as one of the
Leaguers said, 'better than any 81-ton gun ever
manufactured.'

Parnell's Ennis speech was altogether an agrarian
speech. He concentrated himself upon the land, and
told the people how the campaign against landlordism
was to be carried on. But at Galway, on October 24,
he plunged into politics and dealt with the more con-
genial subject of national freedom: 'I expressed my
belief at the beginning of last session that the present
Chief Secretary, who was then all smiles and promises,
would not have proceeded very far in the duties of his
office before he would have found that he had undertaken an impossible task to govern Ireland, and that
the only way to govern Ireland was to allow her to
govern herself.' (Cheers.)

A voice. 'A touch of the rifle.'

'And if they prosecute the leaders of this movement——'

A voice. 'They dare not.'

Parnell. 'If they prosecute the leaders of this
movement it is not because they want to preserve the
lives of one or two landlords. Much the English
Government cares about the lives of one or two landlords.'

A voice. 'Nor we.'

Another voice. 'Away with them.'

Parnell. 'But it will be because they see that behind this movement lies a more dangerous movement to their hold over Ireland ; because they know that if they fail in upholding landlordism here—and they will fail—they have no chance of maintaining it over Ireland; it will be because they know that if they fail in upholding landlordism in Ireland, their power to misrule Ireland will go too.' (Cheers.) Then he uttered one of those sentences which, coming straight from the heart, and disclosing the real thoughts and feelings which animated him, burned themselves into the minds of his hearers. 'I wish to see the tenant farmers prosperous ; but large and important as this class of tenant farmers is, constituting, as they do, with their wives and families, the majority of the people of the country, I would not have taken off my coat and gone to this work if I had not known that we were laying the foundation in this movement for the regeneration of our legislative independence. (Cheers.) Push on, then, towards this goal, extend your organisation, and let every tenant farmer, while he keeps a grip on his holding, recognise also the great truth that he is serving his country and the people at large, and helping to break down English misrule in Ireland.'

The Land League now grew in importance and influence day by day. Money poured into its treasury, not only from Ireland, but from America. Its branches extended all over the country. Its mandates were everywhere obeyed. It was, in truth, nothing more nor less than a provisional Irish Government, stronger, because based on popular suffrage, than the Government of the Castle. 'Self-elected, self-constituted, self-assembled, self-adjourned, acknowledging no superior, tolerating no equal, interfering in all stages with the administration of justice, levying contributions and discharging all the functions of regular government, it obtained a complete mastery and control over the masses of the Irish people.'

So Canning described the Catholic Association. So might the Ministers of the day have described (so in effect they did describe) the Land League.

'Things are now come to that pass that the question is whether O'Connell or I shall govern Ireland'—so said the Irish Viceroy, Lord Anglesea, in 1831. And Lord Cowper might have said in 1880: 'The question is whether Parnell or I shall govern Ireland.'

While Parnell, helped by the Fenian Treasurer Egan[1] and the Fenian Secretary Brennan, was driving the League ahead in Ireland, Davitt was forming branches throughout the United States.

There was still a party in the Clan-na-Gael opposed to the new departure. The Clan-na-Gael man who had come to England in 1878 to see Parnell, and who was then favourably disposed to an alliance between the Revolutionists and the Constitutionalists, had now gone quite round. In addition to his hostility to the policy of Devoy and Davitt, he had formed an intense dislike to Parnell, and was resolved, so far as he could, to break off all relations with the Parliamentarians. Davitt, who always kept himself well

---

[1] Egan has been described by the late Mr. A. M. Sullivan in *New Ireland*. 'He seldom or never made a speech. He aspired to no display on the platform, but was the ablest strategist of the whole campaign, and perhaps, except Davitt, the most resolute and invincible spirit amongst them all.'

posted in the American news, soon learned that things
were not going quite smoothly on the other side of the
Atlantic. In May he sailed for New York, to co-operate
with Devoy in defeating their opponents in the Clan.
The supreme council of the I. R. B. were also aware
that a party of American Fenians led by the Clan-na-
Gael man shared their views about the inadvisability of
working with the Constitutionalists, and they had previously despatched the prominent Fenian of the Craven
Street meeting to defeat Davitt's plans. A meeting of
the council of the Clan was called in New York to hear
both Davitt and this Fenian.

The proceedings were opened by the Clan-na-Gael
man, who moved a resolution severing all connection
between the Clan and the Parliamentarians. Parnell was
not to be trusted. He would simply use them for his own
purposes, and throw them over at the first opportunity.
What were they asked to do? Practically to supply
funds for parliamentary agitation. The thing was
absurd. They would keep their funds for their own
organisation, and concentrate themselves upon it. The
Parliamentarians had everything to gain by uniting
with them. They had nothing to gain by uniting with
the Parliamentarians. That was the Clan-na-gael man's
case. Davitt replied. He said that Fenianism had lost
ground by holding aloof from public movements in Ireland. The Fenians ought to keep themselves in touch
with all that was going on. They should try to influence
every movement and to gain support from all quarters.
The land was the question of the hour. Was it to be
left wholly in the hands of the Constitutionalists? The
farmers would be the friends of the men who helped
them in this crisis of their fate, and no movement could
be successful in Ireland unless the farmers were at its

back. How were they to gain the farmers? By throwing themselves into the land agitation, by identifying their cause with the cause of the tenants.

The prominent Fenian attacked Davitt. He said that the new departure was immoral and impolitic. Fenians and Constitutionalists were to be combined in one movement. There was to be a pretence of loyalty, but in reality treason all along the line. The upshot of this arrangement would be sham loyalty and sham treason. He did not believe in a policy of dust-throwing and lying, but that was the policy of the new departure. The Fenian movement was purely a national movement. If he were to stand absolutely alone, he would resist this dishonest and unholy alliance. 'Freedom comes from God's right hand,' and he, at all events, believed in righteous means as well as in righteous ends.

A division was then taken on the Clan-na-Gael man's motion, and it was defeated. The prominent Fenian had beaten Davitt in 1879. Davitt had his revenge in 1880.

The founder of the Land League, as Davitt has been called, next made a tour throughout the States, forming branches of the League and 'spreading the light.' All his public utterances—and he addressed many meetings—resolved themselves into two main arguments:

1. The cause of the tenant farmers was just in itself and ought to be supported.

2. The destruction of landlordism would lead to the overthrow of the English power in Ireland.

Two extracts may be given from his speeches to illustrate their character. Speaking at Chicago in August, he said, referring to the raid on the 'Juno':

' The convulsion of horror which grew out of it was
because the English Government knew there were men
in Ireland to-day absolutely feverish to clutch hundreds
and thousands of rifles, in order, not only to abolish
Irish landlordism, but to consummate the hopes of
Irishmen by abolishing something else.'

At Kansas City, in September, he said : ' We have,
as you have already been told, declared an unceasing
war against landlordism ; not a war to call on our people
to shoulder the rifle and to go out in the open field and
settle the question that is now agitating Ireland—
although I am not opposed to a settlement of that
nature providing I could see a chance of success—but
for the fourth time during the present century we
have tried a physical struggle with England, and
instead of hurting England we have generally hurt
ourselves.   Now I believe it is far better to meet
on different ground and to do battle in a different
mode.   And in declaring this war against Irish landlordism, in not paying rent in order to bring down
the garrison in Ireland, we know we are doing a proper
work.   We are preparing the way for that independence which you enjoy in this great American
republic.'

In America Davitt formed a fast friendship with
Patrick Ford, the proprietor of the ' Irish World,'
who defended the policy of the new departure, collected funds for the Land League, and preached a
furious crusade against England.

The ' Irish World ' was circulated freely in Ireland,
and it must be confessed that a more inflammable production could scarcely be placed in the hands of the
people.   A few extracts from its columns may be given
to make the point clearer.

'England's mode of warfare. What is it? Ask
the biographer of Cromwell, ask the Ghoorkas of
India, ask the signers of the Declaration of Independence. Listen! She has plundered our seas, ravaged
our coasts, burned our towns, and destroyed the lives of
the people. This is the testimony of the men of '76.
Ask the American historian of the War of 1812. Ask
every unfortunate people upon whom England has
ever breathed her unwholesome breath, and in whose
midst her ruffian soldiery have planted her robber flag.
The answer is all the same.'

In June 1880 the following passage appeared :
'Some think it is an open question whether the
political agent called dynamite was first commissioned
in Russia, or first in Ireland. Well, it is not of much
consequence which of the two countries takes precedence in this onward step towards civilisation. Still,
we claim the merit for Ireland. True the introductory
blast was blown in England, and in the very centre of
the enemy's head-quarters. But the work itself was
no doubt done by one or two Irish hands, which settles
both the claim and the priority.'

In October its correspondent 'Transatlantic' wrote :
'The Irish Land League is accepted by the Irish
people at home and abroad as the faithful friend,
philosopher, and guide. I am thoroughly grieved
to find existing among my American friends, and my
Dublin friends also, a disposition to quarrel with the
trustees of the Skirmishing Fund[1] in New York,
because they advanced 1,000 or 2,000 dollars over a
year ago from the Skirmishing Fund to help to start

---

[1] This fund was formed by O'Donovan Rossa and Ford for the purpose
of employing agents to lay English cities in ashes.—*Report of Special
Commission*, p. 60.

the anti-rent agitation in Ireland. No possible application of a portion of the fund would to my mind be
more legitimate, more in accordance with the desire
of us all to help on towards the deliverance of our
downtrodden people. That little bit of seed, the first
advance from the Skirmishing Fund, has worked as
great a miracle as the grain of mustard seed spoken
of in the Sacred Scripture. Behold now 200 Land
League branches established through Ireland with at
east 500 members in each, and all in full cry against
the land robbers. Behold almost as many more co-
operating branches established in America, Canada,
Australia, and in England, Scotland, and Wales. Will
any man tell me that this movement will die out
without lifting Ireland to a vantage ground on which
she may declare and maintain her separate political
existence? Wait till the numbers of the Land
League branches swell to 300,000. Wait till they
are enlightened with political knowledge, instructed
in military drill, and armed with rifles, bullets, and
buck-shot. One or two years more will work
wonders.

'Don't quarrel, friends, about 1,000 dollars or 2,000
dollars. . . . I pray and urge my friends at home and
abroad to drop the controversy, and to unite against
the common enemies of our people, the landlords of
Ireland and of England, with their forces of armed
men at their backs!'

While Davitt was helping to 'spread the light'[1] in
America the state of Ireland was growing desperate.

---

[1] On May 5 Davitt cabled to Ford: 'Copies of *Irish World* shall be
sent to all parts of Ireland. Bishop Moran, of Ossory (a nephew of
Cardinal Cullen) denounced it and the Land League. May Heaven
open his eyes to the truth; " Spread the light." '

The people in the western districts were starving. ' I must say,' wrote General Gordon, who visited the country in the winter of 1880, ' from all accounts and my own observation, that the state of our fellow-countrymen in the parts I have named is worse than that of any people in the world, let alone Europe. I believe these people are made as we are ; that they are patient beyond belief ; loyal, but broken spirited and desperate ; lying on the verge of starvation in places where we would not keep cattle.' It rained evictions, it rained outrages. Cattle were houghed and maimed ; tenants who paid unjust rents, or took farms from which others had been evicted, were dragged out of their beds, assaulted, sometimes forced to their knees, while shots were fired over their heads to make them promise submission to the popular desires in future. Bands of peasants scoured the country, firing into the houses of obnoxious individuals. Graves were dug before the doors of evicting landlords. Murder was committed. A reign of terror had in truth commenced.[1]

What were they doing at Dublin Castle all this time ? Lord Cowper and Mr. Forster fully realised the gravity of the situation. Neither was quite out of sympathy with the demands of the tenant farmers. Both desired a policy of concession to a certain extent. ' If you pass the Bill ' [the Compensation for Disturbance Bill], Mr. Forster had said in the House of Commons,

[1] The following table will show the increase of evictions and outrages from 1877 to 1880 (inclusive) :

Year	Evictions (Persons)	Year	Agrarian Outrages
1877	. . . 2,177	1877	. . . 236
1878	. . . 4,679	1878	. . . 301
1879	. . . 6,239	1879	. . . 863
1880	. . 10,457	1880	. . . 2,590

'it will put out the fire.' The Bill was not passed.
The fire blazed up with increased and increasing fury.
How was it to be 'put out' now? The House of
Lords would have no concessions. What was the
alternative? Coercion, pure and simple. The Land
League had, in fact, become a rival Government. If
the Queen's authority were to prevail, no choice remained but to crush the League. The question really
was, whether Lord Cowper or Parnell should rule
Ireland, for both the Viceroy and the Chief Secretary
recognised that Parnell was the centre of disturbance.

'When I was in Ireland,' says Lord Cowper, 'we
considered Mr. Parnell the centre of the whole movement. We thought him the chief, if not the only,
danger. We feared him because he had united all the
elements of discontent, because we never knew what he
would be up to, and we felt that he would stop at
nothing. I certainly thought that his aim was separation. I thought that he used agrarian discontent for
separatist purposes. There was very little said about
Home Rule at that time. It was all agrarianism, with
separation in the background, and Parnell was the
centre of everything.

'He had no second, no one at all near him. I
should say that the next man to him was Davitt;
but he was a long way off. Mr. Healy was, I think,
coming to the front then. We thought him clever,
but he did not trouble us much. Mr. Dillon was
better known, and he used to go about the country
making speeches. But our view of him was that
somehow he was always putting his foot in it. Our
attention was concentrated on Parnell. We did not
think he instigated outrages. We thought that he
connived at them. We thought that he would stop

at nothing to gain his end, and, as I have said, we believed his end was separation.   I think he was very English.   He had neither the virtues nor the vices of an Irishman.   His very passion was English, his coolness was English, his reserve was English.'

In September or October Lord Cowper and Mr. Forster came to the conclusion that the Government could not be carried on by the ordinary law.   Still they were reluctant to take extreme measures until it was patent to every law abiding and loyal citizen that extreme measures could alone meet the exigencies of the case.

The suspension of the Habeas Corpus Act was an old familiar 'remedy.'   The officials at Dublin Castle had been accustomed to govern in a state of siege. Landlords, magistrates, police officers, judges, privy councillors—all the loyal and ruling classes—cried out with one voice : 'Suspend the Habeas Corpus Act or the country will be ruined.'   'Everyone,' says Lord Cowper, 'advised us to suspend the Habeas Corpus Act ; the Lords-Lieutenant of Counties, the police, the law officers.   The police said they knew all the people who got up outrages; and that if the Habeas Corpus Act was suspended they could arrest them all.'   Nevertheless, Lord Cowper and Mr. Forster still hesitated.   'We shall first,' they said in effect, 'make an effort to put down disorder by enforcing the ordinary law.   We shall prosecute the Leaguers.   If the jury refuse to convict on the plain facts which we shall produce, then it will be clear to every reasonable and loyal man that the administration of the country cannot be carried on unless we are invested with extraordinary powers.

'If trial by jury breaks down, manifestly the only

remedy is suspension of trial by jury, but trial by jury first.'

Lord Cowper placed his views before the Cabinet and before Mr. Gladstone personally in a series of able communications, some of which I shall now set out :

Lord Cowper to the Cabinet

[Early in October 1880.]

' There has been an immense increase of agrarian crime. Men who have taken farms from which others have been evicted have in many cases been intimidated into throwing them up, and of those who remain a large number are under police protection. Meetings denouncing in strong language the very class which has been subject to this outrage and intimidation have at the same time been held throughout the country, and it seems reasonable to connect the meetings with the increase of crime. In spite of the fact that some of the speakers have dissuaded their hearers from committing murder, and of the suggestion that if freedom of speech were stopped secret associations would derive increased strength, it is my opinion that the meetings cause more crime than they prevent.

' I would preserve freedom of speech to the very utmost as long as it is confined to general subjects, such as abuse of England, abuse of the Government, or advocacy of political measures, however impracticable ; when it has the immediate effect of endangering the lives or property of individuals, it should be stopped. One would wish to check it either by stopping meetings, or only prosecuting the promoters of meetings or the principal speakers. Can this be done ? We might, it is true, have stopped the Charleville meeting, because

a particular farm was named in the placard and the
occupier denounced ; but this mentioning of a name
was a slip which is not likely to be made again. We
could not stop other meetings. As to speeches. No
speech has yet been made in the presence of a Government reporter for which the speaker could be prosecuted.
Government reporters can only be sent to a limited
number of places, and these speakers, knowing that
they are now being watched very carefully, will become
more cautious. Even if the occupier of a farm is
mentioned in a placard, and subsequent to the issue
of that placard throws up the farm, the person responsible cannot be prosecuted, as is evident from the
answer of the law officers to the question about the
Riversdale case. From all this it appears that we shall
probably never have an opportunity of either stopping
a meeting, or prosecuting a speaker, or issuer of a
placard. If we think that agitation ought to be stopped
it appears there is only one possible way. A combination to prevent persons from taking evicted farms or
purchasing stock, &c., is illegal. We have not yet obtained a decided opinion upon the question whether the
Land League is such a combination, but it would appear
to be so. If so, it would also appear that its president
or its leading members could be prosecuted. Such a
course would have the advantage of striking at the
head. It would fix the attention of the whole country
from its announcement till its conclusion and divert
the minds of the leaders of the League from their
ordinary work, such as intimidating landlords and
agents and the takers of farms from which men have
been evicted. It would show the determination of the
Government to stop the present state of things. If
the prosecution failed through the perversity of the

jury, it would give a reason for asking for stronger powers. The prosecution of the Land League, if possible, seems desirable in itself, but its chief recommendation is that it appears to be the only alternative to doing nothing. The proposed new Land Bill will be much more likely to have a good effect if it follows a strong blow against agitation than if it appears to result from it.'

Lord Cowper to Mr. Gladstone

[October 20, 1880.]

'DEAR MR. GLADSTONE,—Though you are in constant communication with Forster, and though he and I take pretty much the same views, perhaps you would not object to an occasional line from me saying what I think and giving what information I can.

'Spencer will have shown you the statistics of crime, and you will have seen that outrages are very numerous, and will have gathered that they will probably increase. But the peculiarity of the present state of Ireland seems to me to lie not so much in the number of outrages as in the general ill-feeling among the tenants. I gather from all sources, including men of Liberal politics, and who would naturally support the Government, such as Colonel Dease, my Chamberlain, Cork's agent, Leahy, and Kenmare's agent, Hussey, that there never has been such a state of panic on one side and lawlessness and ill-will on the other. The police fully confirm this. Of course, what strikes me is the universal sympathy of the population with the criminals, and the impossibility of bringing to justice any one member of large gangs of men who do not even, on some occasions, take the precaution of disguising themselves. This, how-

ever, is not what most impresses those who know the
country, for the difficulty of detecting a criminal[1]
seems always to have existed.   What strikes them
most is the bitterness of feeling against all landlords
and agents, and most of all against all those who have
lately taken farms, even in cases where the previous
tenant had owed three or four years' rent and was himself quite willing to leave.   It seems really to be the
case that in four or five counties none of these classes
feel their lives to be safe, and the mischief is rapidly
spreading.   Tenants are also afraid to pay more than
the Government valuation, or any other sum ordered.
As to this point a crisis will probably arise in about a
fortnight or three weeks.   Most rents are due on
November 1, and will be collected immediately after.
We shall then see what happens.   Many people expect
a general refusal.

  'The state of feeling which I have described is by
the class which suffers from it universally ascribed to
the Land League, and I have been repeatedly assured
that places which were peaceful and contented before
become very different after a meeting.   If this is the
case the population must be very inflammable, but it
certainly is the general impression.   I do not know
whether you were surprised or annoyed by the news of
the impending prosecution having oozed out.   I have
been inclined to look upon it as a lucky accident.   It
would, of course, have been better to have struck at
once, but as this could not be done the announcement
that we intend to strike appears to me the next best
thing.   The knowledge that the Government intends
to do something has, I think, rather moderated the

---

[1] An agrarian criminal.

language of one party, and certainly mitigated the panic of the other.'

On November 2 the Government 'struck.' An information was on that day filed in the Crown Office of the Queen's Bench, Dublin, against the Land League for conspiracy to prevent the payment of rent, to resist the process of ejectment, to prevent the taking of farms from which tenants had been evicted, and to create ill-will among her Majesty's subjects.

The defendants named in the information were: Charles Stewart Parnell, M.P.; John Dillon, M.P.; Joseph G. Biggar, M.P.; T. D. Sullivan, M.P.; Thomas Sexton, M.P.; Patrick Egan (Treasurer), Thomas Brennan (Secretary), Michael O'Sullivan (Assistant Secretary), M. P. Boyton (Organiser), Matthew Harris (Organiser), J. Nally, P. J. Gordon, John W. Walsh, P. Sheridan.

The determination of the Government to prosecute the League produced no effect on Parnell. He knew that a conviction was practically impossible; the jury might disagree; they might acquit him. In either case the League would be triumphant. Two days after the information had been filed he referred to the matter with contemptuous brevity at a public meeting in Dublin.

'I regret,' he said, 'that Mr. Forster has chosen rather to waste his time, the money of Government, and our money in these prosecutions. He has begun in a bad way, and I fear that the result of his attempt to govern Ireland on these lines will be to shatter his reputation for statesmanship which he formerly acquired in another branch. He is surrounded by a landlord atmosphere at the Castle of Dublin, and although he may be able to resist the effect of that atmosphere longer than most men, yet, sooner or later, it is bound to tell on him.'

About the same time he told the people of Limerick, when they presented him with the freedom of the city, that no reliance could be placed 'permanently' on an Irish party at Westminster.

'I am not one of those,' he said in a remarkable utterance, 'who believe in the permanence of an Irish party in the English Parliament. I feel convinced that, sooner or later, the influence which every English Government has at its command—the powerful and demoralising influence—sooner or later will sap the best party you can return to the House of Commons. I don't think we ought to rely too much on the permanent independence of an Irish party sitting at a distance from their constituencies, or legislating, or attempting to legislate, for Ireland at Westminster. But I think it possible to maintain the independence of our party by great exertions and by great sacrifices on the part of the constituencies of Ireland, while we are making a short, sharp, and I trust decisive, struggle for the restoration of our legislative independence.'

I met Mr. Patrick Egan while the legal proceedings were pending. He was full of glee, for he anticipated a crowning victory. 'When this prosecution breaks down,' said he, 'we ought to make Forster an honorary member of the League.' Biggar, however, was seriously angry. 'D——d lawyers, sir,' said he. 'D——d lawyers. Wasting the public money, wasting the public money. Whigs—rogues; Forster d——d fool.'

Lord Cowper scarcely expected that the prosecution would succeed, and warned the Cabinet that they must be prepared to suspend the Habeas Corpus Act:

Lord Cowper to Cabinet [abridged].

'The state of the country is undoubtedly most serious. Nor do the number of outrages by any means represent the [gravity of the situation], and for this reason : that in many places . . . those who would profit [by outrages] are complete masters of the situation, and their temptation, therefore, is removed. Nobody dares to evict. Tenants of evicted farms, even those who have been in possession for more than a year, are daily giving them up. Eighty persons are under police protection. We cannot yet say for certain how far the autumn rents will be paid, but it appears already that in many places tenants have refused to pay more than Government valuation. Landlords will not agree to this, they will evict, and then a great increase of outrages may be expected. It will then be too late to give us extra powers. If they are to be conferred, the decision must be come to at once.

'Her Majesty's Government may well be reluctant to repeat once more the dreary old story of special restrictive legislation for Ireland, the evil of which has so often been exposed. I cannot regard it as an error to have trusted, even for a short period, to the common law for the maintenance of order in this country. And if we could be sure of going through the coming winter with no greater amount of outrage than we have now, large as that amount is, so great is my detestation of coercive measures that I should hesitate to recommend them. But I feel strongly that there is nothing to prevent outrages from largely increasing at any moment both in number and atrocity, and if this should be the case

I should reproach myself for the rest of my life with not having put my opinion on record that, in the present state of feeling, the law is not strong enough as it stands. For the ordinary law to be sufficient to re-press crime it is necessary that the majority of the population be on the side of the injured person, and in the disturbed parts of Ireland the vast majority are, in cases of an agrarian nature, invariably on the side of the criminal. In spite, then, of all my wishes being that we could trust to the ordinary law, I must repeat my conviction that to make up our minds to face the winter without stronger powers would be very danger-ous. If her Majesty decides upon coercive legislation, what form is it to take? . . . The one remedy sug-gested by every landlord and every agent is the sus-pension of the Habeas Corpus Act; and though the opinion of one class, particularly when in a great state of alarm and indignation, should certainly not be held conclusive as to the necessity of strong measures, it may nevertheless, if strong measures are resolved upon, be a good guide as to what direction they should take. The same remedy as to the whole of Connaught except Sligo is recommended by the police inspectors in their answer to a recent circular. Authority would therefore point to a suspension of the Habeas Corpus Act as the proper remedy, and common sense would appear to make the same suggestion. The sudden imprisonment of some of those who are known to instigate or to commit these crimes would strike general terror in a way that nothing else would, for no man would know how far he was suspected or whether his own turn might not come next. . . .'

Lord Cowper to Mr. Gladstone

'November 13, 1880.

'I am more convinced every day and every hour of
the necessity of suspending the Habeas Corpus Act
and having an Arms Bill. The fear of being unduly influenced by the strong current of public feeling in favour
of coercion, and a vivid conception of what a glorious
triumph it would have been to get through the winter
with nothing but the ordinary law, have prevented me
from giving an opinion until the other day, and perhaps
even then made me give it in too undecided a manner.
You have all the statistics before you, and everything
that can explain them ; and, with Mr. Forster at hand
to answer every question and give information of all
kinds, you will very likely think a letter from me
unnecessary. But I write more to relieve my own
mind than anything else. What impresses me most is
the conviction that there is absolutely nothing to prevent sudden outbursts of the worst kind. I do not
know that it is an exaggeration to say that something
like a general massacre of all landlords and agents not
under police protection is a conceivable and possible
event.

'Of course I do not mean that this is probable,
but how can we say it might not happen ? The longer
a suspension is put off, the more doubtful will it be
whether the mischief has not got beyond the stage
in which it can be cured by the arrest of a few important people ; certainly, in order to have the desired
effect more people would have to be arrested now
than a short time ago—and more still in another
month.'

Lord Cowper to Mr. Gladstone

'November 23, 1880

' You know my apprehensions as to an outbreak of crime in this country. I must repeat that there is nothing to prevent this, and if it does take place it will be because the landlords are afraid of exercising their power, and because the greater part of the country is under the absolute dominion of the Land League and all rights of property are at an end.

' The remedy, and the only remedy, for this state of things is, I feel quite sure, the suspension of the Habeas Corpus Act. I have been anxiously considering during the last few days whether, holding this opinion, I am justified in retaining the position of Lord Lieutenant unless this remedy is provided. I am most unwilling to have the appearance of leaving the ship in the middle of the storm. I feel, also, as regards myself, that to resign now would be to put an end for ever to anything in the shape of a public career.

' I had given up all hope of this till your offer to me last May of the high place I occupy made me feel I had an unexpected chance which it would be a great sacrifice for me to forfeit. I can honestly say that it is a great source of pride and pleasure to me to serve in the Government of one whom I have always regarded with such feelings of admiration. What, however, has most weighed with me is a sense of the embarrassment my retirement would cause others.

' I feel that if I went Mr. Forster's position would become almost untenable, all the more so as I know him to hold the same opinion as I do. Putting everything together, I have come to the conclusion that I will not do anything until January, but that if then I see no possibility of changing my mind as to the necessity of a suspension of the Habeas Corpus Act, and if it is not granted, I will place my resignation in your hands.'

Mr. Gladstone to Lord Cowper

'November 24.

'I am persuaded, after reading your letter of yesterday, that in a very difficult case you have arrived at a wise conclusion. For my own part I incline to the belief that an outbreak of secessions from the Government either way, at this particular moment, when the double question of order and of land reform is at issue, would render it impossible for us to effect any good solution of that question in its twofold branches.

'It is with regret, and perhaps with mortification, that I see the question of land reform again assuming or having assumed its large proportions. My desire certainly would have been to remain on the lines of the Act of 1870, if not exactly as it passed, such as (I speak of the occupying clauses) it left the House of Commons. It is needless to inquire in what proportions the scarcity, or the agitation, or the Disturbances Bill, or (last, not least) the rejection of that Bill may have brought about the result; for there it is. I think that on this side of the Channel we feel not less really, if less acutely, than you in Dublin the pain, the embarrassment, and discredit of the present condition of Ireland. Acquiescence in its continuance for even a few weeks seems to me dependent on these conditions :

'1. That the disturbance so largely affecting property and causing terror should not assume the form of a great increase in crime affecting life.

'2. That by means of this delay we put ourselves

in a position to propose with authority as a united Government a remedy applicable to the whole of the mischief.

'The paralysis of very important rights affecting the tenure of land is the special characteristic of the present mischief in Ireland, and it may be right to apply a thorough remedy a little later rather than a partial (indeed, as I think, a very doubtful) remedy a little, and only a little, sooner. What I personally think a very doubtful remedy is a suspension of the Habeas Corpus Act proposed alone, carried after much delay, in the teeth of two-thirds of the representatives of Ireland (without taking British allies into account), and used in order to cope with a wide-spreading conspiracy embracing in certain districts large fractions of the population, and largely armed with means other than material for action. You may rely upon it that, when the time you indicate arrives, the Cabinet will look at the duty of defending proprietary rights without any mawkish susceptibilities, and the suspension, should you and Forster then still see cause to desire it, will be most impartially entertained. For my own part, what I lean to expecting is, that if requisite it will not be sufficient, and that we may have to legislate directly against the Land League, not against its name only, but against the purpose of all combinations aiming at the non-payment of debts and non-fulfilment of contracts at the very least, when these illegal aims are so pursued as to endanger the public security.'

Lord Cowper to Mr. Gladstone

'December 12.

'In my letter of November 23 I said that I had come to the conclusion that if in January I saw no possi-

bility of changing my opinion as to the necessity of a
suspension of the Habeas Corpus Act, and if it was not
granted, I should feel it my duty to place my resignation
in your hands. I am sorry to say that I have not been
able to change my opinion, and all chance of my doing
so may be considered at an end.

'The state of the country becomes worse every day.
Outrages have increased, and the Land League has
taken a much deeper root. . . . I feel very strongly
that Parliament ought to be called together without
delay.'

The day after this letter was written the State trial
began. It lasted twenty days before two judges—Mr.
Justice Fitzgerald and Mr. Justice Barry—and a jury.
At half-past one o'clock on Tuesday, January 25, 1881,
the jury retired to consider their verdict. At half-past
five they returned to court. 'Have you agreed to your
verdict, gentlemen?' asked the clerk of the crown.
'No,' answered the foreman. 'Is there any likelihood
of your agreeing?' asked the judge. 'Not a bit, my
lord,' said the foreman; and he added, amid a burst of
laughter, 'we are unanimous that we cannot agree.'
The jury were sent back to their room for a couple of
hours more; they came into court again at half-past
seven. 'Well, gentlemen,' said the judge, 'have you
agreed?' 'No, my lord,' said the foreman, 'and there
is no good in keeping us here any longer; we'll never
agree.' 'We are ten to two, my lord,' said an indiscreet
juror, with the look of a man who had a grievance; and
the gallery rang with applause. 'Let the jury be discharged,' ordered the judge; 'we shall not force an
agreement.'

Parnell, who was in court, hastened from the scene.

His appearance in the hall was the signal for another outburst of applause, and as he jumped on an outside car and drove rapidly off to catch the boat for England, the crowd on the quay cheered vociferously, shouting 'Long live the Chief!'

'The Land League,' cabled Parnell to the 'Irish World,' 'has scored a victory. The ten to two disagreement of the jury is everywhere accepted as having the force of an acquittal. Thanks to the " Irish World " and its readers for their constant co-operation and substantial support in our good cause. Let them have no fear of its ultimate success.'

Brennan, the secretary of the League, cabled about the same time (February 2) to the 'Irish World': '$1,000 cabled this week by "Irish World" is received.'

The result of the trial was received with a blaze of approbation. Bonfires were lit on every hill, meetings were called in every district, resolutions of triumph and confidence were everywhere passed. The first move of the Government was a blunder. It served only to consolidate the strength of the League.

I shall close this chapter with some account of a non-political function which Parnell attended in the autumn of 1880. I shall let Mr. Horgan, who took a leading part at the function, tell the story.

'In the summer of 1880 I was engaged to be married. One evening I took my intended wife to the House of Commons. She went to the Ladies' Gallery. I had some business to do with Parnell. He and I walked up and down one of the corridors for some time, talking over business matters. That done, I said to him, " Mr. Parnell, I am going to be married." " Quite right, Horgan," said he, placing

his hand on my shoulder; "I am glad to hear it." I
thought I should like to ask him to come to my
wedding, but I didn't know how he would take it.
He was, however, so very pleasant and friendly this
evening that I mustered up courage, and, faith, a good
deal to my surprise, found myself saying, "I would
feel very proud, Mr. Parnell, if you would come to
my wedding." "Certainly, Horgan," said he, in the
most off-hand manner. When he consented to this I
thought I might ask him to do anything. "Mr. Parnell,"
said I, "will you think it presumptuous of me if I ask
you to be my best man?" He looked amused, smiled,
and said quickly, "With pleasure, Horgan; and now
you must introduce me to your intended wife." I told
him she was in the Ladies' Gallery. We went up. I
introduced him. He talked away pleasantly, took her
over the House, said smilingly "he was glad Horgan
was going to have someone to take care of him," and
was altogether perfectly charming. I was married at
the Redemptorist Church, Clapham, on August 7.
Eleven o'clock was the hour fixed for the ceremony.
The rumour had got abroad that Parnell was coming
to the wedding, and the church and the street were
crowded with people anxious to see him. As the hour
approached I felt very nervous, for I thought he might
not turn up, or that at all events he might not turn up
in time. Indeed, I thought I would be a lucky fellow
if he arrived at twelve or one o'clock. I stood at the
church door on the lookout. At about ten minutes to
eleven a carriage and pair dashed up to the door, and
there was Parnell, dressed magnificently and looking so
handsome and dignified. Every head was uncovered
as he stepped out of the carriage, with the air of an
emperor, and walked up to me. "Ah, Horgan," he

said, " you look nervous (which I was very). Come and have a glass of champagne; that's what you want. We have plenty of time." We went to an hotel close by and we had a pint of champagne, which was what I wanted. We then returned to the church. He was very attentive during the ceremony, knelt down, and showed every respect and reverence. Afterwards he signed the register. Then I thought he would dash off, glad to be rid of us. Not a bit of it. He came to the luncheon, entered quite into the spirit of the whole business, and did not leave until my wife and I drove away. There was a great deal of kindness in the man, despite his coldness and reserve. The wedding must have bored him terribly, but he came because it gave pleasure to others.'

CHAPTER XII

COERCION AND REDRESS

BEFORE the State trials had commenced the Cabinet resolved to suspend the Habeas Corpus Act in Ireland. The decision was arrived at reluctantly. Mr. Gladstone was opposed to coercion. Mr. Chamberlain was opposed to it. Mr. Bright detested it. But the demands of the Irish Executive were imperative. The question was practically coercion or resignation; and Bright, Chamberlain, and Gladstone ultimately yielded to the importunities of Dublin Castle. The determination of the Ministers was foreshadowed in the Speech from the Throne:

'I grieve to state that the social condition of [Ireland] has assumed an alarming character. Agrarian crimes in general have multiplied far beyond the experience of recent years. Attempts upon life have not grown in the same proportion as other offences, but I must add that efforts have been made for personal protection far beyond all former precedent by the police under the direction of the Executive. I have to notice other evils yet more widely spread; the administration of justice has been frustrated with respect to these offences through the impossibility of procuring evidence, and an extended system of terror has thus been established in various parts of the country which has paralysed alike the exercise of private rights and the performance of civil duties. In a state of things new in some important respects, and hence with little available guidance from former precedent, I have deemed it right steadily to put in use the ordinary powers of the law before making any new demand. But a demonstration of their insufficiency, amply supplied by the present circumstances, leads me now to apprise you that proposals will be immediately submitted to you for entrusting me with additional powers, necessary, in my judgment, not only for the vindication of order and public law, but likewise to secure, on behalf of my subjects, protection for life and property.'

Thus the Queen's Speech.

Parnell prepared for action. The Government might, he said, carry their coercive measures, but it would be only after a struggle which they should never forget.

In the thick of the fight he cabled to the 'Irish World' : 'The fight the Irish members are making for the liberties of the people is inspiring and strengthening every Irishman. We are now in the thick of the conflict. The present struggle against coercion will, please God, be such as never has been seen within the walls of Parliament.'

The 'Times' once said that Parnell might prophesy with safety, because he had the power of fulfilling his prophecies. This particular prophecy was at all events fulfilled to the letter. In 1883 there was a memorable struggle over Grey's Coercion Bill. Then the debate on the Address lasted five nights, the debate on the first reading six nights, the debate on the second reading two nights, and six nights were spent in committee. That record was now beaten. In 1881

the debate on the Address lasted eleven nights, the
debate on the first reading five, and even then the Bill
was only ' read ' by a *coup de main*. The debate on
the second reading lasted four nights, ten nights were
spent in committee, and two on the third reading.

Forster's case may be stated in a few words. The
Land League, the centre of disturbance, was ' supreme.'
It was necessary its powers should be crippled. They
could only be crippled by investing the Executive with
extraordinary powers. The wretches who committed
the outrages—' village tyrants,' ' dissolute ruffians '—
were known to the police. If the Habeas Corpus Act
were suspended they would all be arrested and the
disorder would be stopped. It gave him the keenest
sorrow, he declared, to ask for extraordinary powers.
This had been to him a most ' painful duty,' he added
with pathetic honesty. ' I never expected I should
have to discharge it. If I had thought that this duty
would devolve on the Irish Secretary, I would never
have held office ; if I could have foreseen that this
would have been the result of twenty years of parliamentary life, I would have left Parliament rather than
have undertaken it. But I never was more clear than
I am now that it is my duty. I never was more clear
that the man responsible, as I am, for the administration of the government of Ireland ought no longer to
have any part or share in any Government which does
not fulfil its first duty—the protection of person and
property and the security of liberty.'

Parnell's answer may be given briefly too. The
public opinion of Ireland was at the back of the
League. The policy of the Government was the
coercion of a nation. The people suffered wrongs.
The Government admitted it. Let these wrongs be

redressed, and peace would be restored; but no amount
of coercion would force the Irish people to submit to
unjust and cruel laws.   Let evictions be stopped and
crime would disappear.   'What a spectacle have we?
Two great English parties united for one purpose only
—to crush, put down, and bully a poor, weak, and
starving nation; a nation they did not attempt to
assist in her hour of famine and suffering.   In this
state of things the duty of the Irish members is plain.
They are bound to use every form of the House to
prevent the first stage of the Bill.   We shall have no
indecent haste.   We must have full and fair discussion;
and the Irish members are the best judges of the extent
and value of the resistance which they ought to make
to the measure of coercion.'

'We are bound to prevent the first stage of the
Bill.'   This was a frank avowal of policy; obstruction,
not argument, was the weapon on which the Irish
leader relied.   Indeed, he never tried to make a secret
of his contempt for argument in the House of Commons.   'Don't embarrass the Government,' was the cry
of the complacent Irish Whig.   'Embarrass the Government' was the mandate of Parnell.

During the six nights' debate on the first reading I
spent some hours with him walking up and down the
corridors of the House.   He was always anxious to
learn anything of Irish history which had any practical
bearing on the issues of the day.   He now wished to
know something of the previous fights over coercion.   I
told him the story of the struggle over Grey's Coercion
Bill.   'By Jove,' he would say, 'that's good—and
O'Connell too!   They are always holding O'Connell
up to me as a model, but you make him out to be as
bad as I am.   Can I get all this in books?   You see I

am very ignorant. I am very quick, though, at picking
up things.' I named some books to him. 'All right,'
he said, 'I will go into the Library and get them. We
will look through them together.' He went to the
Library, and soon returned with the books. We stood
at the little desk close to the door leading into the
Reading-room. He plunged into the books, marking
with blue pencil the passages that specially interested
him. 'Do they allow you to mark books here?' I
asked, observing that he was disfiguring the pages in
the most reckless fashion. 'I don't know,' was the
answer, with the air of a man who thought the question
quite irrelevant. 'By Jove!' he would repeat, 'this is
very good,' and he would once more daub the margin.
'Well, they cannot say I invented obstruction, for here
is O'Connell doing the very thing, and defying everybody.'

A Whig Home Ruler came along, and was about to
pass into the Reading-room, when Parnell suddenly
stopped him.

'Where are you going?' he asked. 'Just into the
Reading-room, Mr. Parnell, to skim over the evening
papers.'

Parnell. 'Don't you think you ought to be in the
House?'

Whig Home Ruler. 'Yes, Mr. Parnell, I will return
immediately.'

Parnell [laying his hand on the Whig's shoulder].
'You will speak against the Bill?'

Whig Home Ruler. 'I would rather not, Mr. Parnell.
I really am not able to speak.'

Parnell [with a faintly humorous glance at me].
'You can move the adjournment of the debate, or move
the Speaker out of the chair. That won't take much.'

Whig Home Ruler [with alarm]. · 'Oh, dear, no, Mr. Parnell, you must excuse me; I never could do it.'

Parnell [tightening his grip on the Whig's shoulder]. 'Mark, you must *vote* against this Bill. I suppose you can do that. It does not need a speech, and the sooner you get back to the House the better.'

Someone else called Parnell's attention off at this moment, and as the Whig, passing into the Reading-room, turned to me and said, 'Desperate man, desperate man,' Parnell returned to the desk.

After a time another Irish member (a moderate Nationalist) came along. Parnell stopped him too. 'Why have you come away?' he asked.

'I have just spoken, Mr. Parnell,' said the member, 'to the motion for adjournment, and I cannot do anything until the division is taken. I cannot speak twice to the same motion.'

Parnell. 'No, but you can help to keep a House and watch what is going forward. I think you should all remain in your places.'

After a little while I saw both the Nationalist and the Whig wending their melancholy way back towards the Lobby.

Another member soon appeared.

Parnell [stopping him]. 'Why are you all coming out of the House? You should remain at your posts. It is impossible to say what may turn up at any moment.'

Member. 'I have just spoken.'

Parnell. 'That does not matter; a speech is not everything.'

Member. 'Here is a telegram which I have just received from the corporation of ——, protesting against coercion.'

Parnell. ' Then go back and read it.'

Member. ' I cannot ; I have already spoken.'

Parnell. ' Then you can give it to someone else to read.   Give it to me.   Come along.'   And both walked off.

Another night while we were together an Irish newspaper reporter came to him and asked : ' Will you speak to-night, Mr. Parnell ? '

Parnell. ' I really don't know.'   Then, turning to an Irish member who had just joined us, ' I have lost the notes of my speech.'

Irish member. ' Where do you think you left them, Mr. Parnell ? '

Parnell. ' I don't know.'   Then, with a roguish twinkle : ' The notes of your speech are tied up with them.'

The Irish member, without asking any more questions, dashed off to the Library, and was soon back again and tearing off in other directions in search of the notes.

' I am sorry for poor F——,' said Parnell, as he looked in an amusing way after him ; ' but it really does not matter whether the notes are lost or not.' On another occasion, when the debate had lasted for several nights, and when the House was thoroughly exasperated, an Irish Liberal who had made one of the ablest speeches against the Bill came up to Parnell and said :

' Will you allow the division to be taken to-night, Mr. Parnell ? '

Parnell. ' I think not.'

Irish Liberal. ' To be quite frank, I have a personal interest in asking the question.   I came up from Liverpool to vote to-night.   I am obliged to be in

Liverpool again to-morrow, and I don't want to have
my journey for nothing.'

Parnell. 'I don't think there will be a division to-
night.'

Irish Liberal. 'When will there be a division?'

Parnell. 'I don't know. It won't be to-night.'

The Liberal pressed Parnell to allow the division
to be taken, urging that there would be plenty of
opportunities on the second reading and in committee
to attack the Bill.

Parnell's simple answer was: 'No, I don't think
there will be a division to-night.'

He did not argue the question. He gave no reasons
for his decision. He merely repeated: 'There will be
no division to-night.'

'Inexorable,' whispered the Liberal to me as he
went off. 'That's the character of the man, and it
gives him his power.'

Mr. Bright made a vigorous speech in support of the
Bill. Mr. O'Connor Power, who was put up to answer
him, failed utterly. I said so to Parnell. 'Your man
failed to answer Bright. Bright ought to be answered.
But he should not be treated as an enemy. His past
services to Ireland ought not to be forgotten. He is
as much our friend now as ever, though he is wrong
on this question.'

Parnell. 'I agree with what you say about Bright.
He ought to be treated in a friendly way. I got one
of our best men to reply to him. I can do no more.'

'Do you think Bright has been answered?'

Parnell. 'Perhaps not. But if O'Connor Power
failed, who is likely to succeed?'

'Bright's speech is very damaging, and it is
ridiculous of your people to try and make light of a

speech which none of them have answered up to the present.'

We walked along the corridor in silence for a few seconds; then Parnell turned round, faced me, and said : 'What does it matter? Do you think that Irish speeches have any effect on that House? You know they mean to pass this Bill. Do you think' (with a sneer) 'that any number of clever and pretty speeches will prevent them? What does it matter who is right about the number of outrages? The question really is, Do the Irish people support the League or the English Government? We all know they support the League, because the League helps them, and they never trust the English Government. If we had not the people behind us we could do nothing. Mr. Forster talks as if *he* represented Ireland, and the House believes him. They believe what they like to believe. We must show them that Ireland supports us, and defies their House. They will get this Bill through, but it will be a big job I can assure you. They have not read it a first time yet. I don't know when they will, unless they break their own rules.'

A few nights afterwards we were walking in one of the corridors. The excitement in the House at this time was intense, and almost every English member was against the Irish party. Parnell was, as usual, calm and self-possessed, and he seemed to enjoy the discomfiture of the enemy. After awhile Lord Granville came along the corridor. Parnell took no notice of him. I said : 'A pleasant face, Lord Granville's.'

Parnell. 'I did not see it.'

Then Lord Kimberley came along. Parnell looked furtively at him as he passed, but said nothing. Soon Lord Spencer came along, following his colleagues.

Parnell turned round and looked after him, saying : 'A
Cabinet Council. I wonder what they are up to now.
They are at their wits' end to get this Bill read a first
time. I wonder what will they do. Something violent
I suspect. I wish I knew.' It was amusing to watch
him as he said this, rather aloud to himself than to me ;
standing in the middle of the passage with folded arms,
handsome, thoughtful face, figure erect and defiant, a
very picture of dignity and authority. Looking at
him one would have supposed that he was the Prime
Minister, bent on upholding law and order, and that the
innocent noblemen at whom he looked so suspiciously
were Land Leaguers conspiring against the State. We
walked once more towards the Library, when three
more Cabinet Ministers approached us. 'I am right,'
whispered Parnell as they passed ; 'it is a Cabinet
Council. I'm off' (with a smile). 'I must get my
people together,' and he disappeared through a side
door.

I wrote out an extract for him to use in his speech on
the Coercion Bill. Mr. A. M. Sullivan, who sat by him
as he read it to the House, afterwards described the
scene to me. 'He made an impressive speech, and was
listened to as usual with much attention. Then he
pulled a piece of foolscap out of his pocket and began
to read its contents. He got through the first two or
three sentences fairly well, but stopped at the fourth.
Ultimately he made it out ; only, however, to find himself hopelessly stuck in the fifth and following sentences.
The House watched him as he turned the paper in
every direction to decipher the illegible words. I felt
quite embarrassed on his account, though he was cool
and unconcerned. I leant forward looking at the
writing over his shoulder. " Mr. Parnell," I said, " I

am accustomed to that handwriting. Will you let me
read the extract for you?" "No," said he, "I will
read it myself," and he stuck to it doggedly until he
read the whole document through. It was the worst
quarter of an hour he had ever had in the House of
Commons.'

I met Parnell the next night. I said: 'I am
afraid I caused you some embarrassment last evening.'
'How?' he replied. 'A. M. Sullivan tells me you could
scarcely make out my handwriting.'

Parnell. 'Not at all. I read it very well and produced a very good effect.'

This was characteristic of him—always ready to
make the best of everything.

Forster's Coercion Bill was introduced on January
24. On the 25th Mr. Gladstone moved that it should
have precedence of all other business. Parnell and the
Irish members fiercely opposed this motion, adopting
the most extreme obstructive tactics, and keeping the
House sitting continuously from 4 P.M. on Tuesday
until 2 P.M. on Wednesday. On Thursday, 27th, the
debate was resumed. On Monday, 31st, the Government declared their determination to close the debate
on the first reading that night. Parnell and the Irish
protested, and prepared for another all-night sitting.
Relays were ordered on both sides, and English and
Irish settled down doggedly to work. The House was
once more kept sitting continuously from 4 P.M. on
Monday until 9 A.M. on Wednesday—forty-one hours.
Then a memorable scene occurred.

On Wednesday morning, February 2, the Speaker
—who had been relieved from time to time in the
discharge of his duties during an uninterrupted sitting
of forty-one hours—resumed the chair, and, review-

ing the incidents of the debate, declared that in the interest of ' the dignity, the credit, and the authority of the House,' he had resolved to stop the further discussion of the Bill, and to call upon hon. members to decide at once on the question of the first reading. This announcement fell like a thunderclap on the Irish party. They were thoroughly unprepared for it ; they had no conception that the debate would be closed in this manner. Accordingly, taken completely by surprise, they did not attempt to resist the Speaker's authority, and the first reading was then put, and carried by a majority of 164 to 19. Immediately afterwards the House adjourned until noon, the Irish members, astonished and perplexed, crying out as they retired : ' Privilege !   Privilege ! '

Mr. Parnell was not present at this scene. He had been at his post until an advanced hour in the morning, and had retired for a brief rest. ' Parnell,' says Mr. Justin McCarthy, ' was not present. He came into the House some time afterwards. The men were complaining of his absence. But there were no complaints when he appeared. Everyone seemed delighted to see him. There was a feeling of relief. He took the whole business very coolly, and said the action of the Speaker should at once be brought under the notice of the House.

The House met at twelve o'clock. The report of the Speaker's *coup* had spread rapidly throughout the West End, and many persons had gathered within the precincts of the House to watch the further development of events. The Lobby was crowded, as usual on great or critical occasions, and the question, ' What will Parnell do now ? ' passed hurriedly around. There was a general impression that any attempt on the part of the Irish members to resist the ruling of the Speaker, or to reopen in any shape the discussion which had been so summarily closed that morning, would be attended with grave consequences, the nature of which, however, no one ventured to define. 'They will be sent to the Tower,' said one bystander. 'Nonsense,' said another. 'Then what will happen?' said the first. 'God knows,' was the reply, 'but the House is not in a temper to stand any nonsense now.'

About twelve o'clock the Speaker passed through the Lobby to take the chair, looking as if nothing out of the ordinary routine of business had occurred. He was soon followed by the Irish party, who marched from the Library through the Lobby in single file with Parnell at their head, looking somewhat perplexed, but combative and defiant. After some preliminary matters had been disposed of, Mr. Labouchere rose, and in a full House, breathless, I think I may say, with expectation, and perhaps anxiety, said in his clear, bell-like voice: 'I wish to ask you, sir, whether, in bringing the debate upon the question which was before the House this morning to a sudden close, you acted under any standing order of the House, and if so, which.' Mr. Labouchere's rising was received with complete silence, and when he resumed his place only a very feeble cheer broke from the Irish ranks. It was plain the Irish members had not yet recovered from the effects of the Speaker's blow, and they were far too anxious and too uncertain as to the issue of the combat to cheer much or heartily. When Mr. Labouchere sat down the Speaker rose, and, folding his gown around him with dignity, said: 'I acted on my own responsibility, and from a sense of duty to the House.' Then a loud and prolonged cheer broke from the Whig and Tory benches—the cheer of men who had been victorious, and were resolved that the fruits of their triumph should not be lost. When the cheering ceased Parnell rose, and his rising was a signal for a cheer, but yet a feeble one, from his followers. He said : ' I venture, sir, to assume it will be proper for me, in consequence of the reply which you have just vouchsafed to the question of the hon. member for Northampton, at once to bring forward, as a matter of privilege, a resolution declaring that the action of the Speaker in preventing further discussion on the Protection of Property and Person (Ireland) Bill this morning was a breach of the privileges of the House.' Parnell resumed his seat, and the Speaker at once rose, and in measured language answered : ' The hon. member having stated the resolution he proposes to submit to the House, I have to inform the hon. member that the resolution he so proposes relates, not to a question of privilege, but to a question of order.' These words were received with another burst of cheering from the Whig and Tory benches ; and the Speaker continued : ' If he thinks proper to bring the matter under the notice of the House in the regular way, he is entitled to do so by notice of motion, but not at the present time and as a question of privilege.' Once more the words of the Speaker were received with Whig and Tory cheers, amidst which he resumed his seat. Mr. Parnell rose again, and again slight Irish cheers greeted him, his followers being desirous of showing their loyalty to him, but feeling that in the present crisis of affairs they really were not in a position to cheer. They had been defeated in the morning, and there did not yet appear the slightest chance of the tide of battle being turned against their adversaries. In these

circumstances they doubtless thought that it did not
behove them to demonstrate too much. Their leader,
addressing the Speaker, said : ' Sir, I respectfully submit for your further consideration that there is at least
one precedent for the course I propose to take.' The
Speaker firmly replied : ' I have ruled that the course
the hon. member proposes to take is out of order.'
Again the Whigs and Tories cheered lustily, and the
Speaker added : ' If he wishes to challenge that ruling
he is entitled to do so by motion.' Parnell rose again ;
but the House had now grown impatient, and cries of
' Order, order ' broke from the benches on both sides
above the gangway, in the midst of which he sat
down. Here The O'Donoghue interposed to ask when
his ' hon. friend would have an opportunity of raising
the question of order '—an interrogatory which was
received with laughter. The Speaker answered, ' That
is a matter for the House itself,' a reply which evoked
another salvo of cheers from the Whigs and Tories.
And now the struggle seemed all over. There were
slight ' movements ' in the House, as if hon. members
were preparing to settle down to business. The
Speaker leant back in the chair and waved his hand
gently in the direction of the Treasury Bench, to indicate to the leader of the House—Mr. Gladstone—that
the coast was at length clear for passing to the ' Orders
of the day.' At this juncture Mr. A. M. Sullivan sprang
to his feet. ' Do I understand you, sir,' he said, with
outstretched hand and in a clear and manly voice, ' do I
understand you, sir, to rule that my hon. friend cannot
as a matter of privilege challenge the course which,
without precedent, you took this morning?' He
paused for a moment, manifestly much agitated, but
quite self-possessed, and then boldly continued : ' In

that case, sir, I rise to move that the House do disagree
with Mr. Speaker in that ruling.' Now, for the first
time, hearty cheers broke from the Irish ranks, mingled
with cries of 'Chair,' 'Order, order,' from other parts
of the House. Mr. Speaker quickly rose and said : 'In
taking that course the hon. member will be disregarding the authority of the Chair, and I must caution the
hon. member that the course he proposes to take will
involve him in the consequences of that proceeding'—
a reply which again called forth shouts of applause
from the Ministerial and Tory benches. Mr. Sullivan,
nothing daunted or disturbed by the minatory words
of the Speaker, replied that there was no member of
the House more ready to bow to the ruling of the Chair
than he, as there were none who more 'totally disre-
garded consequences in the discharge of conscientious
duties.' He was only seeking for advice and direction,
and wished to be instructed and guided by the Speaker
in the course he proposed to take. 'I ask you, sir,' he
said, 'whether it is not a fact that in the Journals and
records of this House there stand motions that the
House do disagree with a particular ruling of Mr.
Speaker on a point of order?' Again there were Irish
cheers, which had scarcely subsided when the Speaker
rose and said : 'I can quite understand that there may
have been motions of that kind made in the House, and
it may be that the hon. member can make such a
motion, but not as a matter of privilege.'

'I did not rise,' answered Mr. Sullivan, 'to make it
as a matter of privilege, but to ask your advice as to
the course proper to take.'

The Speaker replied : 'If the hon. member admits
that it is not a question of privilege his course is quite
clear ; he is bound to give notice of motion.' Once

again the decision of the Speaker was the signal for
Whig and Tory expressions of triumph and exultation.
But these manifestations of feeling did not disconcert
the sturdy Celt, who was now full of fight and quite
indifferent to consequences.

'I thank you, Mr. Speaker,' he said, 'but I wish
further to ask you if it is not a fact that the ruling of
the Chair has been challenged on the instant?'

The great crisis in the contest had now clearly
arrived. The answer of the Speaker to this question
would manifestly decide the issue, and it was accordingly awaited with much anxiety. 'The hon. member,' said the Speaker, 'asks me a question which
at the present moment I am not able to answer
without searching for precedents.' No Whig or Tory
cheer greeted these words, but a ringing shout of
triumph broke from the Irish benches, which was
repeated again and again as Mr. Sullivan rose and,
waving his hand in the direction of his countrymen,
essayed to speak, but in vain, for the plaudits of the
Home Rulers rendered all sounds save their own cheers
inaudible. At length, the cheers gradually subsiding
and complete silence having for a moment supervened,
Mr. Sullivan, raising his voice to its highest pitch and
speaking with great deliberation and firmness, said :
'Then, sir, in order that you may have time to search
for precedents I shall conclude with a motion.' This
declaration was received with another outburst of Irish
applause, which was not in the least checked—but
perhaps rather stimulated—by the rising of the Speaker.
When order was restored, the Speaker, looking grave
and serious, said : 'I caution the hon. member that if
he proposes to move the adjournment of the House with
a view of calling in question what was done this morning

he will be entirely out of order.' This statement was received with ironical laughter by the Irish members, and met by Mr. Sullivan with a pointed and, I think, dignified reply. He said : ' Sir, I am about to move the adjournment of the House, and I trust I shall do so within the strict rules and privileges of the House, and not beyond them.' He then proceeded to deliver a clever speech on the question of adjournment which lasted nearly an hour. He was followed by Mr. Gray, who seconded the motion. In quick succession the rest of the Irish members, supported by Mr. Cowen and Mr. Labouchere, took part in the debate, which dragged on until a quarter to six in the evening, when the House adjourned. Thus the Irish members on Wednesday afternoon gained a victory over the House which was as complete as that gained by the House over them in the morning. Throughout the whole of Wednesday they obstructed the public business, and rendered the work of the Speaker in stopping the debate in the morning inoperative.[1]

The fierce obstruction of the first reading of the Coercion Bill convinced the Government that a drastic change in the Rules of Procedure was necessary to defeat the tactics of Parnell, and they resolved to make this change before the next stage of the measure. Mr. Gladstone accordingly, on February 2, gave notice of a resolution to the effect that if a motion declaring the business urgent should be supported by forty members rising in their places, then the motion should be put forthwith without debate, and if carried by a majority of not less than three to one, the regulation of the business for the time being should remain in the hands of the Speaker.

[1] I have taken the description of this scene (which I witnessed) from *Fifty Years of Concessions to Ireland.*

This resolution was the first order of the day on Thursday, February 3. But before it was reached Sir William Harcourt informed the House that Michael Davitt had just been arrested in Dublin for violating the conditions of his ticket-of-leave.

'What conditions?' asked Parnell; but Sir William Harcourt gave no answer.[1]

Mr. Gladstone then rose to move the 'closure' resolution, but Mr. Dillon interposed to ask further questions relating to Davitt's arrest. The Speaker called on Mr. Gladstone.

Mr. Dillon refused to give way. 'I demand,' he cried out, amid the din which his persistence produced, 'I demand my privilege of speech.'

The Speaker then 'named' Mr. Dillon for wilfully disregarding the authority of the Chair, and on the motion of Mr. Gladstone he was suspended. Called upon to withdraw, he refused to leave his place, and was removed by the Sergeant-at-Arms. Mr. A. M. Sullivan questioned the authority of the Chair in ordering the forcible removal of Mr. Dillon without first seeking the sanction of the House for that course, but the point was quickly overruled.

Mr. Gladstone rose once more to propose his resolution, when Parnell moved that 'the right hon. member be no longer heard.' Another scene of indescribable excitement and confusion followed. The Speaker refused to hear Parnell; Parnell 'insisted' that his motion should be put. The Speaker named him for persisting in a course of 'wilful and deliberate obstruction,' and he was at once suspended on the motion

---

[1] The Government recognised that Davitt was a danger, and simply made the violation of the conditions of the 'ticket-of-leave' a pretext for arresting him. Davitt was immediately taken to Portland, where he remained until May 6, 1882.

of Mr. Gladstone. Thirty-two Irish members refused
to leave the House during the division, and they
were immediately suspended. 'I was sitting quietly
in my room off the Strand,' says Mr. Frank Hugh
O'Donnell, 'when Biggar rushed in and said : "We
have been suspended. Do you run down to the House
and get suspended at once." Of course I rushed off.
As I took my seat Mr. Gladstone was speaking on the
"closure." I at once moved that he should be no
longer heard, and was suspended on the spot.' Other
Irish members who had been away, at the 'grand
scene' strolled in, moved that Mr. Gladstone should
no longer be heard, and were suspended in detail.
The last victim was 'Dick' Power, one of the most
genial and pleasant of men. He was a great friend of
the Sergeant-at-Arms, Sergeant Gossett, and indeed
spent many hours chatting away in that official's room
during dull nights when the House bored him. 'Dick'
having refused to leave his seat during the division on
Mr. O'Donnell's suspension, was named. He declined
to withdraw unless under the pressure of superior
force. The Sergeant-at-Arms appeared, placed his
hand on Dick's shoulder, and asked his old friend to
retire. 'I won't go, Sergeant,' said Dick. 'My dear
Dick,' quoth the Sergeant, 'do come away.' 'Devil a
foot, Sergeant. You'll have to get the police before I
stir.' And he kept the Sergeant on tenterhooks for
several minutes before finally quitting his place. Later
on he might have been seen discussing the whole
question in the Sergeant's room over a friendly cigar.

'Did Mr. Parnell,' I asked Mr. McCarthy, 'seek
the expulsion of the Irish members on this occasion ? '

He answered : ' Parnell certainly forced the running.
Dillon first got into difficulties with the Speaker. He

said to Parnell: "Don't commit the party on my account. Let it be my affair alone." Parnell answered, "Go on, go on," and very soon made the matter a party affair. He did it deliberately. He always believed that the one thing necessary was to cause explosions in the House, and to show how hopelessly strained were the relations between English and Irish.'

The active Irish members having been got rid of, Mr. Gladstone then moved his resolution, which was carried with one alteration—viz., that there should be at least a House of 300 as well as a majority of three to one before ' urgency ' could be voted.

The resolution having been adopted, ' urgency ' was at once declared, and next day, February 4, Mr. Forster moved the second reading of the Coercion Bill.

Despite the revolution in procedure, the Irish still fought vigorously against the measure, and it was not until February 25 that the last stage was passed in the Commons. On March 2 the Bill became law. Briefly, it enabled the Lord Lieutenant to arrest any person whom he reasonably suspected of treasonable practices or agrarian offences, and to keep such persons in prison for any period up to September 30, 1882.

The Irish Executive were now possessed of the powers for which they had asked, and during the spring, summer, and autumn of 1881 hundreds of Land Leaguers were swept into Kilmainham. But the agitation did not abate. Men were readily found to jump into the breach; the places of the suspects were quickly filled; land meetings went on much as usual; the speeches of agitators increased in violence and lawlessness; crime and outrage were rampant—in a word, the policy of the Government was everywhere met with denunciation and defiance, the Land League remaining supreme. The difficulties of the situation, in nowise diminished by the suspension of the Habeas Corpus Act, were fully realised at Dublin Castle, as the following minute of Lord Cowper will show :

Lord Cowper to the Cabinet

' The first point which I will consider is whether it is desirable to break up the Land League. I mean whether it should be declared an illegal association, and the head committee in Sackville Street and the various local committees forcibly suppressed. There is no doubt that in the opinion of many lawyers it is an illegal association, and if our law officers had shared this opinion it might have been a grave question in the early autumn whether it should not have been put an end to. This could hardly be done now without an Act of Parliament, and how long such an Act would take to pass, and how far the business of the session would be interfered with, her Majesty's Ministers are better able to judge than I am. It must be remembered that the Land League has now taken very deep root throughout the country, and that Fenians, Ribbonmen, and bad characters of every description take advantage of its organisation, and are enrolled in its local branches. If the restraining influences of the central body were withdrawn, and the local branches driven to become secret societies, crime, particularly assassination, might increase ; for though the central body gives unity and strength to the movement, it does to a certain extent restrain crime.

' The priests still exercise an extraordinary influence

over the people, as has been shown lately in the most
marked manner by the power they possess of controlling and pacifying the most excited crowd, and to
withdraw the priests from the movement would be an
object for which a great deal of risk might be run.
I have thought it worth while to make these observations, but from recent speeches in both Houses I
infer that her Majesty's Government have come to
the conclusion that the Land League is not to be
broken up.

'Next comes the question of stopping the Land
League meetings. I have already expressed my opinion,
in a minute of December 27, 1880, that they ought to
have been stopped. They did an immense amount of
mischief, and allowing them to go on has been and will
be fixed upon as the chief error of our Administration.
On the other hand, no one can suppose that under any
circumstances there would not have been a vast number
of outrages last year ; and if we had suppressed the
meetings we should have been accused of sitting on
the safety valve, and it would have been said that if
we had allowed a freer expression of opinion and a
constitutional agitation all would have been well.

'I think now that stopping the Land League meetings would be too late, that it would involve too great a
change of front, and that it would be much more
difficult than last year, as the people are better organised
and able to change the time and place of meeting more
rapidly than they could before. We must pursue the
policy we began at the end of the year, drawing a line
at those meetings where there is sworn information
that they would be attended with danger to an
individual.

'Now comes the question of the arrest of indi-

viduals. To strike at the leaders is undoubtedly the
right thing, and this is just what we have been accused
of not doing. But openly teaching the doctrine of
breach of contract, which is their real crime, does not,
unfortunately, enable us to take them up. We are
hampered in our action by an express agreement that
we will not arrest any man unless we can say on our
honour that we believe him to have actually committed
or incited to outrage. This at first prevented us
from attacking the leaders as vigorously as we might
have done, but latterly some of them have been less
cautious, and we have also prevailed upon ourselves to
give a wider interpretation to our powers. For my
part, I should be inclined to interpret them very widely.
It is hardly too much to say that in the present state of
the country everybody who takes a leading part in the
Land League does, by the very fact of so doing, incite
to outrage. And there is now hardly anybody whose
detention policy would demand that I would not
personally arrest. Next to arresting all the leading
men that we can comes the strict enforcement of the
law. Every failure to serve a process, or to carry out
a forced sale, or an eviction, does immense mischief.
Of course, a collision should, if possible, be prevented,
and for this purpose we always endeavour to send an
overwhelming force.

'I may here notice that complaint has been made
of the troops being exposed to stoning without being
allowed to act in return. A certain amount of this
may be unavoidable, but troops, in my opinion, should
never be brought face to face with the mob unless they
are intended to act. It is not fair for the troops,
and it diminishes the moral effect upon the people.
The police should, if possible, be employed in prefer-

ence, as they can use their bâtons, which they are not afraid to use, and which inflict just the right sort of chastisement.

' These are the general principles which are impressed upon each Resident Magistrate, but as to details he must, of course, in each individual instance use his own discretion. I have little more to recommend. The state of the country is very bad, after making every allowance for the exaggeration of the Press. Indeed, these very exaggerations are a proof of the uneasiness of public feeling. One of the worst points is the bad feeling which prevails in the south and west against the military and police. Worse still are the vast mobs which can be collected at a moment's notice.

' In the autumn individual assassination was the great danger. Now, in addition to this is the danger of a sudden overwhelming, by sheer weight of numbers, of small bodies of police or military. One such catastrophe would be of incalculable evil. Besides the disgrace of the authorities, it would lead to after attempts of the same kind, and might actually be the beginning of a small civil war which could not be concluded without such an amount of bloodshed as would cause renewed bitterness of feeling against England for more than one generation. If the troops fire upon the people, as may be necessary at any moment, and loss of life, even indeed that of women and children, is the result, it must be remembered their action may have saved the country from something even more deplorable.'

If the Government had hoped to conciliate the agitators by the introduction of a big Land Bill they were doomed to disappointment. The bitterness caused by the fight over the Coercion Bill and the imprison-

ment of the Land Leaguers intensified the old feeling
of distrust and ill-will, so that when Mr. Gladstone
brought in his sweeping measure of land reform on
April 7 he spoke to unsympathetic Irish benches.
Biggar sat next to Parnell as the Prime Minister proceeded to unfold his scheme.　When he had been on
his feet for about ten minutes—and, of course, before he
had touched the fringe of the subject—the member for
Cavan turned to his colleagues and said, with characteristic abruptness : ' Thoroughly bad Bill.'　A delightfully humorous smile was Parnell's only response.
But Biggar's frame of mind was the frame of mind of
many of the advanced Nationalists.　They wanted a
' thoroughly bad ' Bill because a ' thoroughly bad ' Bill
would not ease the situation.

There always have been certain Irishmen who
believe that a policy of ' remedial legislation ' would be
fatal to the national demand.　' Let the grievances of
the people be redressed,' they say, ' and there will be
an end of Home Rule.'　This was not Parnell's view.
He believed that the spirit of nationality could not be
quenched ; that the claim for legislative independence
would never be given up, whatever the course of
remedial legislation might be.　I once had a conversation with him in the Smoking-room of the House of
Commons on the subject.　It was à propos of a suggestion to appoint grand committees for the consideration
of Irish, English, and Scotch Bills.　Some of the Irish
members thought that the appointment of these committees might be accepted as a substitute for Home
Rule, and accordingly opposed the proposal.　' Irish
nationality,' said Parnell, ' must be very thin if it is to
be given up for grand committees or anything else.
My opinion is that everything they give us makes for

Home Rule, and we should take everything. The better off the people are, the better Nationalists they will be. The starving man is not a good Nationalist.' Upon another occasion a rumour reached me that the Government (Lord Salisbury's Ministry, 1886) intended buying up the Irish railways. I mentioned the fact to an Irish member. ' Oh,' he exclaimed, 'we must not have that. It would settle Home Rule for ever. If the English Government sink money in the country that way, they will take care to keep everything in their own hands.' I told Parnell what his colleague had said. 'I am accustomed to these remarks,' was his commentary. ' All I say is, I hope what you tell me about the intentions of the Government is true. It would be a good business. It would open up the country, bring the people nearer good markets, and develop industry. Home Rule is not to be killed as easily as —— thinks. It would go on even if we lost ——.'

Parnell wanted a good Land Bill, and he was determined to secure the fullest measure of justice which it was possible to obtain for the tenants. ' The measure of Land Reform,' he had said at Ennis in 1880, ' will be the measure of your energy this winter.' The people were energetic with a vengeance, and the Land Bill was a sweeping measure of reform. ' I would strongly recommend public men,' Parnell said in the same Ennis speech, ' not to waste their breath too much in discussing how the land question is to be settled, but rather to encourage the people in making it ripe for settlement.' The people had made it ' ripe ' for settlement. Mr. Gladstone's Bill proclaimed a revolution.

The old power of the landlord was for ever taken

away. He could no longer increase rents at his pleasure, or, indeed, increase them at all. New tribunals [1] were established for fixing rents, and generally for adjusting the relations of landlord and tenant. Increased facilities for the creation of a peasant proprietary were given, and the tenant's right to dispose of the goodwill of his farm was amply secured. The 'three F's'—fixity of tenure, fair rents, and free sale—for which Isaac Butt had agitated in vain (within the law, and without seeking to outrage Parliament or to humiliate English parties), were now wrenched from the Government by one of the most lawless movements which had ever convulsed any country.

'There is no use,' an Irish Unionist member once said in the House of Commons, 'in any Irishman approaching an English Minister on Irish questions unless he comes with the head of a landlord in one hand or the tail of a cow in the other.' It was in this way the Land League came, and we all now know the Land League triumphed. 'I must make one admission,' said Mr. Gladstone in 1893, 'and that is, that without the Land League the Act of 1881 would not now be on the Statute-book.' [2]

The Irish members were fairly astonished at the completeness of Mr. Gladstone's Bill, and some of them were little disposed to accept it.

Parnell's position was one of extreme difficulty. To have wrecked the Land Bill would have been an act of insensate folly ; to have accepted it cordially might have made the Government feel that they had conceded too much, and would certainly have caused divisions in his own ranks. What was he to do?

---

[1] Land courts.
[2] House of Commons, April 21, 1893.

'When in doubt, do nothing,' was one of Lord Melbourne's wise maxims. Parnell resolved to do nothing for the present. Before the first and second reading of the Bill the Easter recess intervened. During that time he kept his own counsel. The general impression was, however, that he meant to support the Bill. 'People whispered: 'Parnell will take the moderate line, he will accept the Bill.' A clique of Parliamentarians prepared to undermine his authority. A convention was summoned in Dublin to consider the situation. Like Parnell, the convention decided to do nothing. Every member of Parliament was to be left free to take any course he pleased, thus leaving the question still open. The second reading of the Bill was fixed for the 25th of April.

A few days previously the parliamentary party met to consider finally what course should be pursued. 'We were all assembled on the appointed day,' says an Irish member. 'As usual, Parnell was not up to time, which gave an opportunity to the malcontents to grumble. At length he arrived, walked straight to the chair, of course, made no apology for being late, sat down, then rose immediately and said: "Gentlemen, I don't know what your view on this question is. I am against voting for the second reading of the Bill. We have not considered it carefully. We must not make ourselves responsible for it. Of course I do not want to force my views upon anybody, but I feel so strongly on the subject that if a majority of the party differ from me I shall resign at once." This was a thunderbolt. It took us all by surprise. The clique who were plotting against Parnell looked perfect fools. He had trumped their card. There was dead silence. "I now move," said Parnell, "that we

do not vote for the second reading." There were some
expressions of dissent, but the motion was carried.
The whole thing was done in less than an hour.
Parnell, neither then nor at any other time, discussed
the question with us.'

Mr. A. M. Sullivan was one of those who had
spoken publicly during the recess in favour of the Bill.
Parnell's decision that the party should abstain from
voting on the second reading came as a surprise to
him, as well as to everyone else. He was not at the
party meeting, but news of what had occurred soon
reached him. Coming into the chambers which we
both occupied in the Temple and flinging himself into
a chair, he said, with some warmth, ' Do you know
what has happened ? ' I said ' No.' He went on :
' Parnell has carried a resolution pledging the party
not to vote for the second reading of the Land Bill.
He forced the party into this position by threatening
to resign. This is a high-handed act. He did not
give us the slightest inkling of what was passing in his
mind. Some of us have made speeches in support of
the Bill. I have myself stated publicly that I would
vote for the second reading. Then Parnell comes without giving us a moment's preparation, and says that
we must not vote for the second reading, or, if we do,
he will resign. The only course open to me is to leave
the party. I will write to Parnell, telling him exactly
what I think, and placing my resignation in his
hands.'

Mr. Sullivan did as he said. Afterwards he had an
interview with Parnell, of which he gave me the following account : ' Parnell is certainly the coolest hand I ever
met. He is never put out at anything, and he never
thinks that you ought to be put out. He is a regular

Englishman. There is not a bit of the Celt in him.
" Vote for the second reading if you think you have
committed yourself. It will make no matter. As a
question of tactics we ought not to make ourselves
responsible for the Bill. Do whatever you think best.
The Bill is safe." That is simply his answer to me.
Parnell may be quite right in holding back. I entirely
appreciate his anxiety not to make himself responsible
for the Bill. What I object to is, that he should keep
us in the dark up to the very last moment, and then
force us into a position inconsistent with our public
declarations.' Some days later Mr. Sullivan said : ' I
never come away from talking to Parnell without feeling
that he knows better than any of us how to deal with
the people on this side. Time always tells in his favour.
Many of us are inclined to be carried away by what we
think a kindly or a generous act. Parnell is never
carried away by anything. He never dreams of giving
the English credit for good intentions. He is always
on the lookout for the cloven foot. He distrusts the
whole lot of them, and is always on the watch. They
have got their match in him, and serve them right.
It is not poor Isaac Butt that they have to deal with, or
even O'Connell. Parnell is their master as well as ours.'[1]

The Land Bill was read a second time on May 19
by 352 to 176 votes, 35 Home Rulers walking out with
Parnell and 24 joining the majority. In committee,
however, Parnell's true designs revealed themselves.
The Bill was to be saved, but the Government were
not to be ostentatiously supported. Whenever the
measure was in danger the Parnellites came to the
rescue. When it was safe they criticised and objected,
and, it must be allowed, improved the Bill. Mr.

[1] Mr. Sullivan did not vote for the second reading.

Heneage, a Liberal, moved an amendment to exclude English-managed estates from the operation of the Act. The Parnellites stood by the Government and saved the clause. Lord Edmond Fitzmaurice moved an amendment to limit the jurisdiction of the Land Court in fixing fair rents to tenancies under 100*l.* annual value. The Parnellites again stood by the Government and again saved that clause too.[1]

On July 30 the Bill was read a third time by 220 to 14 votes. Mr. Parnell again walked out of the House, followed by a handful of friends, while the great bulk of the Irish party supported the Government. Two nights afterwards—August 1—Parnell was suspended for defying the authority of the Chair. On a motion for regulating the business of the House during the remainder of the session he insisted on demanding a day for the discussion of the Irish administration. The Speaker called him to order again and again, but he held on the even tenor of his way. The Speaker warned, Parnell defied the warning. 'The Ministry of the day,' he said, 'of course always gain the sympathies of the powers that be, in this House, and if we may not bring the cause of our imprisoned countrymen before the House, I may say that all liberty and regard of private right is lost in this assembly, and that the Minister of the day has

---

[1] Another shifting of the political kaleidoscope occurred on the proposal of Mr. Parnell that the landlord should not be allowed to force the sale of the tenant's rights except with the consent of the court. The Government, desirous of giving the tenant a fair start with the new Bill, accepted the proposal, but on the protest of Mr. Gibson that the landlord should not possess less rights than other creditors, Mr. Parnell modified his proposal so as to place all on the same footing. These tactics somewhat disconcerted the Conservative leaders, who found themselves on a division supported by only seventy-six members, whilst Mr. Parnell was followed into the lobby by twenty members, including the whole Treasury Bench.—*Annual Register*, 1881.

transformed himself from a constitutional Minister into a tyrant ! ' Here the Speaker named Parnell at once.

Mr. Gladstone. ' I was about to move——'

Parnell. ' I shall not await the farce of a division. I shall leave you and your House, and I shall call the public to witness that you have refused freedom of discussion.'

He was then suspended for the remainder of the sitting.

The Land Bill now passed without further incident through the Commons, was of course ' amended ' in the Lords, and ultimately received the Royal assent on August 22.

An Ulster Liberal has made the following statement to me with reference to the Land Bill :

' At the beginning of the year there was an article in the " Daily News " from which I gathered (rightly or wrongly) that it was the intention of the Government to introduce a strong Coercion Bill and a weak Land Bill. I wrote to the paper saying substantially that if this were the policy of the Government they could not rely on Ulster.

' I met Sir William Harcourt in the Lobby, and he asked me what I meant by writing such a letter. I said that Ulster would have no tinkering with the land question ; that there should be a sweeping measure of reform. Sir William Harcourt asked me to breakfast with him next day, in order that we should talk the matter over. I then told him plainly that unless the Government meant to accept the " three F's " they had better not legislate at all. He expressed no opinion on the subject, but listened quietly to all I had to say. Some time afterwards, when the Bill was introduced, I met him in the Lobby again. He said :

" D——, when you told me that morning we break-
fasted together that nothing less than the 'three F's'
would do, I thought you were mad ; but they are all in
the Bill."

'When the second reading was carried, a number
of Ulstermen met at the Westminster Palace Hotel to
consider what message should be sent to the north.
They had no copy of the Bill, and they asked me to
get one. I went to the Irish office and saw Law (the
Irish Attorney-General). I told him about the meeting
at the Westminster Palace Hotel, and asked for a copy
of the Bill. He said : " The only copy I have is the
one you see on the table, which has my private notes
on it, and of course I cannot give you that." I pressed
him to give it to me, and he finally consented, making
me promise that I would not let it out of my hands.
As he gave me the Bill he said : " Do you see
that ? " pointing to a figure—I think it was 22—on
the Bill. I said : " Yes ; what does it mean ? " " It
means," he replied, " that that is the twenty-second
Bill which has been before us ! " " And, Law," I
asked, " what was the first Bill like ? " " Well may
you ask," he said with a smile. And then I learnt
this moral lesson from my conversation with Law :
that the first Land Bill was an insignificant amendment of the Land Act, 1870, but that as lawlessness
and outrage increased in Ireland the Bill was broadened
until it reached its final dimensions.'

While the measure was going through Parliament
Parnell lent himself to a new project. There was no
organ in the Irish Press which he could absolutely
control. The ' Freeman's Journal ' was in the hands of
Mr. Gray ; the ' Nation ' and ' Weekly News ' belonged
to the Sullivans ; the ' Irishman,' the ' Shamrock,' and

the 'Flag of Ireland' were owned by Mr. Pigott. Parnell resolved to buy out Pigott and start a journal which he could himself command.

To carry out this purpose he formed the 'Irish National Newspaper and Publishing Company, Limited,' purchased all Pigott's papers, dropped the 'Shamrock,' converted the 'Flag of Ireland' into 'United Ireland,' and continued the 'Irishman.'

Mr. William O'Brien was appointed editor of the Land League organs, as 'United Ireland' and the 'Irishman' now became.

While negotiations were pending Parnell wrote to Dr. Kenny on July 9, 1881 :

Parnell to Dr. Kenny

' MY DEAR DR. KENNY,—Mr. O'Brien arrived here yesterday morning. I have had to-day an interview with him, and he has definitely agreed to accept the position at a salary of 400*l*. per annum. He wishes to be permitted to appoint a sub-editor, who will also act as commercial manager, at a salary of 300*l*. to 350*l*. ; and he mentions Hooper, who is at present manager and factotum in general of the " Cork Herald." He thinks that Mr. James O'Connor might have his present salary in a third position on the paper; but he is not quite certain about this—so that it may become desirable to give Mr. O'Connor a hundred pounds or so and let him go. Mr. O'Brien will not be able to undertake the duties for two or three weeks ; so that meanwhile the paper will have to be brought out by Mr. O'Connor. Mr. O'Brien thinks it would tend greatly to insure the success of the paper if it were known that the proprietors were the leading members of the Land League ; and I have, on reconsideration of the question, come to the conclusion that it would be better that our Limited Liability Company should be formed of such members. I would suggest the following names : Yourself, Mr. Egan, Mr. Dillon, Mr. Justin McCarthy, Mr. John Barry, Mr. Biggar, and myself. These names will be fairly representative of the different shades of feeling in the organisation. Mr. Davitt's name should of course be one, but there might be danger of interference from the Government under present circumstances. Kindly say by wire what you think of these names for the Limited Liability Company. Mr. O'Brien is very hopeful of the success of the paper, if determinedly taken in hand by the organisation of the Land League. He thinks that a total capital of 10,000*l*., including the purchase money, will be sufficient. I have also communicated the above names to Mr. Egan.—I am, yours very truly,

'CHARLES S. PARNELL.'

Some difficulties arose in carrying out these schemes, but Parnell brushed them all aside. On July 22 he wrote again to Dr. Kenny :

Parnell to Dr. Kenny

' I have had a good deal of business these last few days, so that I trust you will excuse my tardiness in replying to your letter. I think you were quite right to make the arrangement you have with O'Connor, which I suppose you did after consultation with O'Brien.

' I regret very much that Dillon will not co-operate in reference to the " Irishman " ; but feel sure, when I am able to see him and explain matters fully, he will come round. I do not apprehend any grave results from the position taken up by our friends in Kilmainham in regard to the matter.'

All difficulties were finally got over, and on August 13 the first number of ' United Ireland ' appeared.

With the passing of the Land Bill Parnell's difficulties increased. His American allies, as represented by Ford and the ' Irish World,' did not in the first instance wish the Bill to become law ; they did not wish to see it in force. Parnell was resolved not to quarrel with his American allies, whose contributions filled the coffers of the League. On the other hand, he determined that the Land Act should not be made a dead letter. Indeed, he knew that the tenants would not permit it. What course, then, was he to pursue so that the farmers might reap the full benefit of the Land Act and his American friends be appeased ? He determined to adopt his old tactics of drawing the fire of the English enemy on himself, believing that while English statesmen and publicists blazed at him from every quarter his influence in Ireland and in America would be unimpaired. Next, he determined that the tenants should be prevented from rushing precipitately into the Land Courts, and from abandoning all agitation henceforth. He had little faith in the Land Court *per se.* He believed that the reduction of rents would be in exact proportion to the pressure which the League could bring to bear upon the commissioners. ' By what rule,' I once asked an Irish official ' do the Land Courts fix the rents ? ' ' By the rule of funk ' was the answer. Parnell resolved that the ' rule of funk ' should be rigidly enforced. By the ' rule of funk ' he had got the Land Act. By the ' rule of funk ' he was determined it should be administered.[1] ' I thought at

---

[1] *United Ireland*, September 17, 1881, expressed this idea in unmistakable language : ' The spirit which cowed the tyrants in their rent offices must be the spirit in which the Land Commission Courts are to be approached.'

the time,' said the Ulster Liberal whom I have already quoted,[1] 'that Parnell's policy of trying to keep the tenants out of the Land Courts in 1881 was foolish, and almost criminal. But I now believe he was quite right.' By keeping the tenants back, by looking suspiciously at the Act, by keeping up the agitation, he succeeded in getting larger reductions than would ever have been made if the farmers had rushed into the courts, and if Parnell had taken no pains to control the decisions of the commissioners. In fact it was Parnell who got the Land Act, and it was Parnell who administered it in the south ; though he refused to make himself responsible for it, and even appeared to be hostile to it. He played a deep game and played it with great ability. He kept his whole party together by not cordially accepting the Land Act, and he took pains at the same time to secure the best administration of it in the interests of the tenants.

Mr. Gladstone thought that Parnell was bent on obstructing the Land Act and thwarting the Government. Nevertheless the Prime Minister believed that the Irish Executive ought to pursue a conciliatory policy. On September 5 he wrote to Mr. Forster :

Mr. Gladstone to Mr. Forster

'. . . We have before us in administration a problem not less delicate and arduous than the problem of legislation with which we have lately had to deal in Parliament. Of the leaders, the officials, the skeleton of the Land League, I have no hope whatever. The better the prospect of the Land Act with their adherents outside the circle of wirepullers, and with the

[1] *Ante*, p. 298.

Irish people, the more bitter will be their hatred, and the more sure they will be to go as far as fear of the people will allow them in keeping up the agitation which they cannot afford to part with on account of their ulterior ends. All we can do is to thin more and more the masses of their followers, to fine them down by good laws and good government; and it is in this view that the question of judicious releases from prison, should improving statistics encourage it, may become one of early importance.'

In September an election took place in the County Tyrone. Mr. T. A. Dickson, the Liberal candidate, gained a great victory over Parnell's nominee, the Rev. Harold Rylett, a Unitarian Minister. The result filled Mr. Gladstone with hope.

On September 8 he wrote to Mr. Forster, who had gone abroad for a short holiday :

Mr. Gladstone to Mr. Forster

'The unexpected victory in Tyrone is an event of importance, and I own it much increases my desire to meet this remarkable Irish manifestation and discomfiture both of Parnell and the Tories with some initial act of clemency, in view especially of the coming election for Monaghan. I do not know whether the release of the priest (Father Sheehy) would be a seasonable beginning, but I shall be very sorry if we cannot do something to meet the various friendly and hopeful indications of which the Ulster election is the most remarkable. To reduce the following of Parnell by drawing away from him all well-inclined men seems to me the key of Irish politics for the moment. Though I felt reluctant that anything should be done in your absence, yet I think the impendency of Monaghan election is a fact of commanding importance in the case before us.'

To this letter Mr. Forster replied on September 11, saying that the Tyrone election was certainly a stroke of luck, but reminding Mr. Gladstone that Tyrone was in Ulster, and that 'Ulster is not Connaught or Munster.' Upon the whole he was not disposed to take Mr. Gladstone's advice until there was some more cogent proof of the waning influence of Parnell than the Tyrone election afforded.

On September 14 a great Land League Convention which lasted for three days met in Dublin to consider the situation. There were divided counsels. Some thought that the Land Act should be freely used, others that it should be wholly repudiated. But, under the direction of Parnell, the convention unanimously re-solved on a middle course. The Act was to be 'tested'; certain cases were to be carefully selected for trial. But there were to be no indiscriminate applications to the courts. This resolution simply meant that the Act was to be administered under the control of Parnell. 'Nothing,' said Parnell, 'could be more disastrous to our movement and our organisation, and to your hopes of getting your rents reduced, than any indiscriminate rush of the tenantry into court, and it is with a view to prevent this that we desire to take the tenantry in hand and to guide them in this matter, because, depend upon it, if we don't guide them there will be others that will. If we don't take hold of the Irish tenantry and guide them for their advantage, there will be others who will guide them for their destruction.'

Parnell's policy, however, did not satisfy his American allies, and he was forced to send the follow-

ing explanatory telegram to the President of the Land
League of America :

' Dublin : Sept. 17, 1881.

'The convention has just closed after three days'
session. Resolutions were adopted for national self-
government, the unconditional liberation of the land
for the people, tenants not to use the rent-fixing clauses
of the Land Act, and follow old Land League lines,
and rely on the old methods to reach justice. The
Executive of the League is empowered to select test
cases, in order that tenants in surrounding districts
may realise, by the result of cases decided, the hollow-
ness of the Act.'

On September 26 Parnell attended a Land League
convention at Maryborough, when a number of resolutions were passed endorsing the action of the Dublin
convention, and practically advising the tenants to use
the Act under the direction of the League.

A private meeting of organisers was held some
hours before the convention assembled to consider the
resolutions which were to be submitted to it. 'I well
remember,' says one who was present, 'sitting beside
Parnell at this private meeting. Proofs of the resolutions were handed around. There were fifteen resolutions altogether. Parnell fixed his attention at once on
No. 11, which ran as follows :

' " That the test cases selected for the Land Commission shall not be the most rack-rented tenants, but
rather tenants whose rents hitherto have not been considered cruel or exorbitant."

'Parnell took out of his pocket a blue-ink pencil,
and, having glanced down the proof, turned it over and
wrote on the back :

'"*After the eleventh resolution.*

'"That, pending the result of the test cases selected by the Executive, no member of the League should apply to the court to fix his rent without previous consultation with, and obtaining the consent of, the branch of the League to which he belongs."

'Having written this, he handed me the proof to pass it on to the secretary so that the alteration might be duly made. I looked at it, and said: "This is an interesting document, Mr. Parnell, and I think I will give the secretary a clean copy and, as the lawyers say, 'file the original.'" He smiled, and simply said "It is business." The resolution as amended by Parnell was carried at the convention.'

I cannot say how far this Maryborough meeting affected the action of the Irish Executive, but curiously enough it was on this very day, September 26, that Mr. Forster wrote to Mr. Gladstone suggesting that Parnell should be arrested, adding: 'I think you will do great good by denouncing Parnell's action and policy at Leeds.'[1]

Mr. Gladstone did denounce Parnell's 'action and policy' at the Leeds meeting on October 7, telling his audience that the 'resources of civilisation were not exhausted,' and plainly hinting that they would be used against the Irish leader who [in his efforts to obstruct the operation of the Land Act] stood between the living and the dead, not, like Aaron, to stay the plague, but to spread the plague.'

'Parnell's reply to you,' Forster wrote to Gladstone on October 9, 'may be a treasonable outburst. If the

---

[1] Sir Wemyss Reid, *Life of the Right Hon. W. E. Forster.*

lawyers clearly advise me to that effect, I do not think I can postpone immediate arrest on suspicion of treasonable practices.'

Parnell's reply, made at Wexford on October 9, may or may not have been a 'treasonable outburst,' but there can be no doubt that it was the reply which the occasion demanded—spirited and defiant. He began :

'You have gained something by your exertions during the last twelve months ; but I am here to-day to tell you that you have gained but a fraction of that to which you are entitled. And the Irishman who thinks that he can now throw away his arms, just as Grattan disbanded the volunteers in 1783, will find to his sorrow and destruction when too late that he has placed himself in the power of the perfidious and cruel and relentless English enemy.' Then, turning to Mr. Gladstone's speech, he continued :

'It is a good sign that the masquerading knight-errant, this pretending champion of the rights of every other nation except those of the Irish nation, should be obliged to throw off the mask to-day, and stand revealed as the man who, by his own utterances, is prepared to carry fire and sword into your homesteads, unless you humbly abase yourselves before him and before the landlords of the country. But I have forgotten. I said that he maligned everybody. Oh, no. He has a good word for one or two people. He says the late Isaac Butt was a most estimable man and a true patriot. When we in Ireland were following Isaac Butt into the lobbies, endeavouring to obtain the very Act which William Ewart Gladstone, having stolen the idea from Isaac Butt, passed last session, William Ewart Gladstone and his ex-Government officials were following Sir Stafford Northcote and Benjamin Disraeli into the

other lobby. No man is great in Ireland until he is
dead and unable to do anything more for his country.

'In the opinion of an English statesman, no man is
good in Ireland until he is dead and buried, and unable
to strike a blow for Ireland. Perhaps the day may
come when I may get a good word from English statesmen as being a moderate man, after I am dead and
buried. When people talk of " public plunder " they
should ask themselves who were the first plunderers in
Ireland ? The land of Ireland has been confiscated
three times over by the men whose descendants Mr.
Gladstone is supporting in the enjoyment of the fruits
of their plunder by his bayonets and his buckshot.
And when we are spoken to about plunder we are
entitled to ask who were the first and biggest plunderers. This doctrine of public plunder is only a
question of degree.

'In one last despairing wail Mr. Gladstone says,
" And the Government is expected to preserve peace
with no moral force behind it." The Government has
no moral force behind them in Ireland ; the whole Irish
people are against them. They have to depend for
their support upon a self-interested and a very small
minority of the people of this country, and therefore
they have no moral force behind them, and Mr. Gladstone in those few short words admits that English
government has failed in Ireland.

'He admits the contention that Grattan and the
volunteers of 1782 fought for ; he admits the contention
that the men of '98 died for ; he admits the contention that O'Connell argued for ; he admits the contention that the men of '98 staked their all for ; he
admits the contention that the men of '67, after a long
period of depression and apparent death of national

life in Ireland, cheerfully faced the dungeons and horrors of penal servitude for; and he admits the contention that to-day you, in your overpowering multitudes, have established, and, please God, will bring to a successful issue—namely, that England's mission in Ireland has been a failure, and that Irishmen have established their right to govern Ireland by laws made by themselves on Irish soil. I say it is not in Mr. Gladstone's power to trample on the aspirations and rights of the Irish nation with no moral force behind him. . . . These are very brave words that he uses, but it strikes me that they have a ring about them like the whistle of a schoolboy on his way through a churchyard at night to keep up his courage. He would have you believe that he is not afraid of you because he has disarmed you, because he has attempted to disorganise you, because he knows that the Irish nation is to-day disarmed as far as physical weapons go. But he does not hold this kind of language with the Boers. At the beginning of this session he said something of this kind with regard to the Boers. He said that he was going to put them down, and as soon as he had discovered that they were able to shoot straighter than his own soldiers he allowed these few men to put him and his Government down. I trust as the result of this great movement we shall see that, just as Gladstone by the Act of 1881 has eaten all his own words, has departed from all his formerly declared principles, now we shall see that these brave words of the English Prime Minister will be scattered like chaff before the united and advancing determination of the Irish people to regain for themselves their lost land and their legislative independence.'

Parnell's speech was received with salvos of applause.

He struck the keynote of defiance which suited the temper of the audience. Mr. Gladstone spoke at Leeds as if he had a special mission to stand between Parnell and Ireland. Ireland answered at Wexford repudiating the help of any Englishman, and reminding the Prime Minister that whatever she had got from England she had got by the strength of her own right hand.

On the evening of the Wexford meeting two Irish members dined with Parnell. ' We felt,' one of them has since said to me, ' that he was bound to be arrested after this speech, and we thought that he ought to give us some instructions as to the future in case our suspicions should prove correct. P——— (the other member) suggested that I should ask him for instructions. I suggested that P——— should be the spokesman. In fact neither of us quite liked the job, not knowing exactly how he would take it. We all three sat down together. P——— and I were like a pair of schoolboys, anxious to get information but afraid to ask for it. It was a comical situation. P——— kept kicking me under the table to go on, and I kept h'ming and hawing, and beating about the bush, but Parnell, who was not at all inclined to talk, could not be drawn.

' At length I plucked up courage and said : " Do you think, Mr. Parnell, that you are likely to be arrested after your speech to-day ? " " I think I am likely to be arrested at any time—so are we all. A speech is not necessary. Old Buckshot [1] thinks that by making Ireland a jail he will settle the Irish question." Then

---

[1] ' Buckshot' was a nickname given to Mr. Forster in reference to the kind of ammunition which the constabulary were ordered to use in case of being obliged to fire on the people. The name was scarcely appropriate to Mr. Forster, because the buckshot had been ordered by his predecessor. I once pointed this out to Parnell. He said : ' I believe so ; but Forster uses the buckshot, so it comes to the same thing. It is a very good name for him.'

there was a pause. After a little while I returned to
the charge. "Suppose they arrest you, Mr. Parnell,"
I asked, "have you any instructions to give us ? Who
will take your place ? " "Ah ! " he said deliberately,
looking through a glass of champagne which he had
just raised to his lips. "Ah, if I am arrested Captain
Moonlight [1] will take my place." '

On Tuesday, October 11, Mr. Forster crossed to
England, having previously arranged with Sir Thomas
Steele, the Commander-in-Chief of the Forces in Ireland,
that in the event of the Cabinet consenting to the
arrest of Parnell he would wire the one word 'proceed.'

On Wednesday, October 12, the Cabinet met.
Parnell's arrest was decided on. Forster immediately
wired to Steele, 'Proceed.' [2]

Meanwhile Parnell, who had returned to Avondale
on Tuesday, came back to Dublin on Wednesday night,
intending to address a meeting next day in Naas, County
Kildare. He was to have left the Knightsbridge
terminus at 10.15 A.M. On Wednesday night he told
the boots at Morrison's Hotel to call him at half-past
eight in the morning. I shall let Mr. Parnell himself
continue the narrative.

'When the man came to my bedroom to awaken
me, he told me that two gentlemen were waiting below
who wanted to see me. I told him to ask their names
and business. Having gone out, he came back in a
few moments and said that one was the superintendent
of police and the other was a policeman. I told him
to say I would dress in half-an-hour, and would see

---

[1] The threatening notices which used at this time to be served on
landlords and obnoxious tenants were generally signed ' Captain
Moonlight.'

[2] Sir Wemyss Reid, *Life of the Right Hon. W. E. Forster.*

them then. He went away, but came back again to
tell me that he had been downstairs to see the gentlemen, and had told them I was not stopping at that
hotel. He then said I should get out through the
back of the house, and not allow them to touch me.
I told him that I would not do that, even if it were
possible, because the police authorities would be sure
to have every way most closely watched. He again
went down, and this time showed the detectives up to
my bedroom.'

The rest of the story is told by the 'Freeman's
Journal.'

'Mr. Mallon, the superintendent, when he entered
the bedroom, found Mr. Parnell in the act of dressing,
and immediately presented him with two warrants. He
did not state their purport, but Mr. Parnell understood
the situation without any intimation. The documents
were presented to him with gentlemanly courtesy by
Mr. Mallon, and the honourable gentleman who was
about to be arrested received them with perfect calmness and deliberation. He had had private advices
from England regarding the Cabinet Council, and was
well aware that the Government meditated some *coup
d'état*.

'Two copies of the warrants had also been sent to
the Knightsbridge terminus, to be served on Parnell
in case he should go to Naas by an early train.
Superintendent Mallon expressed some anxiety lest a
crowd should collect and interfere with the arrest, and
requested Mr. Parnell to come away as quickly as
possible. Mr. Parnell responded to his anxiety. A cab
was called, and the two detectives, with the honourable
prisoner, drove away. When the party reached the
Bank of Ireland (to the former memories and future

prospects of which Mr. Parnell had, but a fortnight previously, directed the attention of many thousands), five or six metropolitan police, evidently by preconceived arrangement, jumped upon two outside cars and drove in front of the party. On reaching the quay at the foot of Parliament Street a number of horse police joined the procession at the rear. In this order the four vehicles drove to Kilmainham. This strange procession passed along the thoroughfares without creating any remarkable notice. A few people did stop to look at it on part of the route, and they pursued the vehicles, but their curiosity was probably aroused by the presence of the force rather than by any knowledge that after a short lull the Coercion Act was again being applied to the *élite* of the League. They stopped their chase after going a few paces, and at half-past nine o'clock Mr. Parnell appeared in front of the dark portals of Kilmainham.'

'We arrested Parnell,' Lord Cowper said to me, 'because we thought it absurd to put lesser men into jail and to have him at large. Furthermore, we thought that his test cases would interfere with the working of the Land Act.'

And how were things going on inside Kilmainham at that moment ? One of the 'suspects' shall answer. 'I was in Kilmainham,' he says, 'several months before Parnell came. There was a little clique among the "suspects" who were always finding fault with Parnell, complaining of his moderation, and saying that he wanted to work the Land Act and to unite with the Liberal party. Upon one occasion a "suspect" was about to be discharged on account of ill-health. It was suggested that he should see Parnell and "stiffen his back," and make him face the Government. I

asked this "suspect," when we were alone, what he
would say to Parnell. He answered: "I don't know.
I suppose he will talk me over in half-an-hour."

'When it became known that a convention would
be held in September to discuss the Land Act these
malcontents came together to consider what message
they would send to the assembly. I remember they
met in an iron shed in the ·recreation yard. One of
them began the proceedings by taking a box of matches
out of his pocket and saying, " Here is the message I
will send to the convention—a box of matches to burn
the Land Act." This kind of thing was always going
on, and Parnell's "moderation" was a constant theme
of conversation. One morning there was unusual
bustle in the jail. A warder came to my room. I said:
"Anything extraordinary going on. Is the Lord
Lieutenant coming to see us?" He grinned and
answered: " Mr. Parnell has come. He is in the cell
below." My first feeling was to laugh outright. Here
was the man whom the malcontents in Kilmainham
condemned for his moderation, and now the Government had laid him by the heels like the rest of us.
I sent a message to the Deputy Governor to ask for
permission to see Parnell. He consented at once.
I went downstairs and found Parnell in a cell 12 feet
by 6, sitting in a chair. " Oh, Mr. Parnell!" I said,
" have they sent you here too? What have you
done?" "Forster thought," he answered, "that I
meant to prevent the working of the Land Act, so he
sent me here to keep me out of the way. I don't know
that he will gain anything by this move."

' The room looked miserable, and I thought I
might improve its appearance and brighten it a bit by
putting a beautiful green baize cloth, which had been

specially worked for me by friends outside, on the bare
table at which Parnell sat.   I went up to my cell and
brought down the cloth.   " This, Mr. Parnell," I said,
" will be better than nothing," and I put the cloth on
the table, feeling very proud of myself.   " Have you any
good cigars ? " asked Parnell.   " Certainly," I answered.
" I have a box of splendid cigars upstairs," and away I
went for them.   When I came back I found Parnell
sitting once more by a bare table, and my beautiful
green baize cloth was huddled up in a corner on the
floor.   I gave Parnell a cigar, and then, looking round
the room, I said : " What have you done with my
beautiful green cloth, Mr. Parnell ? "   " Ah ! " he said,
lighting a cigar, " green is an unlucky colour."   Then,
puffing it, " This is a very good cigar." '

While Parnell was spending his first days in Kilmainham Mr. Gladstone was holding high festival in
London.

A few hours after the Irish leader's arrest the
freedom of the City was presented to the Prime
Minister.   The news had spread that a decisive blow
had been struck at the Irish conspiracy by the arrest
of the chief criminal, and when Mr. Gladstone rose
to address the meeting he was received with significant cheers.   ' Within these few minutes,' he said
in solemn accents and amid dead silence, ' I have been
informed that towards the vindication of the law,
of order, of the rights of property, and the freedom of
the land, of the first elements of political life and
civilisation, the first step has been taken in the arrest
of the man ——.'   Here he was interrupted.   The great
meeting rose *en masse*, frantic with excitement and joy,
and rounds of applause rang again and again throughout
the hall, until the speaker himself was astonished, and

perhaps startled, at the savage enthusiasm which this announcement called forth. When the cheering at length ceased he finished his sentence—'who has made himself prominent in the attempt to destroy the authority of the law, and substitute what would end in being nothing more nor less than anarchical oppression exercised upon the people of Ireland.'

'Parnell's arrest,' says the biographer of Mr. Forster, bearing strange testimony to the power of this extra-ordinary man, ' was hailed almost as though it had been the news of a signal victory gained by England over a hated and formidable enemy.' This description is as true as it is pithy. Indeed, the defeat of a foreign fleet at the mouth of the Thames could scarcely have excited a greater ferment than the simple announcement that Charles Stewart Parnell was safe and sound under lock and key in Kilmainham. The British Empire breathed once more.

How was the news of Parnell's arrest received in Ireland? A cry of indignation and anger went up from almost every part of the country. In many towns and villages the shops were closed, and the streets wore the appearance of sorrow and mourning. In Dublin there were riots, and the people were bludgeoned by the police. Everywhere there were manifestations of discontent and irritation. It may indeed be said without exaggeration that scarcely since the Union was the name of England more intensely detested than during the four-and-twenty hours following Parnell's arrest.

At the Guildhall, as at Leeds, Mr. Gladstone, in denouncing Parnell, assumed the *rôle* of the saviour of Ireland. But the memory of Cromwell was not more obnoxious to the Irish people than the personality of the Prime Minister at this moment. It was the old story. Public opinion in England went in one direction, public opinion in Ireland in another. The solitary individual who regarded the whole proceeding with the most perfect equanimity was the prisoner himself. In the course of the day a reporter from the 'Freeman's Journal' called to interview him. He ended the interview, with one of those significant sentences which displayed his faculty for always saying the thing that best suited the occasion : 'I shall take it as evidence,' he said, 'that the people of the country did not do their duty if I am speedily released.'

In his cell at Kilmainham Parnell was a greater power in Ireland than the British Minister, surrounded by all the paraphernalia of office and authority.

CHAPTER XIII

KILMAINHAM

THE League's answer to Parnell's arrest was a manifesto calling upon the tenants to pay no agrarian rents, under any circumstances, until the Government had restored the constitutional rights of the people.

This document was inspired by Ford and Egan, written by William O'Brien, and signed by Parnell, Kettle, Davitt, Brennan, Dillon, Sexton, and Egan.[1] All the prominent Leaguers were not in favour of the policy of the No Rent manifesto. Mr. O'Kelly was opposed to it, and his views were shared by Mr. Dillon, who was sent back to Kilmainham (for a second time) a few days after Parnell's arrest. Indeed, the very day that Mr. Dillon arrived the document was under consideration. As he entered the room the conspirators were sitting in council. Parnell exclaimed : 'Here is Dillon ; let us see what he says about the manifesto.' The manifesto was handed to Mr. Dillon, who condemned it on the instant. 'A strike against rent,' he said,

[1] On the introduction of the Coercion Bill Egan retired to Paris, and there attended to the financial business of the League. On October 17 Ford wired to him : 'Communicate with Parnell if possible, consult with your colleagues, then issue manifesto "No Rent."' Egan replied : 'Your suggestion is approved. Prompt measures are now in preparation to prepare a general strike against rent. The manifesto will be issued throughout the land. It is the only weapon in our hands.' Davitt's name was signed by Brennan, Davitt being in Portland.

' cannot be carried out without the help of the priests, and the priests cannot support so barefaced a repudiation of debt as this. Rome would not let them.' Parnell, who was really opposed to the manifesto, but reluctant at the moment to run counter to Ford and Egan, used Dillon's opposition as a pretext for re-opening the whole question. 'That,' he said, 'is serious. I think we had better carefully reconsider the whole question. We will read the paper over again.' This was done, Parnell still holding the scales evenly balanced, and throwing his weight neither upon the one side nor the other. At length a vote was taken. The majority of those present approved of the manifesto, which was accordingly issued and published in 'United Ireland' on October 17. It fell absolutely flat. It was condemned by the bishops and priests and ignored by the people. The arrest of Parnell had thrown the movement into the hands of the extremists. The No Rent manifesto was the result.

Parnell was fond of telling a story which tickled his peculiar sense of humour anent this manifesto and his own arrest. In the County Wexford there was a respectable farmer and a man of moderate political views named Dennis ——. He subscribed to the funds of the Land League, but took no further part in its work. He was, in fact, what in Ireland is contemptuously called an 'Old Whig.' Like many persons who sympathised little with the operations of the League, he had an intense admiration for Parnell. The arrest of the Irish leader was a shock to him. The one man of sense and moderation in the movement had been flung into jail, the one restraining hand had been paralysed—such was the wisdom of the

British Government. So reasoned Dennis ——, and so reasoning he resolved to make a protest on his own account.

A Land League meeting was convened in his own district. He determined to attend it. The day of meeting came. Dennis put in an appearance. The 'boys' were astonished and delighted to see him, and everyone said, 'Dennis must take the chair.' Dennis emphatically declined the most unexpected honour thus thrust upon him. But the chance of holding a Land League meeting under such respectable auspices was not to be thrown away. Despite all remonstrances, Dennis was borne to the chair amid popular acclamations. Strong resolutions were proposed, violent speeches were made, and a paper, which made the chairman's ears tingle, though he did not take it all in at once, was read. Then he was called upon to put the resolution to the meeting and to read the paper. He read the paper. It took his breath away, but he went through manfully to the end. The paper was the 'No Rent' manifesto, and the resolution pledged the meeting to support it. Three days afterwards Dennis found himself inside Kilmainham. The mildest-mannered man in Wexford was within the grip of the law. That was not all. Dennis was at first much shocked by the conversation of some of his fellow 'suspects.' He did not appreciate the good stories of the Leaguers. Gradually, however, he became reconciled to them. Finally, he began to retail them. At length the crisis arrived. One day he approached Parnell in the recreation yard. 'Mr. Parnell,' said he, 'I would like to have a word with you.' 'Certainly, Dennis,' said Parnell. They walked apart. 'Then'—as Parnell would say, telling the story—'Dennis came very close to me, put his lips very

close to my ear, and, holding up a copy of the
" Freeman's Journal " at the same time, whispered :
" Another blackguard swept." '   A landlord or a tenant
had been shot for disobeying the popular decrees.
Dennis had become completely demoralised under the
coercion *régime*.   The ' Old Whig ' had been converted
into a rampant Land Leaguer.

Apart from the inevitable monotony of a prison,
life in Kilmainham was not severe.   The place itself,
for a jail, is not particularly repulsive.

Passing the portals, which are dark and gloomy, you
enter a magnificent hall, through the glass roof of
which, on the day in August 1897 when I visited it,
the sun shone brightly.   In this cheery-looking place
there was scarcely a suggestion of a prison.   A number
of little rooms—cells about twelve feet by six—rising
in three storeys, open off this central hall, and you
ascend to the top by iron staircases.   I went into one
of the cells.   A prisoner was working hard making
sacks ; he was bound to get through a certain
number in the day, and he plied his needle with fierce
industry.   He was a forbidding-looking individual, and
eyed the warder and myself rather savagely.   Yet he
had literary tastes, and a book by Rolf Boldrewood
rested on a little shelf in his cell.   The man was in
for theft.   I learned subsequently that it was in this
cell that Parnell slept his first night in Kilmainham.
He was, however, immediately transferred to good
quarters in another part of the building.   They consisted
of two large rooms, one of which he used by day, the
other by night.   Nothing could be more comfortable
within the walls of a prison.   The day room was
indeed excellent—large and plenty of light.

It has sometimes been said that Parnell chafed

more than any of the suspects under the prison treatment. I asked one of the warders if that were so.
He said : 'Not at all. He was a delicate gentleman,
but he bore up as well as any of them.' Parnell himself did not complain of his treatment in Kilmainham.
One night, shortly after his release, when a scratch
dinner had been prepared for him in the house of a
Dublin friend, the hostess apologised, saying : 'This is
worse than Kilmainham.' 'Ah well, come,' he said
smiling, 'Kilmainham was not so bad after all.'

One of his favourite recreations in jail was chess.
All the 'suspects' used to meet in the central hall,
and there Parnell would be often seen playing chess
with one of his comrades. 'I often played with him,'
says one of these. 'He was not a scientific chess
player, and he clearly had very little practice. I used
always to beat him, and I am not a good player ; but
his play was characteristic. He was very slow in
making moves. As soon as he had decided on some
course, instead of moving the piece slowly, as people
who think slowly generally do, he would pounce upon
it and rap it energetically down on the spot he wanted,
suddenly developing some fierce movement of attack.
When he was stopped he would relapse into a state of
thoughtfulness once more until he had worked out
another plan of assault ; then he would again move
rapidly and energetically until he was brought to a
standstill again.'

On April 10, 1882, Parnell was allowed to leave
Kilmainham to visit his sister, Mrs. Thomson, whose
son was dying in Paris. It was whispered at the time
that this was merely an excuse to get out of prison ;
that Parnell's nephew was not dying ; even some malig-
nant spirits went so far as to say that he had no

nephew. The following letter will dispose of these slanders :

Parnell to Mrs. Dickinson

' 8, Rue Presbourg, Paris: April 17, 1882.

' MY DEAR EMILY,—I shall be sure to call to see Theodosia and Claude before I return to Ireland, but cannot fix the day just yet. I will wire him the day before. Delia is much cut up by her dreadful loss, but is somewhat better now ; my being here has done her a great deal of good. It appears Henry used to live in an apartment of his own, and it was quite by accident that they discovered he was ill. In the first ten days it did not seem to be much, but the fever then went to his head, and after a week's constant delirium the poor fellow died. He used to devote himself entirely to music, composing, &c., and it is thought that his brain was injured or weakened by dwelling too much upon this one subject, and so was unable to stand disease.

' Your affectionate brother,

' CHARLES S. PARNELL.

' P.S.—I am sorry to hear Theodosia is not looking at all strong.'

A few days afterwards Parnell returned to Kilmainham.

Mr. Forster's Coercion Act had now been twelve months in force. It had proved an utter failure ; and, to do Mr. Forster justice, no one was more painfully conscious of the fact than he. His confessions of failure are indeed pathetic. ' I can never do now what I might have done for Ireland,' he sorrowfully admits as early as June 1881, and he adds, ' it is seriously to be thought whether after the Land Bill is passed I ought not to get out of it all.'

In September he writes again : 'Up to now, Limerick, West Cork, Kerry, and the Loughrea district of Galway have been as bad as ever.'

In October Mr. Gladstone, in the innocence of his heart, was anxious that law-abiding citizens in Ireland should be sworn in as special constables. There is a touch of humour in Mr. Forster's reply, though it also affords a curious commentary on the complex state of affairs in Ireland. ' As regards special constables, one of the first questions I asked months ago was, why could we not have them? I was soon convinced that in Ireland they are impossible ; in the south and west we cannot get them, and in the north Orangemen would offer themselves, and we should probably have to put a policeman at the side of every special to keep him in order.' In November he writes again : ' I am sorry to say there is a turn decidedly for the worse, and we are going to have a most anxious winter. . . . We have more secret outrages and attempts to murder ' ; and he concludes sorrowfully : ' If we could get the country quiet I should be anxious to leave Ireland. While we are fighting for law and order I cannot desert my post ; but this battle over and the Land [Act] well at work, I am quite sure that the best course for Ireland, as well as for myself, would be my replacement by someone not tarred by the Coercion brush.' [1]

The early months of 1882 still found Ireland the prey of anarchy and disorder.[2] On April 12 Mr. Forster wrote to Mr. Gladstone : ' My six special magistrates all bring me very bad reports. These are confirmed by

[1] Sir Wemyss Reid, *Life of the Right Hon. W. E. Forster.*

[2] The Irish Government seems to have lost its head over the anarchical condition of the country ; and Mr. Clifford-Lloyd, one of the special magistrates, issued an insane circular to the police stating that

constabulary reports.   The impunity from punishment
is spreading like a plague.'

On April 19 Lord Cowper wrote to the Cabinet :

Lord Cowper to the Cabinet

'The returns of agrarian crime during the last two
years are before the Cabinet.   They have been presented in every kind of shape, and comparisons may be
made by weeks, by months, and by quarters.   The
increase of murders and other serious outrages is
fluctuating, and not uniform, but this increase is very
serious, and for this reason new legislation is demanded.
With regard to this fluctuation, I may remark in passing
that after any very great crime, towards which any
considerable attention has been attracted, there appears
generally to be a lull.

'For instance, since the murders of Mr. Herbert
and Mrs. Smythe [1] there were very few outrages for
nearly a fortnight.   This seems to point towards
proving that a strong organisation still exists, and
that the Land League is not so completely broken
down as was imagined.   This is, I am afraid, very
much owing to the fact that since the imprisonment or
dispersion of the men who led it the work has been
taken up by women.   We know that women go about
the country conveying messages and encouraging disaffection, and that they distribute money in large
quantities both by hand and by letter.

if they should ' accidentally commit an error in shooting any person on
suspicion of that person being about to commit a murder,' the production of the circular would exonerate them.   This document—which, as
the *Annual Register* says, was practically authority ' to shoot on sight '—
had ultimately to be withdrawn.—*Annual Register*, 1882, p. 187.

[1] On April 2 a most sensational agrarian murder was committed.
Mr. Smythe, while driving with his sister-in-law, Mrs. Henry Smythe,
was fired at.   The shot missed him, but hit and killed Mrs. Smythe.

' My own idea, looking solely to the state of things
in this country, would have been to treat the women
exactly like the men, both as to the ordinary law and
as to arrest under the Protection of Person and Property
Act ; and to have made no more difference between the
two sexes than a magistrate or judge would in the case
of stealing a loaf of bread or a pair of boots. I am
aware, however, that the feeling of the British public
and of the House of Commons must be consulted, and
if the arrest of women would raise such a storm as to
render the renewal of the Act impossible this may be
sufficient reason for not acting as I should wish. The
returns of outrage of themselves appear to demand new
measures. But they are not the only mode by which
we should judge the necessity for these. If I am asked
what other means of judging there are, I answer,
" general opinion, as far as it can be collected, of those
likely to know."

' The Irish Press of all shades of political feeling is of
one mind as to the serious state of the country. I have
seen many landlords, agents, and others. I have seen
many of the judges, and their personal accounts more
than confirm what they have said in public. Above
all, I have seen resident magistrates, inspectors, and
sub-inspectors, who come to the Castle almost every
day from all parts of the country to recommend arrests ;
and the general, I may say universal, opinion is that
the amount of intimidation is as serious as it can be,
and that a sudden increase of agrarian crime at any
moment, to any extent, is quite possible.

' But it is hardly necessary to go further than the
printed reports of the six special resident magistrates,
who have charge of the worst part of the country. It
must be remembered that these six men are picked out

from more than seventy of their class, that each one
of them is known to be of exceptional ability, and that
their experience is drawn from separate districts. They
all concur in their views of the deplorable state of the
country and the utterly crushing intimidation which
prevails, and we know what this intimidation may at
any time produce. They agree also as to the necessity
for further legislation, and their recommendations are
substantially the same.

'In addition to the renewal of the Protection of
Person and Property Act for another year, these
recommendations are as follows :

' 1. Increase of summary jurisdiction.

'This is the point to which I should personally
attach the highest importance of all. A resident
magistrate, and in serious cases a special resident
magistrate, should be present.

' 2. Special commission to try agrarian cases in
certain districts without jury. Unless the judge can
be compelled to act there will be difficulties about this.
If so it will be all the more necessary that, under
No. 1, twelve months' imprisonment with hard labour
could be given as recommended by Messrs. Plunkett,
Clifford-Lloyd, and Blake.

' 3. Improvement of Arms Act, so as to make one
warrant do for a whole townland and allow search by
night ; also power to search for papers.

'4. Power to tax districts for payment of extra police,
and for compensation for death or injury to the person.

' 5. Power to arrest strangers and persons at night.

' As I consider the present question to be whether
any fresh legislation is required, and in what general
direction, I do not enter into more minute particulars.
I content myself with saying that in my opinion legis-

lation is required, that it is required at once, and that every day during which crime can be committed with impunity will make the dealing with it more difficult.'

This minute of Lord Cowper's bears witness to the failure of Mr. Forster's policy. The last state of Ireland was worse than the first. ' If you are arrested, who will take your place ? ' Parnell was asked after the Wexford meeting. ' Captain Moonlight will take my place ' was the answer. Captain Moonlight had taken his place in earnest. The National Land League had been suppressed immediately on the publication of the ' No Rent ' manifesto. Its place was at once taken by the Ladies' Land League, an organisation formed some twelve months previously on the suggestion of Mr. Davitt to meet the very contingency which had arisen.

The ladies very soon outleagued the League. Lord Cowper, as we have seen, said on one occasion that the central executive of the Land League did exercise some controlling influence over the wilder spirits in the country districts. But no controlling influence was exercised now. Things went from bad to worse.

The total number of agrarian outrages for the ten months—March to December 1880—preceding the Coercion Act was 2,379. The total number for the ten months—March to December 1881—succeeding the Coercion Act, 3,821. When one classifies these outrages the case appears even worse.

Ten months preceding Coercion Act

Homicides	Firing at the person	Firing into dwellings
7	21	62

Ten months succeeding Coercion Act

Homicides	Firing at the person	Firing into dwellings
20	63	122

In the first quarter of 1881 there was one murder; in the first quarter of 1882 there were six. The total number of cases of homicide and of firing at the person in the first quarter of 1881 was seven; in the first quarter of 1882, thirty-three.

The total number of agrarian outrages in October 1881, when the Land League was suppressed, stood at 511; in March 1882 the figure was 531. But it is unnecessary to dwell further on these details. The utter breakdown of the Coercion Act is beyond dispute.

'Everyone,' says Lord Cowper with perfect frankness, 'advised us to suspend the Habeas Corpus Act—the lords-lieutenant of counties, the police, the law officers. The police led us quite astray. They said they knew all the people who got up the outrages, and that if the Habeas Corpus Act was suspended they could arrest them. Of course we found out afterwards that the police were mistaken.'

Some two years after the events with which I am now dealing I called one morning on Mr. Bright at his apartments in Piccadilly. He was sitting at the table, wrapped in a dressing-gown and reading Plowden's 'History of Ireland.' 'Ah!' he exclaimed, 'they say I have lost all interest in Ireland since I voted for coercion, as they call it; still I have been reading this book all the morning. The history of Ireland has always interested me.' After some talk about Irish history the subject of coercion came up again. 'They call it coercion,' he said, 'but they forget the coercion of the Land League.'

'Their coercion, Mr. Bright,' I said, 'is at all events more effective than yours. Mr. Forster's Act was a complete failure. I felt very sorry that you voted for the Bill. I heard your speech in support, and I didn't like it.'

Mr. Bright (with a smile, and stroking his chin with his finger). 'I dare say you didn't. What would you have? Remember, I voted for coercion before. The position I have always taken has been that you cannot resist the demand of the Minister who is responsible for the administration in Ireland, though you may say, as I have certainly said, that other remedies must be applied.'

I said : 'The Minister in this case was wrong.'

Mr. Bright. 'Well, yes' (getting up and throwing some coal on the fire and then turning his back to it, looking withal a noble figure, as he there stood with leonine head, venerable grey hair, and dignified bearing). 'The suspension of the Habeas Corpus Act,' he continued, 'had been successful in the case of the Fenians ; we supposed it would be successful in the case of the Land League. That was the mistake. The League was a bigger organisation. It extended all over the country. The arrest of the leaders did not affect it : the local branches were too well organised. For every man who was arrested there was another ready to take his place. Our information was wrong. The conspiracy was more widespread and more deeply rooted than we were led to suppose. It was not a case for the suspension of the Habeas Corpus Act.'

I said : 'The policy was inexcusable.'

Mr. Bright. 'To be fair you must consider the circumstances under which the policy was adopted. Put yourself in the place of a Cabinet Minister. Suppose the Lord Lieutenant and Chief Secretary—the men, mark, who are responsible for the government of the country, the Executive—suppose they tell you that they will resign unless you give them the powers they demand, what would you say?'

I made no reply.

Mr. Bright. 'You don't answer, but what you feel inclined to say is, "Let them resign."'

I said: 'Exactly.'

Mr. Bright. 'If you say that, it shows that you cannot put yourself in the place of a Cabinet Minister. Resignations are very serious things for a Government. They are not to be lightly accepted. There is another point. Suppose you could not get anyone to fill their places. I do not say it was so; it did not come to that. I put the case. No. I admit the policy was a failure, or, at least, not as successful as we anticipated it would be. But under the circumstances, in face of the representations of the Irish Government, it was impossible to avoid trying it. Remember, too, that if we had not passed a Coercion Act we could not have got a good Land Bill through. That was a consideration which weighed much with me, and I think with all of us.'

The failure of Mr. Forster's policy was patent to all. What was now to be done? The Irish Executive had no misgivings on the point. More coercion; that was *their* remedy. The Protection of Person and Property Act, which would expire in September, should be renewed, and a new Crimes Bill passed. These were the proposals of Lord Cowper and Mr. Forster. But Mr. Gladstone was little disposed to plunge deeper into a policy which had been tried and which had failed. All along it had been his wish rather to let the 'suspects' out than to keep them in, and the thought uppermost in his mind at this crisis was, 'Is there any chance of a *modus vivendi* with Parnell?'

Mr. Chamberlain also had been against coercion from the beginning; he had been Forster's enemy in the Cabinet during the whole period of the Chief Secretary's term of office, and he was now determined to thwart the efforts of the Irish Executive in committing the Government any longer to a policy which had been marked by failure. Mr. Chamberlain was energetically supported in the Press by Mr. John Morley, then editor of the 'Pall Mall Gazette.'

'We knew,' said Lord Cowper, 'that Mr. Chamberlain and Mr. Morley were working together to thwart Mr. Forster,' and Lord Cowper was right. But this was not all. The Tories were suddenly seized by a virtuous fit, and cried out against coercion too. 'The present measures of coercion,' said Mr. Gorst on March 28, 'have entirely failed to restore order in Ireland. The assizes just concluded show that the amount of crime was more than double what it was in all the various districts last year; in almost every case the juries failed to convict, and therefore there must be some new departure on the part of the Government.'

A Conservative member, Sir John Hay, gave notice of motion:

'That the detention of large numbers of her Majesty's subjects in solitary confinement, without cause assigned and without trial, is repugnant to the spirit of the constitution, and that to enable them to be brought to trial jury trials should, for a limited time in Ireland, and in regard to crimes of a well-defined character, be replaced by some form of trial less liable to abuse.'

Mr. W. H. Smith proposed 'to ask the First Lord of the Treasury if the Government will take into their consideration the urgent necessity for the introduction of a measure to extend the purchase clauses of the Land Act, and to make effectual provision for facilitating the transfer of the ownership of land to tenants who are occupiers on terms which would be just and reasonable to the existing landlords.'

Here were the Tories apparently condemning coercion and proposing an alternative policy.

A peasant proprietary had always been Parnell's solution of the Land question. A peasant proprietary was now the solution of Mr. W. H. Smith. Were the Tories going to outflank Mr. Gladstone? Was the old parliamentary hand going to be checkmated? There never existed a parliamentary tactician on whom it was more difficult to execute a flank manœuvre than Mr. Gladstone, and he had no notion now of allowing the Opposition to pose as the enemies of coercion and the friends of the Irish tenants at his expense. Indeed, the Tory manœuvres served only to strengthen the hands of the anti-coercionists in the Cabinet, and to stimulate the Prime Minister in his eagerness to end the Forster *régime*.

While Whigs and Tories were thus playing the usual party game, regarding Ireland merely as a pawn on the chess-board, Parnell sat in his spacious room in Kilmainham revolving the whole situation in his mind. ' And what a room ! ' said a friend who visited him at this time. ' The table strewn with everything, newspapers, books, magazines, light literature, Blue Books, illustrated periodicals, fruit, addresses from public bodies, presents of every description, all lying in one indiscriminate heap before him, and he supremely indifferent to their existence.'

' You have everything here, Mr. Parnell, except a

green flag,' said an admirer; and Parnell smiled at this
delicate allusion to one of his many superstitions.
'How is the No Rent manifesto working, Mr.
Parnell?' said another visitor. 'All I know about it
is that my own tenants are acting strictly up to it,' was
the grim answer.

Reports of the state of the country reached him
almost every day. Indeed, he knew all that was going
on as well as, perhaps even better than, Mr. Forster.
Ireland was in a state of lawlessness and anarchy.
Lawlessness and anarchy which served only to embarrass the British Minister mattered little to Parnell.
Lawlessness and anarchy which served to embarrass
himself mattered a great deal. The country was drifting out of his hands, and drifting into the hands of
reckless and irresponsible men and women whose wild
operations would, he felt sure, sap his authority and
bring disaster on the national movement. It was quite
time for him to grasp the reins of power once more, and
to direct the course of events. His release from prison
became, in fact, a matter of paramount importance.
How was he to get out? I have said that the thought
uppermost in Mr. Gladstone's mind was how to bring
about a *modus vivendi* with Parnell. The thought
uppermost in Parnell's mind was how to bring about a
modus vivendi with Mr. Gladstone. It occurred to the
Irish leader that a treaty might be made on the basis
of doing something more for the Irish tenants. He
had pointed out the defects of the Land Act, he had
dwelt on the importance of dealing with the question
of arrears, and he now thought that this question
might be made the ground of some arrangement
whereby the present intolerable and (it seemed to him)
insane condition of affairs would be ended.

Parnell, as has been already mentioned,[1] had left
Dublin for Paris on April 10. At Willesden Junction he
was met by Mr. Justin McCarthy, Mr. Quin, and Mr.
Frank Byrne. They had organised a public demonstration, which, however, Parnell avoided, saying that he did
not consider himself free by the terms of his release to
take part in any political proceedings. That same
evening he had a long conversation with Mr. Justin
McCarthy on Irish affairs. 'I told him,' says Parnell,
'that the tenants, all of them who could pay their rents,
had done so and obtained good reductions, and that there
only remained those who could not pay—the smaller
tenants in arrears. That the "No Rent manifesto"
had been practically withdrawn, as when the [new]
Land Bill was drafted[2] it had been withdrawn from
circulation, and no further attempts made to get the
tenants to refuse to pay their rents; and that now the
thing was to press Parliament for some legislation to
assist the small tenants, some 100,000 in number I
suppose, who were unable to pay their rents and who
were threatened with evictions. I told him that if
these tenants were evicted on any large scale the result
would be great increase of crime and terrible suffering,
and that I had every reason to believe that the state of
the country, and the crime in the country, was entirely
due to the inability of those small and poor tenants to
pay their rents, and that in self-protection they were
going about, or their sons were going about, banding
themselves together to intimidate the larger tenants
from paying, or that they had been doing so, and that
an Arrears Act would have an immediate effect in

---

[1] *Ante.* p. 323.
[2] A Bill drafted by Parnell in prison for the amendment of the
Land Act of 1881.

producing tranquillity and restoring peace in the country.' [1]

On April 11 he saw Captain O'Shea (an Irish Home Rule member of Whig proclivities, who was in touch with the Government), and repeated what he had said to Mr. McCarthy. That night Parnell crossed to Paris. Captain O'Shea immediately put himself in communication with Mr. Gladstone and Mr. Chamberlain, apparently suggesting the feasibility of some arrangement by which the 'suspects' might be released and an Arrears Bill passed. Subsequently he received the following letters:

Mr. Gladstone to Captain O'Shea

'April 15, 1882.

'Dear Sir,—I have received your letter of the 13th, and I will communicate with Mr. Forster on the important and varied matter which it contains. I will not now enter upon any portion of that matter, but will simply say that no apology can be required either for the length or freedom of your letter. On the contrary, both demand my acknowledgments. I am very sensible of the spirit in which you write; but I think you assume the existence of a spirit on my part with which you can sympathise. Whether there be any agreement as to the means, the end in view is of vast moment, and assuredly no resentment, personal prejudice, or false shame, or other impediment extraneous to the matter itself, will prevent the Government from treading in that path which may most safely lead to the pacification of Ireland.

'Truly yours,
'W. E. Gladstone.'

---

[1] Special Commission, Q. 58,758, *et seq.*

Mr. Chamberlain to Captain O'Shea

'April 17, 1882.

'MY DEAR SIR,—I am really very much obliged
to you for your letter, and especially for the copy of
your very important and interesting communication to
Mr. Gladstone. I am not in a position, as you will
understand, to write you fully on the subject, but I
think I may say that there appears to me nothing in
your proposal which does not deserve consideration. I
entirely agree in your view that it is the duty of the
Government to lose no opportunity of acquainting
themselves with representative opinion in Ireland, and
for that purpose that we ought to welcome suggestions
and criticism from every quarter, and from all sections
and classes of Irishmen, provided that they are animated by a desire for good government and not by
blind hatred of all government whatever. There is one
thing must be borne in mind—that if the Government
and the Liberal party generally are bound to show
greater consideration than they have hitherto done for
Irish opinion, on the other hand, the leaders of the
Irish party must pay some attention to public opinion
in England and in Scotland. Since the present
Government have been in office they have not had
the slightest assistance in this direction. On the
contrary, some of the Irish members have acted as if
their object were to embitter and prejudice the English
nation. The result is that nothing would be easier
than at the present moment to get up in every large
town an anti-Irish agitation almost as formidable as
the anti-Jewish agitation in Russia. I fail to see how
Irishmen or Ireland can profit by such policy, and I

shall rejoice whenever the time comes that a more hopeful spirit is manifested on both sides.

'Truly yours,
'J. CHAMBERLAIN.'

Mr. Gladstone at once put Mr. Forster in possession of O'Shea's communications. The Irish Secretary seems to have been quite sympathetic on the question of arrears; but he did not see his way to the release of Parnell. He would not bargain with the Irish leader. He would not allow himself to be undermined by Mr. Chamberlain and Mr. Morley. He looked upon the whole business as an underhand proceeding, quite in keeping with the attempts which had been constantly made to thwart him in his Irish administration, and he resolved to take no part in negotiations which had been begun over his head.

'Forster himself,' says Lord Cowper, 'thought ultimately that Parnell would have to be let out on certain conditions. It was the way the thing was done rather than the thing itself to which he objected.'

On April 18 Parnell wrote a characteristic letter, making an appointment with Mr. McCarthy, but saying nothing of the business in hand.

Parnell to Justin McCarthy

'8 Rue Presbourg, Paris: Tuesday, April 18.

'MY DEAR MCCARTHY,—I hope to pass through London next Sunday, and will try to look you up at your house in Jermyn Street. Have had a bad cold since I have been here, but am nearly all right again. With best regards to all friends,

'Yours very truly,
'CHARLES S. PARNELL.'

Parnell to Mr. Justin McCarthy

'Saturday [April 22, 1882].

'MY DEAR MCCARTHY,—I have arrived in England, and will call to see you to-morrow afternoon some time. I cannot at present give you the exact hour, but would it be too much to ask you to remain at home after three o'clock? I trust you will have some news of result of Cabinet to-day.[1]

'Yours very truly,
'C. S. P.'

On Sunday afternoon Parnell discussed the whole situation with Mr. McCarthy. He had previously seen Captain O'Shea, who expressed the hope that, as a result of the negotiations then going on, the 'suspects' might be permanently released. 'Never mind the " suspects," ' he said; 'try and get the question of the arrears satisfactorily adjusted, and the contribution made not a loan, but a gift on compulsion. The Tories have now adopted my views as to peasant proprietary. The great object to be attained is to stay evictions by an Arrears Bill.'[2]

On April 24, as we have seen, Parnell was back at Kilmainham. On the following day he wrote to Mr. McCarthy:

[1] 'It was not,' says Sir Wemyss Reid in his *Life of Forster*, 'until the 22nd [of April] that the Cabinet took up the Irish question, Mr. Forster having by this time returned to London.'—Vol. ii. p. 428.

[2] There were 100,000 tenants in arrears, and consequently unable to avail themselves of the benefit of the Land Act. These tenants could all be evicted. Parnell's object was to get a Bill which would practically wipe out these arrears. See *Annual Register*, 1882, p. 21.

Parnell to Mr. Justin McCarthy

[Confidential]

'Kilmainham : April 25, 1882.

'MY DEAR McCARTHY,—I send you a letter embodying our conversation, and which, if you think it desirable, you might take the earliest opportunity of showing to Chamberlain. Do not let it out of your hands, but if he wishes you might give him a copy of the body of it.

'Yours very truly,

'CHARLES S. PARNELL.'

The body of the letter ran as follows :

'We think, in the first place, no time should be lost in endeavouring to obtain satisfactory settlement of the arrears question, and that the solution proposed in the Bill standing for second reading to-morrow (Wednesday) would provide a satisfactory solution, though the Church Fund would have to be supplemented by a grant from Imperial resources of probably a million or so.

'Next, as regards the permanent amendment of the Land Act, we consider that the rent-fixing clauses should be extended to as great an extent as is possible, having in view the necessity of passing an Amendment Bill through the House of Lords ; that leaseholders who have taken leases, either before or since the Act of 1870, should be permitted to apply to have a fair rent fixed ; and that the purchase clauses should be amended as suggested by the Bill the second reading of which will be moved by Mr. Redmond to-morrow.

'If the Government were to announce their intention of proposing a satisfactory settlement of the arrears difficulty as indicated above, we on our part would

make it known that the No Rent manifesto was withdrawn, and we should advise the tenants to settle with
their landlords. We should also then be in a much
better position than we were ever before to make our
exertions effective to put a stop to the outrages which
are unhappily so prevalent.

'If the result of the arrears settlement and the
further ameliorative measures suggested above were the
material diminution of outrage before the end of the
session, and the prospect of the return of the country,
after a time, to something like a normal condition, we
should hope that the Government would allow the
Coercion Act to lapse, and govern the country by the
same laws as in England.'

Mr. Chamberlain acknowledged the receipt of this
communication in the following letter:

Mr. Chamberlain to Mr. Justin McCarthy

'April 30.

'MY DEAR McCARTHY,—Many thanks for your
note, with the extract from Mr. Parnell's letter. I will
endeavour to make good use of it. I only wish it could
be published, for the knowledge that the question still
under discussion will be treated in this conciliatory
spirit would have a great effect on public opinion.

'You may rely on me at all times to do my best to
help forward the solution of the Irish problem, and, in
spite of past failure and past mistakes, I am still
hopeful for the future.

'Yours very truly,
'J. CHAMBERLAIN.'

About the same time Parnell wrote to Captain
O'Shea:

Kil. Treaty

Parnell to Captain O'Shea

'Kilmainham : April 28.

' I was very sorry that you had left Albert Mansions before I reached London from Eltham, as I had wished to tell you that after our conversation I had made up my mind that it would be proper for me to put Mr. McCarthy in possession of the views which I had previously communicated to you. I desire to impress upon you the absolute necessity of a settlement of the arrears question which will leave no recurring sore connected with it behind, and which will enable us to show the smaller tenantry that they have been treated with justice and some generosity.

'The proposal you have described to me as suggested in some quarters of making a loan, over however many years the payment might be spread, should be absolutely rejected, for reasons which I have already fully explained to you. If the arrears question be settled upon the lines indicated by us, I have every confidence—a confidence shared by my colleagues— that the exertions which we should be able to make strenuously and unremittingly would be effective in stopping outrages and intimidation of all kinds.

' As regards permanent legislation of an ameliorative character, I may say that the views which you always shared with me as to the admission of leaseholders to the fair rent clauses of the Act are more confirmed than ever. So long as the flower of the Irish peasantry are kept outside the Act there cannot be any permanent settlement of the Land Act, which we all so much desire.

' I should also strongly hope that some compromise might be arrived at this session with regard to the amendment of the tenure clauses. It is unnecessary

for me to dwell upon the enormous advantages to be
derived from the full extension of the purchase clauses,
which now seem practically to have been adopted by all
parties.

' The accomplishment of the programme I have
sketched would, in my judgment, be regarded by the
country as a practical settlement of the land question,
and would, I feel sure, enable us to co-operate cordially
for the future with the Liberal party in forwarding
Liberal principles; so that the Government, at the
end of the session, would, from the state of the country,
feel themselves thoroughly justified in dispensing with
further coercive measures.

' Yours very truly,
' C. S. PARNELL.'

On April 30 Captain O'Shea called on Mr. Forster
at his residence in Eccleston Square, and showed him
this letter.   Mr. Forster has given us a detailed account
of the interview :

' After carefully reading [the letter] I said [to
Captain O'Shea] : " Is that all, do you think, that
Parnell would be inclined to say ? "   He said : " What
more do you want?   Doubtless I could supplement
it."   I said : " It comes to this, that upon our doing
certain things he will help us to prevent outrages," or
words to that effect.   He again said : " How can I
supplement it ? "   referring, I imagine, to different
measures.   I did not feel justified in giving him my
own opinion, which might be interpreted to be that of
the Cabinet, so I said : " I had better show the letter to
Mr. Gladstone, and to one or two others."   He said :
" Well, there may be faults of expression, but the
thing is done.   If these words will not do I must get

others; but what is obtained is "—and here he used
most remarkable words—" that the conspiracy which
has been used to get up boycotting and outrages will
now be used to put them down, and that there will be a
union with the Liberal party ; " and as an illustration of
how the first of these results was to be obtained, he
said that Parnell hoped to make use of Sheridan and
get him back from abroad, as he would be able to help
him put down the conspiracy (or agitation, I am not
sure which word was used), as he knew all its details
in the west.   (This last statement is quite true.
Sheridan is a released suspect, against whom we have
for some time had a fresh warrant, and who under
disguises has hitherto eluded the police, coming back-
wards and forwards from Egan to the outragemongers
in the west.)   I did not feel myself sufficiently master
of the situation to let him know what I thought of this
confidence ; but I again told him that I could not do
more at present than tell others what he had told me.
I may say that in the early part of the conversation he
stated that he (O'Shea) hoped and advised—and in this
case he was doubtless speaking for Parnell—that we
should not to-morrow—I suppose meaning Tuesday—
" pledge ourselves to any time for bringing on fresh
repressive measures."   He also said that he had persuaded Parnell to help to support a large emigration
from the west, and that Parnell had told him that he
had a good deal of conversation with Dillon, and had
brought him round to be in full agreement with himself
upon the general question.'

Mr. Forster immediately sent Parnell's letter and
the above account of his own interview with Captain
O'Shea to Mr. Gladstone.   ' I expected little from these
negotiations,' was the Irish Secretary's comment upon

the whole transaction.   But Mr. Gladstone was highly
gratified.   'This,' said he, ' is a *hors d'œuvre* which we
had no right to expect, and I rather think have no
right at present to accept.   I may be far wide of the
mark, but I can scarcely wonder at O'Shea saying " the
thing is done."   . . .   On the whole Parnell's letter is,
I think, the most extraordinary I ever read.   I cannot
help feeling indebted to O'Shea.' [1]

The thing *was* done.   On May 1 the Cabinet met
to discuss the prospective policy in lieu of coercion.
After the meeting of the Cabinet Mr. Gladstone wrote
to Lord Cowper :

Mr. Gladstone to Lord Cowper

' MY DEAR COWPER,—In consequence of the altered
position of the No Rent party, further attested to us by
important information which (without any covenant)
we have obtained, the Cabinet has discussed anxiously
the question whether the three members of Parliament [2]
now in prison should be released, with a view to further
progressive release of those not believed to be impli-
cated in crime upon careful examination of their cases.
No decision has been absolutely taken, but the Cabinet
meets again to-morrow at twelve, and it is probable
that a telegram may be sent to you requesting you to
give directions for the immediate liberation of the
three.   The information we have had in the briefest
words is shortly this : we know that Parnell and his
friends are ready to abandon " No Rent " formally, and
to declare against outrage energetically, intimidation
included, if and when the Government announce
a satisfactory plan for dealing with arrears.   We have

---

[1] Sir Wemyss Reid, *Life of the Right Hon. W. E. Forster.*
[2] The three were Parnell, Mr. O'Kelly, and Mr. Dillon.

already as good as resolved upon a plan, and we do not know any absolute reason why the form of it should not be satisfactory.

'Sincerely yours,
'W. E. GLADSTONE.'

On May 2 Mr. Gladstone telegraphed in cypher to Lord Cowper:

'Matters being settled here for immediate action and on a footing named in last telegram to sign and give necessary directions for the three forthwith.'

To this Lord Cowper wired in reply:

'I should much prefer, for reasons I will give by letter, that your intention should be carried out by my successor. But I will obey orders if insisted on.'

This letter, giving the reasons, ran as follows:

Lord Cowper to Mr. Gladstone

'Vice-Regal Lodge, Dublin:

'May 2, 1882.

'MY DEAR MR. GLADSTONE,—The proposed release of the three members of Parliament so took me by surprise that I have hardly been able to form a deliberate opinion about it. Nothing but a series of formidable objections has yet occurred to me. This is the way in which the circumstances present themselves to my mind. These men have been imprisoned for a gross violation of the law. They follow this up with a violation still grosser, the No Rent manifesto. There is at this moment a great amount of bad outrage. We know or suspect that this is instigated by the prisoners. At the same time their organs in the Press taunt us with having put under restraint the only people who have power to stop it. We, apparently despairing of restoring order ourselves, let them out on condition that they will help us and will refrain for the future, not from the conduct for which they were imprisoned, but only from the more outrageous policy to which they have after- wards committed themselves, and even this they are only willing to do in return for fresh legislation in favour of the tenant.

'There may be another side to the question, but, as I am not able to grasp it, you will understand my objections to being the instrument of their release.

'Yours very truly,

'COWPER.'

Mr. Gladstone wired immediately :

'Your signature, if required, as it would be after resignation, would be merely ministerial and without political responsibility. When do you come to London? I quite understand your letter, as it shows me, to my surprise, that you have had no previous information.'

This terminated the correspondence.

Lord Cowper immediately signed the order of release, and Parnell (with his colleagues, Mr. O'Kelly and Mr. Dillon) walked forth a free man once more. All Ireland, outside the loyal corner of Ulster, hailed the liberation as a national triumph, and a shout of victory went up from one end of the land to the other. The Irish Executive had been beaten. The Prime Minister, who but seven months before had announced Parnell's arrest with such dramatic effect to an excited English meeting, had now flung the Irish agents of the Government over and made peace with the invincible agitator. Mr. Forster, rightly appreciating

the omnipotence of Parnell, described this situation
thus :

'A surrender is bad, but a compromise or arrangement is worse. I think we may remember what a
Tudor king said to a great Irishman in former times :
"If all Ireland cannot govern the Earl of Kildare,
then let the Earl of Kildare govern all Ireland." The
king thought it was better that the Earl of Kildare
should govern Ireland than that there should be an
arrangement between the Earl of Kildare and his
representatives. In like manner, if all England cannot
govern the hon. member for Cork, then let us acknow-
ledge that he is the greatest power in all Ireland to-day.'

On his release Parnell hastened to Avondale,
whither he was accompanied by an Irish member, who
shall describe the scene of his arrival at home :

'I went to Avondale with Parnell after his release
from Kilmainham. When we arrived at the place all
the old servants rushed out to see him. They were
crying with joy. I was horribly affected, and began to
cry myself. Parnell was absolutely unmoved. I
thought he was the most callous fellow I had ever
met. An old woman rushed out and seized him by
the hand, kissed it, covered it with tears, and said :
"Oh, Master Charley, are you back to us again?" He
was like a statue. He made some casual remark as if he
had been out for a morning walk, and passed through
them all into the drawing-room, where Mrs. Dickinson
was. I hung back, as I did not like to be present at the
meeting between brother and sister, but Parnell said :
"Come along." Mrs. Dickinson was as icy as himself.
She got up calmly as he entered, and said quite
casually : "Ah, Charley, is that you? I thought they
would never let you back again."

'*Parnell.* "Well, what did you think they would do to me?"

'*Mrs. Dickinson.* "I thought they would hang you."

'*Parnell* (smiling). "Well, it may come to that yet."

'That was the whole greeting. They then talked about family affairs.'

It has been said that there was no Kilmainham treaty. Well, it is idle to quibble about words. There was a Kilmainham treaty, and these, in a single sentence, were its terms. The Government were to introduce a satisfactory Arrears Bill, and Parnell was to 'slow down' the agitation. 'One of the most sagacious arrangements,' says Mr. Healy, commenting on Parnell's conduct, 'that ever enabled a hard pressed general to secure terms for his forces.'

CHAPTER XIV

THE NEW RÉGIME

ONE of the first results of the Kilmainham treaty was
the resignation of Lord Cowper and Mr. Forster. On
May 4 Mr. Forster made his explanation in Parliament.
The substance of what he said may be given in a few
sentences. The state of Ireland did not justify the
release of Parnell without a promise of ' amendment ' [1]
or a new Coercion Act. He darkly hinted at a bargain
between the Prime Minister and the agitator, but did
not dwell on the subject. While he was in the middle
of his speech, and just as he had uttered the following
words : ' There are two warrants which I signed in
regard to the member for the city of Cork '—Parnell
entered the House. It was a dramatic scene.

Deafening cheers broke from the Irish benches,
drowning Forster's voice, and preventing the conclusion of the sentence from being heard.

Parnell quickly surveyed the situation, and, bowing
to the Speaker, passed, with head erect and measured
tread, to his place, the victor of the hour.

One can easily imagine his feelings when Mr. Gladstone rose to answer Mr. Forster. ' To divide and govern '
had always been the policy of the English in Ireland.

---

[1] On the lines already indicated, *ante*, p. 328.

Parnell was now applying that policy to the English themselves. Seven months before Mr. Gladstone and Mr. Forster had been united in sending him to prison. They were united no longer.

The English in Ireland never more thoroughly appreciated the importance of dividing their enemies, while standing shoulder to shoulder themselves, than did this man, who was so English in temperament and in method. To see English parties at sixes and sevens while he commanded an unbroken phalanx was the central idea of his policy. He now saw the Prime Minister rise to fight his battle, which was, in truth, the battle of the Prime Minister too.

What a revolution ! Mr. Gladstone and Parnell in the same boat and Mr. Forster flung to the waves. Mr. Gladstone's reply was simple and courteous. In brief it came to this. The circumstances which had warranted the arrest no longer existed ; in addition, he had an assurance that if the Government dealt with the arrears question the three members released would range themselves on the side of law and order.

Parnell followed, saying :

'In the first portion of his (Mr. Gladstone's) speech the idea conveyed was that if the hon. members for Tipperary and Roscommon (Messrs. Dillon and O'Kelly), along with myself, were released we would take some special action with regard to the restoration of law and order. I assume that the right hon. gentleman has received information from some of my friends to whom I have made either written or verbal communication with regard to my intentions upon the state of this Irish question. But I wish to say emphatically that I have not in conversation with my friends or in any written communication to my friends entered into the question of the release of my hon. friends and myself as any condition of our action. (Mr. Gladstone, "Hear, hear.") I have not, either in writing or verbally, referred to our release in any degree whatsoever, and I wish to call attention to the first statement of the Prime Minister in order to show that it conveyed—although I am sure the right hon. gentleman did not intend it should do so—the reverse of that fact. ("No, no," from Mr. Gladstone.) Still, sir, I have stated verbally to more than one of my hon. friends, and I have written, that I believe a settlement of this arrears question—which now compels the Government to turn out into the road tenants who are unable to pay their rents, who have no hope of being able to pay their rents, for which they were rendered liable in the bad seasons of 1878, 1879, and 1880—would have an enormous effect in the restoration of law and order in Ireland—(Cheers)—would take away the last excuse for the outrages which have been unhappily committed in such large numbers during the last six months, and I believed we, in common with all persons who desire to see the prosperity of Ireland, would be able to take such steps as would have material effect in diminishing those unhappy and lamentable outrages.' (Ministerial and Irish cheers.)

And so the discussion practically ended on May 4, to be resumed, however, some time later with more bitterness and rancour. In the interval a terrible tragedy occurred. On May 6 the new Lord Lieutenant (Earl Spencer) made his state entry into Dublin. The new Chief Secretary (Lord Frederick Cavendish) took part in the pageant. Afterwards he drove on an outside car to the Chief Secretary's Lodge in the Phœnix Park. On the way he met the Under-Secretary (Mr.

Burke), alighted, and both walked together through the
park. As they came opposite the Viceregal Lodge
about 7 P.M. a band of assassins fell upon them and
stabbed them to death. These men belonged to a
murder society, self-called the 'Invincibles,' which
had sprung up under Mr. Forster's *régime*[1] for the
purpose, as one of them said, of ' making history ' by
' removing ' obnoxious political personages. Mr. Burke
and Lord Frederick Cavendish were their first victims.
The assassins were ultimately arrested and hanged.[2]
The ' Annual Register ' of 1882, in giving an account
of this horrible transaction, says : ' It is even more
painful to know that from the Viceregal Lodge Lord
Spencer himself was looking out of the windows,
and saw with unconcerned eyes the scuffle on the road
some hundred yards away, little thinking that what
seemed to be the horseplay of half a dozen roughs was
in reality the murder of two of his colleagues.'

This statement is inaccurate. Lord Spencer did
not see the ' scuffle.'

Here is his Lordship's recollection of what happened :
' It is said that I saw the murder. That is not so. I
had asked Cavendish [3] to drive to the park with me.
He said he would not ; he would rather walk with
Burke. Of course, if he had come with me it would
not have happened. I then rode to the park with a
small escort, I think my aide-de-camp and a trooper.
Curiously enough, I stopped to look at the polo match
which Carey described, so that he and I seem to have

---

[1] Forster's own life was frequently in jeopardy, and he seems to
have had some miraculous escapes.—Sir Wemyss Reid, *Life of the Right
Hon. W. E. Forster.*

[2] One of the ' Invincibles,' Carey, turned informer. He was afterwards shot by a man named O'Donnell, on board ship off Cape Colony.
O'Donnell was arrested, and brought to England and hanged.

[3] On hearing that Burke had already set out for the park Lord
Frederick Cavendish took the car to overtake him.

been together upon that occasion. I then turned towards the Viceregal Lodge. The ordinary and more direct way for me to go was over the very scene of the murder. Had I so gone the murder would not probably have been committed. Three men coming up would have prevented anything of that kind. But I made a slight *détour*, and got to the lodge another way. When I reached the lodge I sat down near the window and began to read some papers. Suddenly I heard a shriek which I shall never forget. I seem to hear it now ; it is always in my ears. This shriek was repeated again and again. I got up to look out. I saw a man rushing along. He jumped over the palings and dashed up to the lodge, shouting : " Mr. Burke and Lord Frederick Cavendish are killed." There was great confusion, and immediately I rushed out ; but someone of the Household stopped me, saying that it might be a ruse to get me out, and advising me to wait and make inquiries. Of course the inquiries were made and the truth soon discovered. I always deplore my unfortunate decision to make that *détour*, always feeling that if I had gone to the lodge by the ordinary way the murder would have been prevented. I have said that I did not see the murder, but my servant did. He was upstairs and saw a scuffle going on, but of course did not know what it was about.'

The news of the crime sent a thrill through the land. Agrarian outrages were common enough. But political assassination was something new.[1] ' Had the Fenians anything to do with it ? ' a correspondent of an American paper asked Kickham. ' I don't know,' was

---

[1] The object of the assassins was to kill Burke. Lord Frederick Cavendish was killed simply through the accident of his being with Burke.

the answer; ' but if they had they were Fenians seduced
by the Land League.'   Candour compels me to say that
it was the murder of Lord Frederick Cavendish which
produced a real feeling of sorrow and of shame among
the people.   He was a stranger.   He had never up to
that hour taken part in the government of the country.
He was an ' innocent ' man.   An old Fenian—a hater of
the Land League and all its works—told me the
following anecdote, which I think fairly illustrates Irish
popular feeling : ' I went into a shop,' he said, ' in New
York a few days after the murder to buy something.
I said casually to the man behind the counter : " This
is bad work."   He agreed, and denounced the crime in
strong language.   Here, at all events, thought I, is a
man who has escaped the influence of the Land
League.   I turned to leave, and as I got to the door
he added : " What harm if it was only Burke ?   But to
kill the strange gentleman who did nothing to us ! "
That was what he thought about it, and no doubt that
was what a great many other Irish people thought
about it too.'

What thought Parnell ?   There cannot be a question that he was profoundly moved by the event.   It
was not easy to startle him, to take him by surprise.
But the Phœnix Park murders did both.   An outburst of agrarianism would probably have produced
no effect upon him.   The reports which he had
received in prison rather prepared him for that.
Here, however, was a new development for which he
was not prepared, and the exact meaning and extent of
which he did not on the instant grasp.   As a rule, no
man was so ready in cases of emergency.   Now he
collapsed utterly.   He read the news in the ' Observer '
on Sunday morning, and went immediately to the

Westminster Palace Hotel, where he found Davitt.
'He flung himself into a chair in my room,' says
Davitt, 'and declared he would leave public life. "How
can I," he said, "carry on a public agitation if I am
stabbed in the back in this way?" He was wild.
Talk of the calm and callous Parnell. There was not
much calmness or callousness about him that morning.'

Later in the day he called on Sir Charles Dilke
with Mr. Justin McCarthy.

'Parnell,' says Sir Charles, 'called upon me with
Mr. Justin McCarthy the morning after the Phœnix
Park murders. I never saw a man so cut up in my
life. He was pale, careworn, altogether unstrung.'

'On the Sunday after the Phœnix Park murders,'
says Mr. Gladstone, 'while I was at lunch, a letter was
brought to me from Parnell. I was much touched
by it. He wrote evidently under strong emotion. He
did not ask me if I would advise him to retire from
public life or not. That was not how he put it. He
asked me what effect I thought the murder would have
on English public opinion in relation to his leadership
of the Irish party. Well, I wrote expressing my own
opinion, and what I thought would be the opinion of
others, that his retirement from public life would do no
good; on the contrary, would do harm. I thought his
conduct in the whole matter very praiseworthy.'

Mr. John Redmond gives the following 'reminis-
cence': 'I was in Manchester the night of the Phœnix
Park murders. I heard that Cavendish and Spencer
had been killed. I went to the police station to make
inquiries, but they would not tell me anything. I made
a speech condemning the murder of Cavendish, saying
the Government was the real cause of the crime. The
"Times" reported my speech with the comment that

I said nothing about Burke. Parnell spoke to me on the subject. I told him that I did not know that Burke had been killed when I made the speech. He said, " Write to the ' Times ' and say so." I wrote to the " Times." They did not publish the letter.' [1]

A manifesto [2] signed by Parnell, Dillon, and Davitt (who had been released from Dartmoor on that very May 6) was immediately issued ' to the Irish people,' condemning the murders, and expressing the hope that the assassins would be brought to justice. It concluded with these words : ' We feel that no act has ever been perpetrated in our country during the exciting struggles for social and political rights of the past fifty years that has so stained the name of hospitable Ireland as this cowardly and unprovoked assassination of a friendly stranger, and that until the murderers of Lord Frederick Cavendish and Mr. Burke are brought to justice that stain will sully our country's name.'

When the House of Commons met on May 8 Parnell was in his place, looking jaded, careworn, anxious, and depressed. He had won a great victory. He had beaten the Irish Executive. He had drawn the Prime Minister to his side. He had obtained a promise of more concessions, and there was every prospect that the policy of coercion would be abandoned. His success was complete, and now all was jeopardised by a gang of criminal lunatics. He had, so to say, hemmed in the British forces opposed to him, only to find on his flank an enemy whose power for mischief he could not at that moment gauge.

The murders were the one topic referred to in Parlia-

---

[1] The *Times* subsequently explained that they did not receive the letter.

[2] The manifesto was written by Davitt.

ment on that 8th of May. Parnell made a short,
manly, straightforward speech, condemning the outrage
in unqualified terms, saying that it was a deadly blow
dealt to his party, and expressing the fear that, under
the circumstances, the Government would feel constrained to revert to the policy of coercion—a deplorable
prospect.

The Government did revert to the policy of coercion.
On May 11 Sir William Harcourt (the Home Secretary)
introduced a 'Crimes Bill,' based practically upon the
lines laid down by Lord Cowper in his letter to Mr.
Gladstone already quoted.[1] In certain cases (*inter alia*)
trial by judges or by magistrates was substituted for
trial by jury, and power was given to the Executive to
summon witnesses and to carry on inquiries in secret,
even when no person was in custody charged with
crime. Mr. Forster had his revenge. The assassins of
the Phœnix Park had, for the moment, placed him in a
position of triumph. They had in a single hour done
more to subdue the spirit of Parnell than he during
the whole of his administration. The Irish members,
of course, opposed the new Coercion Bill, opposed it
even with energy; but it was clear all the time that
they, and Parnell especially, fought under the shadow
of the crime of May 6. While keenly criticising the
details of the measure and rebuking the Government
for this backward step, he spoke rather in sorrow than
in anger. There was a touch of pathos, a tone of
dejection, in his speeches which sounded unusual and
strange. Mr. Gladstone especially he treated with
the utmost gentleness; nor did he attempt in any way
to conceal the bitterness of his conviction that the
Phœnix Park murders strengthened the hand of the

[1] *Ante*, p. 328.

Government and weakened his own. He looked and spoke like a man under a cloud. An extract from one of his speeches on the Bill will perhaps suffice to show the character of them all. On May 29 he said : ' We have been contending against the right hon. gentleman (Mr. Gladstone) for two years. We have found him to be a great man and a strong man. I even think it is no dishonour to admit that we should not wish to be fought again in the same way by any-body in the future. I regret that the event in the Phœnix Park has prevented him continuing the course of conciliation that we had expected from him. I regret that owing to the exigencies of his party, of his position in the country, he has felt himself compelled to turn from that course of conciliation and concession into the horrible paths of coercion.'

Nevertheless, the struggle over the measure was protracted. There were many scenes. There was an all-night sitting, and eighteen Irish members were suspended.

Finally the Irish withdrew from the contest, pro-testing : ' That inasmuch as the Irish parliamentary party have been expelled from the House of Commons under threat of physical force during the consideration of a measure affecting vitally the rights and liberties of Ireland, and as the Government during the enforced absence of the Irish members from the House pressed forward material parts of the measure in committee, thus depriving the representatives of the Irish people of the right to discuss and to vote upon coercion proposals for Ireland ; we, therefore, hereby resolve to take no further part in the proceedings in committee on the Coercion Bill, and we cast upon the Government the sole responsibility for a Bill which has been urged

through the House by a course of violence and subter-
fuge, and which, when passed into law, will be devoid
of moral force and will be no constitutional Act of
Parliament.'

While it was going through the House Mr. Gladstone brought in the Arrears Bill. As the one measure
was based on lines laid down by Lord Cowper, the other
was based on lines laid down by Parnell. During his
incarceration in Kilmainham he had practically drafted
the Bill. Mr. Healy tells a story *à propos* of this
subject which curiously illustrates how Parnell's super-
stitious instincts never deserted him :

'While the Kilmainham treaty was in preparation,
and the late Mr. W. E. Forster's throne in Dublin
Castle was being sapped by his prisoner from the jail
hard by, Mr. Parnell skilfully hit on the idea of availing
himself of the introduction of an amending Land Bill,
for which the Irish party had won a Wednesday for
a second reading debate, as the public basis of his
arrangement with Mr. Gladstone. The Bill was afterwards moved by Mr. John Redmond, in April 1882, and
one of the clauses became the Government Arrears Act
of that year. To frame such a measure in prison legal
help of course was necessary, and Parnell asked Mr.
Maurice Healy to visit the prison and discuss the matter,
which he did for several days.

'Even at so early a date after the passage of the
Land Act of 1881 that enactment had been riddled by
the judges in provisions vital to the tenants' interest.
There was, therefore, a great outcry for amendments, and
various proposals were discussed in turn in the prison.
One suggestion, however, which my brother made Mr.
Parnell refused to adopt. He was pressed again and
again as to its necessity, but into the Bill he would not

allow it to go. The enemies of the alleged agrarian *jacquerie* in Ireland little supposed that at its head was a moderate, almost conservative, leader, averse, except when driven to it by the "stokers" of the movement, to lend his approval to extreme demands. Indeed, later on, as his power increased, he grew still more moderate, so that Mr. Biggar once said of him, musingly, "I wonder what are Parnell's real politics!" At all events, by Easter 1882 Mr. Parnell, having obtained a fortnight's release on parole, had effected an understanding with Mr. Chamberlain, who was acting for the anti-Forster section in the Cabinet, and he was extremely anxious for some compromise. He was, therefore, unwilling that the proposed Land Bill should be weighted with unacceptable provisions, so the measure took shape without the clauses which his young adviser recommended. After some days a draft was got ready to be sent across to Westminster, where it was urgently required, as the Bill had to be printed and distributed the following Wednesday. When all was completed a fair copy was taken up to the prison, lest any final revising touches should be required before being posted. Clause by clause the great prisoner went over his Bill, until at last the final page was reached. Then he turned over the leaves again and counted the clauses. Suddenly, having contemplated the reckoning, he threw the manuscript on the table as if he had been stung. "Why," said he, "this will never do!" "What is the matter?" said his solicitor, in alarm. "There are thirteen clauses," said Mr. Parnell; "we can't have thirteen clauses." "But is there anything out of order in that?" asked the other, wondering whether some point of parliamentary practice could be involved. "No," said Mr. Parnell sternly; "but what Bill with thirteen clauses could have any chance? It would be horribly unlucky." This was a staggerer for the draftsman. Not even the treaty with Mr. Chamberlain and the promise of favourable consideration of the Bill by the Cabinet could induce the wary prisoner to risk a defiance of his boyhood's teaching. His amazed adviser then asked what was to be done—could any clause be omitted? It was late in the afternoon, post hour approached, and another day's delay might prevent the draft reaching the Queen's printers in London in time for distribution to members before the second reading. The humour of the situation did not at all strike the legal mind at this crisis. A hasty dissection of the Bill was made, but only to disclose that it could not well be shorn of a clause. What could be hit upon? There in bewilderment and anxiety stood the statesman and draftsman in her Majesty's prison at Kilmainham, eyeing each other in despair in the darkening cell as the minutes to post hour slipped away. At last a gleam flashed from Mr. Parnell's eyes, half ironical, half triumphant. "I have it," said he. "Add that d——d clause of yours, and that will get us out of the difficulty." It was an inspiration, and so it was done.'[1]

This Arrears Bill (which became law in July and applied only to tenancies under 30*l*.) provided that the tenants' arrears should be cancelled on the following conditions:

1. That the tenant should pay the rent due in 1881.

2. That of the antecedent arrears he should pay one year's rent, the State another.

---

[1] *Westminster Gazette*, November 2, 1892. 'This clause,' says Mr. Healy, 'though not adopted then, was ultimately embodied in the Tory Land Act of 1887.'

3. That the tenant should satisfy a legal tribunal of his inability to pay the whole of the arrears.

We have seen how Mr. Healy describes Parnell as a man of moderate and even conservative tendencies. The description is true. Never was a revolutionary movement led by so conservative a politician. He was not violent by choice. He was only violent through necessity. When the exigencies of the situation demanded, he never hesitated to raise a popular storm. When the occasion required, he was the first to throw oil upon the troubled waters. At this crisis he desired a calm in public affairs, because the country had got out of hand and he wanted a lull to take his bearings afresh and to shape the future course of the agitation.

On May 6 he had gone to Dartmoor to meet Davitt. They travelled to London together. 'All the the way,' said Davitt, 'he talked of the state of the country, said it was dreadful, denounced the Ladies' Land League, swore at everybody, and spoke of anarchy as if he were a British Minister bringing in a Coercion Bill. I never saw him so wild and angry; the Ladies' Land League had, he declared, taken the country out of his hands, and should be suppressed. I defended the ladies, saying that after all they had kept the ball rolling while he was in jail. "I am out now," said he, "and I don't want them to keep the ball rolling any more. The League must be suppressed, or I will leave public life."

'In August we met at Dublin. The Ladies' League wanted 500*l.* I called on Parnell, at Morrison's Hotel, and asked him for a cheque for that amount. "No," he said, "not a shilling; they have squandered the money given to them, and I shall take care that they get no more." I said: "But, Mr. Parnell, their debts must be

paid whatever happens." But he would not discuss the
matter. I left him in a bit of a temper, and would not
come back when he sent Dillon for me later in the day.
Next day, however, I saw him again. He gave me
the cheque. "There," said he, "let those ladies make
the most of it. They will get no more money from me,
and let the League be dissolved at once." '

I believe the Ladies' Land League was never
formally dissolved, but it died of inanition, for Parnell
stopped the supplies.

The Land League had been suppressed by the
Government.

The Ladies' Land League was practically suppressed
by Parnell.

There was now no public organisation. It was
necessary to found one. Parnell, however, moved
slowly. He had made the Kilmainham treaty. He
wished to keep it. 'There is one thing about the man,'
said Mr. Forster, 'of which I am quite sure—his word
can be relied on.'

It was difficult for him to keep the Kilmainham
compact, for the Crimes Act, which violated the letter
if not the spirit of the treaty, exasperated the people
and made the Government intensely unpopular. Nevertheless Parnell kept his word. 'What are your intentions?' said Mr. Dillon, who thought that the land
agitation should still be carried on with fierce energy.
'Do you mean to carry on the war or to slow down the
agitation?' 'To slow down the agitation,' said Parnell,
with emphasis.

Mr. Davitt wished Land Nationalisation to be made
a plank in the new platform.

Parnell said 'No.'

'He was,' says Mr. Davitt, 'opposed to a fresh

land agitation, and wished to keep solely on the Home
Rule tack.'

Brennan (who with Davitt and Egan made the
working triumvirate of the Land League) denounced
Parnell privately for his moderation, said his days of
usefulness had gone by, and ultimately left the country
in disgust. Before leaving he had asked Parnell to
send him on a mission to Australia. Parnell refused
point blank, and sent Mr. Redmond instead. Egan
(who had already left Ireland) used all his influence to
keep the agitation on the old lines, but in vain. No one
could prevail against the inexorable Chief.

On August 16 he was presented with the freedom of
the City of Dublin. He asked permission to sign the
roll in private. He wanted no public demonstration,
but the corporation insisted on it. He then made a
short speech, warning his audience that an 'Independent Irish Party' could not be maintained 'for any
length of time' in the English House of Commons,
and urging them to concentrate their energies on that
'great object of reform which has always possessed the
hearts of the Irish people at home and abroad, I mean the
restoration of the legislative independence of Ireland.'

Afterwards he went to Avondale and Aughavanagh
to enjoy a brief period of repose. Mr. John Redmond,
who joined him at the latter place, tells the following
anecdote à propos of Parnell's relations with his people
in the country. 'One day,' says Mr. Redmond, 'we
were walking up a mountain, and we met an old man,
a tenant on the property, named Whitty. "Whitty,"
said Parnell, "you have been on the land for many
years, you never pay me any rent, and all I ask you is
to keep the sheep off the mountains when I am out
shooting, and, you old villain, you don't even do that." '

'Used he to talk politics to you?' I asked Mr. Redmond. 'No,' he answered, 'his conversation was principally about sporting. He was always looking for gold in Wicklow. Gold, sport, and the applied sciences were his subjects out of Parliament.'

In October the new organisation was founded.

'On the Sunday previous to the convention,' says Mr. Healy, 'I went in the evening to Morrison's Hotel with the draft constitution, which Parnell wished to talk over. This was in the month of October 1882. I found him in bed, and apparently poorly enough. Seeing this I suggested postponing the work of revision. "Oh, no," said he; "it is nothing." After a pause he added, musingly, "Something happens to me always in October." This remark fell from him as if he were announcing a decree of fate, and struck me intensely. October, in Mr. Parnell's horoscope, was a month of "influence," and he always regarded it with apprehension.

'In October 1879 he became President of the Land League, which was then started for the first time, and he was commissioned to visit America to spread the new movement and collect funds. In October 1880 the agrarian agitation in Ireland culminated, and the Government commenced the State prosecutions of that year. Curiously enough, in the same month of that year, for some occult reason, Mr. Parnell divested himself of his beard and made himself almost unrecognisable by the people. In October 1881 he was arrested, and arrested, strange to say, on October 13. In October 1886 he sickened almost to death in the critical autumn following the rejection of the Home Rule Bill. In October of that year also the Plan of Campaign, as he complained, was published by Mr. Harrington without

his authority or that of the Irish party.   The result was
the enactment of the perpetual Coercion Act of 1887
and the eviction of many tenants, whose fate deeply
affected the Irish party in their decision in Room 15
against Mr. Parnell's leadership.   Strangest of all, in
view of his premonitions, is the fact that it was in the
month of October that he died so unexpectedly in 1891.
A belief that a particular month might be " influential "
would probably react with depressing effect on physical
health at the critical period and thus weaken the
resisting power at that time.   Nevertheless, the stoutest
disbeliever in unseen influence will deem the coinci-
dences noteworthy.

    ' On this Sunday of October 1882, while I worked
away at the draft constitution of the National League
in Morrison's Hotel, the sick man lay with his face to
the wall, replying composedly now and again as to the
points which remained to be settled in it.   I wrote at a
table by his bedside, on which four candles stood
lighted.   Hours passed by, and being engrossed in the
work I did not heed the fact that one of the candles
was burning to the socket and finally spluttered itself
out.   A stir from the patient aroused me, and I looked up.
With astonishment I saw that Mr. Parnell had turned
round, raised himself in the bed, and, leaning over my
table, was furiously blowing out one of the remaining
candles.   " What on earth is that for ? " said I, amazed
at this performance.   " I want more light than that."
His eyes gleamed weirdly in their pale setting as he
answered : " Don't you know that nothing is more
unlucky than to have three candles burning ? "   Almost
petrified, I confessed that I did not.   " Your constitution, then, would have been very successful," said he
with quiet sarcasm, and he turned his face to the wall

again, evidently persuaded that his intervention alone
had averted some political catastrophe.   The conviction
which he threw into his words, the instant motion to
quench the unlucky candle at some inconvenience to
himself and without a warning to me, the strange seer-
like face, and the previous forebodings about October,
made up a situation which felt almost awesome.   It
would have been as irreverent to smile as it would be
to scoff in the presence of believers at the worship of
their unknown gods.   Afterwards I learnt that three
candles are lit at wakes in Ireland around a corpse—
possibly in some distant way to symbolise or reverence
the Trinity.'[1]

On October 17 the convention met.   Parnell pre-
sided.   The National League was formed.   Home Rule
was put in the forefront.   Land reform, local self-
government, parliamentary and municipal reform came
after.   The President announced the policy of the
future in a brief and pithy speech.   H said : 'I wish
to affirm the opinion which I have expressed ever since
I first stood upon an Irish platform, that until we obtain
for the majority of the people of this country the right
of making their own laws we shall never be able and
we never can hope to see the laws of Ireland in
accordance with the wishes of the people of Ireland, or
calculated, as they should, to bring about the permanent
prosperity of our country.   And I would always desire
to impress upon my fellow countrymen that their first
duty and their first object is to obtain for our country the
right of making her own laws upon Irish soil.'   Then,
turning to the subject of land, he added : 'I wish to
re-affirm the belief which I have expressed upon every
platform upon which I have stood since the commence-

---

[1] *Westminster Gazette*, November 3, 1893.

ment of the land agitation—that no solution of the land question can be accepted as a final one that does not insure the occupying farmers the right of becoming owners by purchase of the holdings which they now occupy as tenants.'

Home Rule and a peasant proprietary were, then, the principal planks of the new platform.

Later in the year Parnell sent Mr. Redmond to Australia and to America to collect funds for the League. Mr. Redmond had some strange experiences. 'When I arrived at Sydney,' he says, 'the Phœnix Park murders were the talk of the colony. I received a chilling reception. All the respectable people who had promised support kept away. The priests would not help me, except the Jesuits, who were friendly to me as an old Clongowes boy. The man—a leading citizen— who had promised to take the chair at my first meeting would not come. Sir Harry Parkes, the Prime Minister, proposed that I should be expelled the colony, but the motion was defeated. The Irish working men stood by me, and in fact saved the situation. They kept me going until telegrams arrived exculpating the parliamentary party. Then all the Irish gradually came around and ultimately flocked to my meetings. I collected 15,000l. and went to America. Fenians did everything for us there. Without them we could have done nothing. I addressed a great meeting at the Opera House, Chicago. Boyle O'Reilly was in the chair. There were 10,000 people present. It was a grand sight. It was grand to see the Irish united as they were then. I was escorted to the meeting by the Governor and the Mayor, and the streets were lined with soldiers, who presented arms as we passed.'

During the winter Parnell addressed a few meetings

in the country, speaking with studied moderation, and showing clearly that it was his wish to keep things quiet for the present. Alderman Redmond, who travelled with him by train to one of these meetings—from Waterford to Dungarvan and back—has given me the following note of a conversation which took place between them :

'I found Parnell a pleasant companion. He did not like talking, but he listened to you with great attention. I said : " Mr. Parnell, how do you think Home Rule is getting on ? " " Very well," he answered. " If the people pull steadily together we shall get it in a few years."

'*Alderman Redmond.* " Surely, Mr. Parnell, the English people are strongly opposed to Home Rule. You will take a long time to bring them round."

'*Parnell.* " They were strongly opposed to Catholic Emancipation, but they had to come round in the end. O'Connell had nothing like our power ; he stood almost alone. We have only to fight and stick together, and we will win. We must not yield an inch. You get nothing from the English by yielding."

" *Alderman Redmond.* " But, Mr. Parnell, some people think that we are not fit for Home Rule, that we would misuse it. They say all this in the North."

'*Parnell.* " The North certainly show us a bad example, for they exclude Catholics from all power there. There might be difficulties in working Home Rule at first, but the good sense of the country would make things right after a time. Even the fears of the North would soon be set at rest."

'*Alderman Redmond.* " How would you make Ireland prosper under Home Rule ? "

'*Parnell* (laughing). " Well, I will ask you another

question. How can any country prosper that has not
the management of its own affairs, of its own income ?
Do you think England would prosper if she were to
allow France to take care of her purse ? The income
of Ireland is nearly 8,000,000l. a year. Where does it
all go to ? England can do, is doing, what she likes
with it. An Irish Government could keep down expenses. Take the one item of police. We could save
a million under that head alone. We do not want the
costly establishments of England."

'*Alderman Redmond.* "What would you do with
the landlords ? "

'*Parnell.* "I would treat them fairly and honestly.
I would encourage them to live quietly among their
own people. I would give them a fair share of parliamentary honours, and I would make them happy in
their own country, which they are not at present."

' In returning from Dungarvan to Waterford I said
to him, " Well, Mr. Parnell, you made a good, sensible
speech to-day." He replied, " I hate public speaking,
and always feel nervous before and after I get on a
public platform." '

Mr. William Redmond (who had been in Kilmainham with Parnell) made a 'treasonable' speech in
Cork towards the end of the year 1882, and subsequently left Ireland. Soon after his departure a
warrant was issued for his arrest. Learning this, he
wrote to Parnell, expressing his wish to return and
' face the music.' Parnell replied :

Parnell to Mr. William Redmond

' House of Commons : December 6, 1882.

' DEAR MR. REDMOND,—Your letter of the 1st
instant to hand, and I am strongly of opinion that you

ought not to return. You should carry out your
original programme of going to Nice and looking after
your health.   If you were to come back now you would
be certain to be sentenced to a period of imprisonment
with hard labour, and in any case the state of your
health will be in a better position to face a prosecution
when you return than it is now.   I hope, however, that
the matter will have blown over by then.

'Yours very truly,

'CHAS. S. PARNELL.'

Mr. Redmond ultimately joined his brother in
Australia. When he returned the matter had blown over.[1]

The year 1882 marks one of the darkest periods
in the land agitation in Ireland.   The following table,
submitted by Sir Charles Russell to the Parnell Commission, speaks volumes : [2]

AGRARIAN CRIME FOR THE WHOLE OF IRELAND

—	Two years, 1880-81. Average for two years.	Total in 1882 alone.
Murders	12½	26
Firing at persons . .	45½	58
Incendiary fires and arson .	283	281
Cattle outrages . . .	128	144
Threatening letters . .	1,764	2,009
Firing into dwellings .	105	117
Totals . .	2,338	2,635

[1] 'I was at Parnell's house, Ironsides, Bordenstown, in 1882,' says
Mr. William Redmond, 'when Fanny Parnell died. She died very
suddenly. One day she went out for a walk. She returned in a great
state of excitement with a copy of the *New York Herald* in her hand.
It was the time of the Egyptian war, and there was a rumour of an
English defeat. I remember well seeing Fanny burst into the drawing
room, waving the paper over her head, and saying, "Oh, mother, there is
an Egyptian victory. Arabi has whipped the Britishers. It is grand."
That was the last time I saw Fanny Parnell alive. Next day she died
quite suddenly.'
[2] Sir Charles Russell's speech before the Parnell Commission,
p. 294.

It was especially a year of sensational murders. In January, the Huddys, Lord Ardilaun's bailiffs, were killed. In February, Bernard Bailey, an informer, was shot dead in a crowded thoroughfare in Dublin. In March, Joseph McMahon, another informer, was killed. In April, as has been said, Mrs. Smythe was shot dead in open day while driving in a carriage with her brother-in-law from church.[1] In May, the Phœnix Park murders took place. In June, Mr. Walter Bourke, a land agent, Mr. Blake, another land agent, Mr. Keene, a land steward, and Mr. McCausland were killed. In August, the Joyce family were killed at Maamtrasna, because it was said that they knew the murderers of the Huddys and might give evidence against them. In November, an unsuccessful attempt was made to assassinate Mr. Justice Lawson. In the same month, Field, who had served on a jury which had convicted a prisoner charged with the murder of a policeman, was stabbed almost to death just outside his house in North Frederick Street, Dublin. The country reeked with blood. Mr. Forster had hoped to restrain the 'dissolute ruffians' of Ireland. In truth, he had, unwittingly, let them loose.

No man was more deeply concerned by the distracted condition of Ireland in 1882 than Parnell. He was not 'alarmed' because English public opinion was 'shocked.' He had no faith in the fine moral sense of the English. 'Much the English care,' he had said, 'for the shooting of a few landlords in Ireland.' He looked upon the English as a nation of hypocrites. 'They murder and plunder,' he would say, 'all over the world, and then they howl when somebody is killed in Ireland, because the killing is of no use to them.' He

[1] The bullet was intended for her brother-in-law.

would as soon have thought of favouring a plan for the construction of a railway to the moon as appealing to the moral sense of England. Therefore, when moderate men used to say to him, 'Mr. Parnell, you ought to restrain your people; nothing shocks a law-abiding community like the English so much as lawlessness,' he would simply smile. His one idea of dealing with the English was to put them in a tight place. He felt that English party leaders thought as much and no more of the 'morality' of the 'moves' in the game of politics than a chess player thinks of the morality of the moves in a game of chess. An English statesman was to him an individual who would risk his soul to sit on the Treasury bench. It was the duty of the Irish agitator to see that the English statesman should sit on the Treasury bench only on *his* conditions. An outburst of lawlessness in Ireland was regarded by Parnell simply with a view to its effect on the national 'movement.' And, in his opinion, at this moment there was every danger that the extreme wing of his army might, under the evil influences of men who gained the upper hand while he was in jail, run amuck, which could only end in the disorganisation and collapse of the National cause.

Mr. Dillon and Davitt did not see eye to eye with Mr. Parnell. The former, as I have said, was of opinion that the land agitation ought still to be kept at fever heat. The latter thought that there ought to be a new development of that agitation in the direction of land nationalisation. Parnell differed from both and would not yield a jot to either. Mr. Dillon was much incensed and threatened to resign his seat in Parliament. Parnell did not want this. He did not wish to see the smallest rift within the lute; but he would not give way. It was about this time that Mr. Dillon went to Avondale to

ask him point blank if he meant to 'slow down' the
agitation. On receiving his Chief's answer, delivered
with inexorable precision, and acting on the advice of
his medical attendant, Mr. Dillon sailed for Colorado
and troubled Parnell no more.

Davitt's opposition was a more serious affair. He
was a power. He had the 'Irish World' at his back.
He could easily have formed an anti-Parnellite party in
America. He could not, of course, have driven Parnell
from the position of Irish leader, for all Ireland was
now solid for the Chief—the Church, the farmers, and
many of the rank and file of the Fenians, who had,
contrary to the direction of the supreme council, joined
the Land League—but he could have made divisions
in the ranks. The 'Irish World' was only too ready
to dethrone Parnell, whom Ford disliked for his moderation and his strength. Had Davitt only spoken the word
there would probably have been an internecine struggle
full of peril to the national interests. Parnell knew
this well. The one thing he detested was a quarrel
with any set of Irishmen. But he felt that, at all costs,
the Extremists should be taught that he was master.
He would take money from his American allies. He
would remain in alliance with them. But the direction
of the national movement should rest in his hands, and
in his hands alone. He had no notion of allowing his
American auxiliaries to boss the situation, and that they
meant to boss it he had not a particle of doubt. America
should help, but should not lead Ireland. That was
the principle on which he acted.

His feelings towards Davitt were friendly. He had
always the warmest sympathies for a man who had
suffered so much for Ireland. He always recognised
the power and the usefulness of the political convict.

Davitt, we know, was the connecting-link with America, and Parnell's policy was to curb, not break with, the Americans. Davitt had therefore to be kept by his side, while Davitt's pet scheme of Land Nationalisation had to be flung to the winds. It was in the manipulation of affairs of this nature that Parnell excelled. In such cases the charm of his personality, the strength of his character told. He did not conquer you by argument. He threw over you the spell of irresistible fascination, or impressed you with an uneasy sense of relentless authority. I have said that, 'had Davitt only spoken the word there would probably have been an internecine struggle full of peril to the national interests.' He did not speak it. He made no attempt at revolt. He tried to convert Parnell to his views. He failed and submitted.

'Parnell and I differed seriously,' says Davitt, 'but we remained fairly good friends almost to the end.'

From 1882 onwards there was constant friction between Parnell and the Extremists. Nevertheless he held all the Nationalist forces together; he presented an unbroken front to the common enemy. It is dangerous for an Irish leader to be 'moderate.' He runs the risk of exposing himself to the fatal charge of 'Whiggery.' Yet in his 'moderate' days this charge was never levelled at Parnell. Why? Simply because he never won, never wished to win, the applause of the British public. Butt's fate was sealed the moment he fell in any degree under English influence, the moment English cheers in the House of Commons became pleasant to his ears. Parnell never fell in the slightest degree under English influence, and he avoided an English cheer as a skilful pilot would keep clear of the breakers on a rock-bound coast. He did nothing to please Englishmen at the expense of any Irishman ; indeed, he did nothing to please them at all. This gave him his strength. He was asked upon one occasion to move a resolution in public condemning outrages. ' No,' said he ; ' I dislike outrages as much as any man, but I am not going to act police for the English Government.' ' Why do you not keep your young barbarians in order, Mr. Parnell ? ' a friend said to him one night in the House of Commons. ' Ah ! ' said Parnell, ' I like to see them flesh their spears.'

It was in his moderate days that Parnell spoke the following words, which sank deeply into the Fenian mind : ' I do not wish to attach too much importance to what can be gained by the action of your members in the House of Commons. Much good has resulted, and much good will result, from an independent parliamentary representation, but I have never claimed for parliamentary action anything more than its just share of weight.'

' Extreme ' or ' moderate,' Parnell held his ground because the Irish, ' at home and abroad,' were convinced —and he took good care never under any circumstances to weaken the conviction—that he was ever the unchanging enemy of England.

END OF THE FIRST VOLUME